Being and Organizing in an Entangled World

Sociomateriality and Posthumanism

Published by Mayfly Books. Available in paperpack
and free online at www.mayflybooks.org in 2022.

ISBN (Print) 978-1-906948-57-3
ISBN (PDF) 978-1-906948-58-0
ISBN (ebook) 978-1-906948-59-7

Being and Organizing in an Entangled World

Sociomateriality and Posthumanism

Stephen Allen

Book endorsements:

Readers of this ambitious text should prepare for an adventure. Although Allen frames the book as 'creative academic writing', it is much more than that: an experiment in representing in linguistic form the phenomenon being explored – entanglement. That entanglement quickly encompasses the reader themself, the materials physically supporting them, the trees outside the window gazing in – until the very way in which we are connected, interconnected, and completely reliant on one another, both human and more-than-human, becomes a matter of fact rather than speculation. What Allen has accomplished here is breath-taking.

Donna Ladkin - Professor of Leadership and Ethics
Antioch University, USA

In this engaging book, Stephen Allen writes in accessible terms about our shared responsibilities to lead and change organizations towards greater sustainability, using a language based on relationality, sociomateriality and posthumanism. The book provides a welcome addition to an emerging literature that attempts to reshape business school thinking in response to socio-ecological crises currently faced.

Emma Bell - Professor of Organisation Studies
The Open University, UK

Table of Contents

Acknowledgements

I am not going to write one of those long acknowledgements sections that thanks just about everybody that I have ever met. If the acknowledgements look too long in the books I read I tend to skip them. Firstly, thanks to Gina, my wife-partner, and Rosina, our daughter. To Gina, for being there, and for allowing me to use her painting as the front cover image. And, Rosina for maintaining her excitement about book writing as a worthwhile endeavour. Secondly, I would like to thank Toni Ruuska and Steffen Boehm at MayFly Books for believing in my proposal and that I could deliver on it, as well as their calm and supportive editing. As well as Mihkali Pennanen who has done such wonderful work with the layout and typesetting. Thirdly, the friends-colleagues who I managed to convince to read earlier drafts and to give me feedback amongst all the other things that they need to do in their lives. Their suggestions have informed many improvements, thanks very much to Judi Marshall, Jerzy Kociatkiewicz and Victor Friedman. In particular, thanks to Judi whose assiduous reading and careful commenting were so helpful. I have done my best to respond to all the suggestions I have received, even in the face of my moments of book writing fatigue, although of course I take responsibility for any shortcomings and inadequacies that you might find on these pages. Particularly in relation to any expectations you might have about grammar! As part of my final reviewing I did read the whole book through aloud which has hopefully meant that the most unkempt sentences are now sufficiently tidy. Fourthly, to the trees opposite our house that I can see through the window next to where I have been doing almost all of the typing. Thanks for being nearby and providing perches and sustenance to all the creatures, mainly birds, that I have been able to watch whilst working at my computer. The significance of some of these beings have become written into the book. Finally, thank you to my IT equipment for mainly doing what I expected of it, when I expected it. The collective work of all those hidden wires and microchips allowed both Open Office, the word processing software I used, and Zotero, which manages my references, to run as they were intended. Without these technologies things may well have been a disaster as I can barely read my own hand writing, so producing this book would probably have been impossible!

PART ONE:
Purposes, assumptions and scene-setting

Chapter 1

Introduction

A note about beginning

This is a book about experimenting with thinking-being, with the writing-learning which constitutes it part of that experimenting. What this means is that throughout I attempt to show the situatedness and contingency of assembling it. Doing so is about trying to develop and express a perspective and its associated dilemmas. The perspective is about searching for possibilities of giving voice to voiceless more-than-human others. It is a perspective that gathers together and extends streams of thinking and writing that I have been wandering around with, physically and metaphorically, over the past ten years or so.

My purposes for writing this book involve exploring how it might be possible to navigate some dense theoretical territories (in particular posthumanism and sociomateriality) in ways that can make the assembled words feel pleasurable and worthwhile reading. By trying to creatively weave together a variety of ideas I want to offer a challenging and grounded perspective which can help others to reflect on the (un)sustainabilities of our current predicaments. And, most importantly prompt imaginings of other possibilities for responsible-being and organizing.

Fundamentally, in the face of ecological emergencies writing this book is part of searching with vulnerable optimism for ways of collective (human and other-than-human) flourishing. The perspective offered can not be regarded as some desirable 'end point', rather a potentially useful pebble within rivers of many others' writing and action which modestly seek something else, something better and something hopeful for us all. It is meant to be a troubling but tactile pebble that can prompt us to re-see, re-think and re-act.

You are here

On the pages that follow I will attempt to assemble letters into words, words into sentences, sentences into paragraphs, and paragraphs into chapters to create a book. The book will be the text that I have typed, and images pasted in, that are printed onto numbered pages which are fastened together within a cover. Or, the book will appear as a digital file which can be read by some form of computer device that will enable the text and images to be displayed on a screen.

If you are reading these words then 'it' happened, the book is in your hands, or is on a screen in front of you. Somehow you became aware that this book existed, and somehow it found its way to you. Maybe you know me and are reading it out of some sense of duty, or curiosity about what I have been up to in my tapping away at a computer keyboard for all that time. Or, maybe somebody (dare I suggest!) recommended the book to you, and so you are diligently reading it, possibly feeling slightly disgruntled, because there are so many other possible books you could be looking at. Those other books might well appear much more exciting to you, with snappier titles and authors names that you recognise. Also, you are likely not short of things to read. I am just imaging you looking at those other books still sitting expectantly on your shelves, or desk, or by your bed, waiting to be picked up. Or, maybe you took pity on me at some talk related to the book, perhaps you thought I sounded a bit downbeat as not many people seemed that interested in what I had spent quite some time producing. You felt compelled to take one of the printed copies home with you that I had been lugging around with me. Or, maybe this book just popped up on an internet search engine and you have clicked on it, opening up a digital version for a quick glance. You are feeling eager to dismiss it as irrelevant to your searching so that you can continue on through the mountain of other reading which could be relevant to what you are seeking. Or, maybe it was just there to hand right in front of you, in a library, charity shop or discarded somewhere and your reflex was to pick it up and take a look.

Before we get going I want to make a couple of brief comments about what you will find on these pages. My hope is that you will stay with me throughout the chapters, but it can feel like there is so much to do these days. Much to draw our attention in other directions. Hang on a minute, I think my phone just beeped! The general idea is that Part 1 will ground us, in as an accessible way as I can make it, in some of the key ideas and concepts which set up what I am attempting to offer. Part 2 is more about 'the core' of the perspective that I develop, with Part 3 the 'what next?' section. So if you are in a hurry, maybe somebody who has a decent grasp of some of the key terms (e.g. sociomateriality and posthumanism) then you may well want to speed onto Part 2. However, my hope is that you may take time, i.e. that is does not feel too much like (hard) work, and that you just want to get to the end as quickly as possible. Although with the best will in the world I am not a celebrated literary figure like Kazuo Ishiguro or Ursula K Le Guin – not that I find it easy to feel like I have understood their books. So I have included sub-headings throughout the chapters in an attempt to help readers to be able to dot around more easily. Oh, and it may jar but I am quite into 'conditionality', which means at times that I am often very (perhaps overly) tentative about claims to knowing things in my writing. The conditionality goes with the territories of ideas that we are going to explore. Also, I do have some 'unconventional' grammar in my writing (potentially some verb-less sentences!), that is just what I tend to do in text assembly to make things sound right to me. Sorry, I must have missed those English grammar lessons when they tell you the right way to write. And, just to mention my hoped view of a reader would be more chilling out in a comfy chair, than sat at a desk anxiously thumbing or scrolling the pages with one eye on the clock.

It is also important to be up front that this book is not written in what might be regarded as 'conventional' academic prose. Although you are likely already picking that up from these opening paragraphs. This is a book which I would, perhaps slightly boldly, call a creative piece of academic writing. This is because, we will consider the situatedness and contingency of assembling this book, doing so is important to 'opening up the writing' and expressing the perspective offered. However, something notable in the text so far may well be the inclusion of 'I' which is often disparaged in academic writing.

The expulsion of 'I' is generally about notions of being 'scientific', 'detached' and 'objective' (these notions are considered in Chapter 2), ideals which as we will explore are very much at odds with the perspective I am going to offer. It is fair to say that creative academic writing is not always welcomed with open arms. For example, when I sought to 'package' some pieces a text from this book into a conference paper it seemed to be met with bewilderment more than excitement by its audience. The conference paper probably did not do what was expected of it i.e. a thorough review of literature with a keen focus on how what it offers adds to some very specific debates. Instead as this book does it creatively roved around between writer impulses endeavouring to 'break the mould' in its searching for something different, challenging and exciting. The conference paper appeared to land more as a bemusing 'mash-up' than some pieces of carefully crafted writing for prompting reflection and imagination. Writing creatively is risky because it puts you in tension with was is appropriate and expected as 'academic'. We will explore more about these potential tensions in later chapters.

There will be in-text citations, although we have not had any so far, there are some coming soon. My attempted creative writing approach does not remove a need for making connections to and referencing other texts. Admittedly having in-text citations (e.g. Smith, 2020) may well feel very much from the preserve of 'conventional' academic writing, that as I have mentioned, I am seeking to disassociate from in my approach to writing this book. However, in-text citations are in this book because there is a very practical need to draw upon, connect with, and acknowledge others writing in developing the perspective that I will offer. 'Footnote referencing' is a possible option whereby you have superscript numbers next to pieces of text which relate to a bibliography at the end. By doing things that way you do alleviate the inclusion in-text citations as they are replaced by those quite endearing little numbers (e.g. '[1]'). Which means that at first glance a page of text could be mistaken for that of an enticing fiction novel. There are benefits to doing footnote referencing, although I am not totally sure my Zotero reference management software, with its various 'plug-ins' and 'extensions', which handles the in-text citing on my behalf, is completely au-fait with such things. Also, doing referencing that way means that the names of authors whose writings you are connecting to are relegated to 'the back', and so somewhat hidden and obscured. Perhaps I am being over sensitive here, but the acknowledgement of others is inserted 'behind your text' so your reader is not distracted by these names of others (unless they thumb or scroll to the back pages). Anyway, like it or not, there will be names and years with brackets in the text in this creative academic writing endeavour.

Qualities of 'good' books

Whatever way you have found yourself here to be reading, eagerly or not so eagerly, the first paragraphs of this book, from what I understand the general idea is that we (author-reader) get along well enough via the text and images so that you keep reading. I understand that getting along well enough involves your interpretations of the text and images satisfying your interests enough (or is successfully distracting you from something else that you want to avoid doing, like the ironing or washing up!) so that you can appreciate reading it as an enjoyable and worthwhile use of your time. It sounds a simple enough relationship, but as a reader I notice that I do often approach books with some pretty high expectations.

When starting to read a book I can feel excited that this could be *the* book, the one that I just want to shut out everything else and give my full attention from the first to the last page. In reading the pages contained between the book's covers (so far I can not contemplate trying to read whole books on a computer screen) I have some over-hyped and unrealistic expectations that this could be the one. That the assembled text will transform my understanding of being-in-a-world in new and wonderful ways. Books I am referring to here are non-fiction and what might likely be described as associated with, the already mentioned, category called 'academic'.

Academic is a category which is given a strong whiff of pointlessness by the online Cambridge Dictionary in which the definition includes: 'based on ideas and theories and not related to practical effects in real life'. Unfortunately, I have not managed to make it through many fiction books as I tend to read short sections at a time, typically before going to sleep at the end the day, and get easily lost and frustrated in the multitude of names of characters and places written about. Some examples of academic books which I have read, that I would point to the copy on my bookshelf as particularly significant and offer an excited recommendation to others include: Edward Goldsmith's (1996) 'The way: an ecological world view'; Kenneth Gergen's (2009) 'Relational being: beyond self and community'; and, John Law's (2004) 'After method: mess in social science research'. I don't imagine that you will find these books on any bestseller list, with tens of thousands of copies in circulation, but that is in many ways part of their attraction, you have to hunt them out. They are not trying to tell you of their existence via a poster advertisement at a train station or bus stop. Or, placed on full display so that you almost trip over them on the way into your local book shop. My moments of encountering and reading these books happened over a decade ago during studying fulltime for a doctorate and so I was expected, and it was legitimate, to spend days reading a whole book. Also, I had time to search and find them amongst the reams of writings that are available. Admittedly, these three books I have mentioned are all written by men, who were/are located in Britain or the US, but please bear with me I promise there is more diversity in my influences.

These three books are well written in the sense that they explore, explain and exemplify the perspectives that they develop. By perspectives I mean that through engaging with philosophies of how we understand ourselves, and can know about being-in-a-world, they raise questions about dominant or taken-for-granted viewpoints. And, in doing so offer new attentions and ways of making sense. For example, in Gergen's (2009) book he explores and explodes the concept of bounded separate human selves with private experiences. He does so by considering the implications of, and possibilities for, understanding all action and knowledge as produced through relating and participating with other people. These books are exciting to read as I, the reader, am challenged to reflect on what might be understood as 'conventional thinking', that I have likely 'taken-for-granted', and so am unsettled to reflect on how I might need to re-see my everyday existence. Consequently, such writing can be understood to be at a radical edge of, taking some words from Law (2004), pushing us to question and 'extend visibility' through offering new perspectives that can help us to notice the blinkers and assumptions that we impose on how we understand our world and the possibilities that we have for action. In the case of Goldsmith (1996), he draws sharp contrasts between different historically and geographically located peoples to bring forward 'peculiarities' of contemporary societies' relationships with 'nature', 'ecologies' and the 'nonhuman' world. For example, how modern societies can elevate ideas of economic growth to become a guiding principle, that is ignorant of feedbacks between societies and the bio-physical world which enables and sustains economic activities.

These three books, as part of attempting to put across to readers that they need to pay attention and keep reading, seek to draw you in with compelling narratives, and by setting out issues of significance, that together we need to overcome. However, a key quality of the writing is about raising questions and offering a perspective, rather than asserting to have *the* perspective on knowing what to do about the topics being considered. The use of 'technical' terms and language means that these books are most easily associated with the category of writing called 'academic'. Some of the words and terms used within these books means that the writing will exclude people who would not see themselves as associating, or being able to associate, with 'academic'. Other people might see such titles as leisure reading, but to associate with them in this way you would likely have participated in some university education in English (or another language in to which a book has been translated). What this means is that 'technical' terms as being exclusive is a potential issue for authors.

To write as clearly and as straight-forwardly as possible is a good aim, although it is not often so clear cut as to what that might involve given the unknown variety of readers, and their potential for interpreting texts. Some words that are written to offer certain meanings and explain certain phenomenon, will not often be used in daily exchanges, and so will appear exotic and obscure to many. A glossary does help (for example, Law (2004) offers one that I appreciated as part of interpreting his book) and I was considering including one in this book. The idea with a glossary is that it should help orientate you if you feel lost with a term which has been dropped in with limited introduction and explanation. However, it could have the effect of being overly controlling upon how the text might be interpreted (i.e. by suggesting this is *the* meaning which you as reader must adhere to). Consequently, glossary presentations of definitions could well mask some important differences in meanings which have been attributed to the terms written about. Also, the convention is for glossaries to be organized alphabetically into a list, this can give an encyclopedia-like impression. In the end I decided against a glossary as I want to try to take care with giving 'good' explanations in the 'main text', avoiding sending you off, to find the glossary, either on some page turning mission, or scrolling adventure if you are reading a digital copy, from which you might not return.

Where I have been hoping to get to by writing about these other books, is that there are qualities that I desire in how they have been put together which are important for how I am seeking to assemble this book. Significantly, there is a need to challenge the already mentioned sentiment of the Cambridge dictionary which attaches notions of 'academic' with ideas of detached theory which are 'not related to practical effects in real life'. Such sentiment can be connected with the not uncommonly used phrase that 'it's all academic' which is typically used when people want to suggest that something is meaningless to whatever is about to happen. This is very important for positioning what I am attempting to offer in this book. I am critically approaching social and organizational theory as a perspective, model or lens that we can use to help us to understand and make sense of a given situation, organization, community etc. This is quite different from ideas about theory offering an abstract or comprehensive representation of reality, or a prescriptive way to be or do things right.

Some comments on writing about theory and truth

When a theory is understood as a perspective we can appreciate its offering us a metaphorical pair of glasses to pick up and look at the world through. Based on the assumptions and suggested dynamics of how things happen, according to a theory, we can interpret situations and phenomena, with the potential to extended our visibility on realities. For example, we could apply a theory of personality, associated with psychological analysis, which suggests that we can understand peoples' actions, and how they might work with others, based on the 'type of person' that they are. For instance, you might hear somebody saying 'my team mate is quiet and not contributing to the group discussion because she is an introvert'. We can appreciate a theory of personality to be based on assumptions such as: people have relatively static characteristics which constitute a personality; there are various distinctive types of personality; and, these types can be identifiable based on how a person responds to a questionnaire. So whilst we might not agree with the assumptions associated with this theory, personally I do not, we can appreciate that this theory is a perspective or lens that we can apply to make sense of a particular situation or issue, and from applying it we can reflect upon its value for developing our understanding. Our reflection can then inform what we might do next with this new understanding, which will likely depend on our (dis)agreement with the assumptions which underpin the theory.

We may disregard or embrace a theory of personality, but the critical work it can do is to help us to reflect on the assumptions we have about how things happen. Or, what might be a 'good' way to act in a given moment. Or, what is the 'right' decision to make. Which means that far from being irrelevant to 'real life', we can appreciate academic theory as highly relevant to reflecting upon taken-for-granted assumptions which inform how we value and make sense of, and take action, within the world. As Ann Cunliffe suggests in her work on being critical:

> "In examining [our] assumptions, we can uncover their limitations and possibilities, become less prone to becoming complacent or ritualistic in our thoughts and actions, and develop a greater awareness of different perspectives and possibilities" (Cunliffe, 2004, p. 408)

In this book a key quality of what I am doing is offering a not *the* perspective. This means that whilst I will likely get carried away at times with the words that I am assembling and the theory that I am offering, like all viewpoints or perspectives mine has weaknesses and limitations. This is because, from how I am critically understanding theory and theorising, that is unavoidable. Significantly, as Gregory Bateson suggests in the following quotation theory is not truth:

> "Let us say that truth would mean a precise correspondence between our description and what we describe, or between our total network of abstractions and deductions and some total understanding of the outside world. Truth in this sense is not obtainable. And even if we ignore the barriers of coding, the circumstance that our description will be in words or figures or pictures but that what we describe is going to be in flesh and blood and action – even disregarding that hurdle of translation, we shall never be able to claim final knowledge of anything whatsoever." (Bateson, 1979, p. 27)

If I was understanding theory as truth this would be offering *the* perspective, but a perspective is part of a much more modest project in which assumptions are recognised and limitations are unavoidable. For example, I very much like Puig de la Bellacasa's (2017) notion of being 'critically speculative'. A notion that she describes as "an indecisive critical approach, one that doesn't seek refuge in the stances it takes, aware and appreciative of the vulnerability of any position" (Puig de la Bellacasa, 2017, p. 7). As with the qualities that I have suggested within those three books, mentioned above, which I found significant, similarly in this book I want to raise questions and challenge assumptions. Specifically, about how we can be responsible, and organize responsibly, in ways that pay attention to sustainability issues (including climate change and extinctions of species). In doing so, I hope to prompt imaginings and extensions of visibility about meanings of being human. The general idea is that by noticing and questioning our assumptions, we enhance our understandings about our potential responsibilities and consider what we might do.

I do get fed up when authors try to offer *the* perspective. For example, I recently read Malm's (2018) book 'The progress of this storm: Nature and society in a warming world', that was recommended to me, which in many places I enjoyed and learnt quite a lot. However, I had an ongoing annoyance with what I was reading being presented as *the* perspective. I don't know Malm, I have never met him, but from my reading of his book it gave me a jarring sense of 'my perspective is right, his/her perspective is wrong'. I am sorry to disappoint you if you want the 'right answers' from these pages to your questions, that is not possible. However, I do hope to offer writing about a perspective that is in some way enjoyable to engage with and helps you to pause at moments and question how you see the world and understand yourself within it.

I feel a pressure to hone a compelling narrative that will help us right through to the end of the book. However, as Gergen writes, in one of those three books I noticed as personally signifiant, we do not want to reproduce ideas of an "individualistic tradition" which "portrays the author as one whose mind is fully coherent, confident and conflict free" (2009, p. xxv). My high and likely unrealistic expectations for the books that I start to read involves the author needing to show me some care. In particular, what I am looking for is that if I am being attentive to their writing, I do not feel left to wallow in paragraphs which appear to be incomprehensible or un-connectable to the preceding words or images. Admittedly such a position, offering a 'compelling narrative', does seem to assume the possibility for a narrative to be communicated that guides readers safety through the text, with connected assumptions that the meanings of the text can be controlled by the author. For some time various writers connected with ideas of post-structuralism have argued that reading is ultimately up to the reader, as the reader interprets and creates meanings from the text (e.g. Latour, 1988; Sandywell et al., 1975; Steier, 1991). Post-structuralism might well have been one of those words I would have probably put in a glossary. If it is a new 'one on you' I would not get too anxious about it, I do not plan to type it much more.

You could probably spend the rest of your life reading about post-structuralism and its varieties, but to give it some faint definition here it is very generally a 'movement' or 'stream of writing' about how "knowledge cannot escape its limits" (Williams, 2013, p. 1). Some of those limits have already been suggested, such as with the quote above from Gregory Bateson.

On offering a compelling narrative I agree that meanings cannot be controlled and have elsewhere argued for understanding writing in relational ways, including referring to 'writing-reading' (Allen, 2019c). However, in writing I feel a need to respect and take care towards any readers. You could compare this to a metaphor of showing a visitor around your home. Taking care of the visitor would not involve them left on the door step needing to navigate past a locked door on their own. Or, leaving them in the lounge whilst you wander off into the garden without any attempted explanation as to how the showing them around might continue. Or, indeed if the showing around has ended and you are now moving on to some other activity, such as having dinner, a cup of coffee or some wine. In this process of showing visitors around you can not determine what meanings they might attach to your home and what it contains, but you can try to make sure that they get through the tour and do not have to perform any death-defying leaps to find their way to the food and drinks. Some people might like getting lost. Although, to continue the metaphor, that may well depend on the size of your home, but not offering a way to the next room or activity, or a suggestion that potentially getting lost is okay and part of the tour or activities that you have planned for them, is lacking some care.

For example, I recently took a book out the university library, which I was looking forward to reading as it was about the concept of 'presence', which I was writing about at the time and wanted to develop some understanding about meanings that had been attributed to this idea. One evening I had specifically planned to start to read the book. However, sitting comfortably on the sofa with a cup-of-tea to hand, and some background music on, I became aware that I somehow did not feel very welcomed into the writing in the book. To use another metaphor, it was like being sat on the margins of a group of people in bar or cafe, and despite your attempts to engage with the chat it was clear that a very particular conversation was going on, and this had been going on for some months and years, and frankly it was probably best that you just drink up and go home early. So that was what I did, after much sighing and puffing out of breath, thumbing backwards and forwards between enticingly titled chapters I slung the book on the floor, and picked up something else to look at. Defeated and deflated that I could not glean anything from the book, which related to ideas on which I was not a total novice, feeling an excluded and unwanted reader. That was the meaning that I attribute to that book. I do not assume that is what the writer intended, but that was the effect. Maybe you do not find great interest in carrying on reading this book, perhaps even at this very early stage you are already starting to wonder about how many more paragraphs you want to put some more of your time into. However, as discussed above I do not assume that I can control what you might take away from this book, but at a minimum I would like you to leave it feeling that you were made to feel welcome, part of a conversation. You were able to join in the conversation as you wanted, and although perhaps you did not much like the paragraphs that you were offered, or what you were shown, you were taken through a perspective that added something helpful to your sense of being-in-a-world.

There is quite a lot of advice out there on 'how to write', and some people make a living out of it. When I have been in situations where advice is being given about writing and how to write then somebody is likely to say something like "be clear about who your audience is". Certainly, if you are writing a book and are having conversations with possible publishers they want you to know your 'market'. How is your assembling words on to pages – which the publisher advises on and arranges to be printed and fastened together by a cover, or into an e-book file for distribution – going to be a commercial success? What other ideas of success could there possibly be! Well I suppose it is fair enough they need to pay editors salaries, printing and promoting, and you probably cannot sensibly envisage writing a book for everybody, particularly if it has sociomateriality and posthumanism in the title!

In very general terms the potential audience for this book would be somebody who is interested in considering how to make sense of and take action on sustainability issues. Their interest would involve wanting to engage in books as part of gaining detailed appreciations of the complexities of understanding and acting on the issues involved. If writing an 'academic book' is understood to involve developing a new theoretical perspective then it is very hard for this book not to be associated with that category, as this is what I have outlined as my primary offering. There are, as mentioned already, going to be some 'technical terms', but I have told you I am committed to trying to explain myself as well as I can. However, in response to the advice about knowing your audience I don't have a particularly clear suggestion about who this is. Admittedly books are most physically present and normal objects in sites of education such as universities, colleges and schools, as well as libraries and bookshops. Which means that for many people books are not physically present in the spaces in which they exist, and hence imagining involvement with a book, even of an e-book variety, is beyond what some might understand to be a viable or desirable activity.

I do not want this writing to be exclusive, but then that is quite rich given that I included words such as entangled, sociomaterial, posthuman and anthropocene in the original proposal that I developed for publishers. Ultimately my writing will need to be comprehensible to family members, as a key test of the explanatory quality of the assembled words. Fundamentally, if I do not manage that then I could well be significantly negatively impacting my most likely readership! Also, I would likely feel a bit defeated if undergraduate students that I was teaching felt that the book was somehow beyond their ability to understand its main messages, although perhaps many of them with so much other available text and media, might well not be that onboard with book reading.

You are doing what?

The decision to write a book is not an obvious choice for many academics in Britain these days, which does seem a strange situation. A book is not something that is often seen to have much value. Upon mentioning that you are writing a book your head of department may well look at you with some disbelief, followed with questions such as: 'What as well as needing to do everything else that you are expected to achieve in relation to research grants, articles in top ranked journals and teaching excellence, you want to write a book?'. 'Are you sure you have thought about this carefully?'.

When there is the research count up every six years or so in Britain through the 'Research Excellence Framework', the assessment of your writing is substantially about the journal articles which you have published, for exemplifying 'global significance'. Consequently, writing a book is most likely categorised as something extra to what universities' expect academic work to involve. At worst writing a book could be regarded as career threatening. Although if, having stolen your nerve in the face of colleagues raised eyebrows you have managed to write the book, it is somehow understood to be a 'good' book that gains some 'international recognition' of your work, and consequently your institution, then that may transform the book into being understood to be writing that could be legitimately valued as worthwhile academic work. There is of course the flip side to that, it may not! Alternatively, you may not care what others think about your book writing decision, it just felt like a good idea at the time.

The significant opportunity of writing a book is that it offers the writer much greater space to explain and develop ideas and perspectives than a journal article or book chapter. Whilst there is variety in the openness of different journals for creativity and non-formulaic approaches to writing. In the area of Organization Studies which I associate my work with, the focus can feel to be on squeezing the last drop out of each sentence to pack as much as possible into the space allowed for a journal article. There is much variety between journals, but to characterise what a journal article looks like they are about 9000-words long, involve positioning the research in relation to a particular topic and question of significance, describing how the study was completed, presenting and analysing the findings, and explaining how the study has extended our understanding to develop associated theories. The general aim of these collected parts is to bring them all together in a convincing way to show how the writing is developing active debates in a particular area of research. The results of these conventions is some less than enthralling texts. Of course slower explanations through a longer book with a much more flexible format may well not make reading a much more interesting endeavour. However, the pages of text that are allowed in a book (when I originally mentioned to publishers about potentially writing a book anything less than 80'000 words was indicated to be too short) offer a much more expansive canvas to hopefully be able to paint a much richer and engaging picture. Then, maybe, at least one square centimetre of the canvas can be a seen as a work of art! That is my hope.

I previously wrote a short piece about the need to challenge accepted conventions of academic journal article writing, which I shared with Amanda Sinclair who has written about developing new forms of writing (e.g. Grey & Sinclair, 2006; Sinclair, 2010). Sinclair's reply to me via email included:

> "I agree with the sentiments expressed in the short piece you sent to me. My own frustration with academic writing arises from a mixture of things. The way my heart sinks when I read awful, formulaic writing and my own desire not to cause that suffering in others. The thrill I feel when I read funny, surprising and arresting writing and my desire to try to do that too – to give people pleasure."

Writing to give people pleasure, rather than causing suffering seems quite an obvious target for the text that you may produce. However, as Martin Parker who also responded via email to the same piece of writing suggested:

> "Is most academic writing written to be widely read? I doubt it. My sense is rather that it is produced in response to the need to publish, the need to have items on a CV which in turn drives appointment, promotion, institutional rankings, salary and so on. Academic writing is, in that sense, not about what is written, but about the fact that it is written, and then counted, tabulated, and monetized."

From Parker's quote he indicates some of the ways in which writing is about suffering in the sense that it is about surviving at being-an-academic amongst a constellation of measurement devices and performance criteria. Consequently, Sinclair's suggestion that writing needs to be about pleasure for the reader, and likely inter-connectedly for the writer, can be recognised as quite a radical purpose. However, as discussed above, a book has different writing possibilities to a journal article. As explored so far a book is frequently set aside from journal articles as something else, something additional, because it tends not to be interpreted as core academic writing work. It floats precariously aside the battleships of academic performance criteria. If a book does not become a big hit, then those raised eyebrows of your head of department, might well turn-into utterances of "I told you so..". Of course those performance criteria only matter if you care about getting a job, and following that promotion and increasing salary. It can be hard to be ambivalent about promotion and a growing pay cheque, as those are some of the clearest symbols of recognition for your efforts. I would like to say that I am immune, but they seem somehow impossible to remove from my field of vision. However, writing a book, this book, does feel quite a subversive move, which probably sounds quite ridiculous if you have avoided being dipped into the worlds of academia. What is more, to attempt to write a book, in that category of 'academic', that you, the reader, are hoped to find pleasure is perhaps outlandish.

Writing-to-learn

Can I learn how to write to give some pleasure to readers who find themselves reading these pages? Of course I cannot give you any guarantees that you will learn something as I have no idea what you might know. However, at least somebody is going to learn something, because I am writing to learn. This is another apparently benign statement that could be shocking for some. Writing to learn! Surely you write because you know something and writing is a process of ordering those ideas to convey them to other people? Well sorry, as I tap away here on this keyboard creating the first drafts of this chapter I really don't have a clear sense of where this book is going, and that is why I am writing it. I wrote a plan which included a paragraph explaining what each chapter will include. Doing that was for the publishers as it is generally a good idea to start with some sort of sketch. However, I am excited about writing a book to learn, who knows what will emerge along the way. For example, the piece in the above paragraph about book writing sitting somewhat adrift from the performance metrics of academia because it is so often seen as something other, something extra, I found my way to whilst bringing those words together. So it is fantastic to wonder about what else I might learn on the way. As already suggested writing that is 'internationally significant' and articulating 'substantial theoretical developments' that gets published in highly regarded journals and gains lots of citations in others' writing can bear very little connection to the potential pleasure it offers to readers. Consequently, a book that we might regard as a 'good' and 'worthwhile' read, in the category of 'academic', can be a rarity. For both our sakes let us hope this book has a glimmer of a chance as being interpreted by others as one of those rarities.

As well as the exciting potential to learn about book writing, getting to the end of the project (I would assume that many attempts do not quite manage it) offers something of an enticing 'end product'. In its printed form a book involves pages bound between two covers, it is an object that can become physically present on a desk or on the shelf. Lots about working, inside and outside of academia, is largely invisible and intangible for others. For example, all the preparatory hours of effort attempting to craft relevant and engaging teaching materials and activities, which will likely be covered in a few minutes and then quickly become something that happened, of the past with little trace. Or, a stream of conversations and email exchanges with a student about how they might approach some of the challenges which they understand as part of their life. That stream of exchange, although there is some record, they do not retain any form, the student moves on, their interpretations of the challenges change, their situation evolves, other issues or opportunities take their attentions. So work can often be hidden and immaterial, nothing to show for it. A printed book you can hold it, turn the pages and when you throw it onto your desk it makes a noise on contact. If you put too many books in a bag they require some effort to pick up and move elsewhere. There is something physical, it materialises the work into an object. Whereas with those celebrated journal articles, mentioned above, they tend only to appear on a screen, and quickly closed and potentially forgotten about, it is rare these days to have a bound copy of the latest issue of a journal to thumb through.

Heavy books

I am not advocating that we need more tree cutting and paper copies of texts. Although the substantial material inputs that are required to enable the ongoing availability of digital copies of a text are neither 'clean' nor 'benign'. For example, the servers and data-centres which enable the internet connectivity to a digital article, and the components of the device which enable showing the text on a screen containing an array of metals, like those known as tin and tantalum (e.g. Simpson, 2012). As well as the significant use of water for cooling in some data-centres (e.g. Mytton & Ashtine, 2021). The use of such matter as we will go on to explore can really matter for ideas of sustainability. However, the physical presence of a book that you have written is an exciting outcome, 'something to show for it all' as it were. Albeit a micro-version of those wealthy people who want their name emblazoned on the side of a new big shiny building. A possible fear of being forgotten, of not being understood to have done anything that is particularly worthwhile. I suppose a book says "I was 'ere and look I did do something, it even has my name on the front". I better move on before I get too worried about this book writing being an overly egotistical endeavour and decide to call the whole thing off!

A couple of years ago I moved some books from my home to my office at the university. We had moved house to be in the same city as where I worked, and it no longer made sense to have the books at home. What I discovered when I moved about twenty of these books, wheeling them in a folding shopping trolley around the hilly streets of Sheffield, a city in northern Britain, to my office, was that they are heavy things. The shopping trolley still carries scars, with some parts of its metal and plastic frame bent out of shape from the substantial weight it carried. A realisation of the physical burden involved in carrying printed books around does take some of the edge off my enthusiasm to potentially add additional weight to somebodies' shelves. However, that sense is tempered with the, as mentioned, moments of being able to point to this object that sits and is seen on a shelf, a materialisation of work. A permanence to its presence until the next clear out, or some emergency fuel for a fire on a cold night!

A book can of course be too long. When I have picked up and begun reading a bit of a tome I can not help but wonder if the author could not have made things somewhat more concise. At least set themselves something of a word-limit. Maybe a weighty tome on your selves can be seen by some as a representation of their imagined weighty intellect, and so the bigger the better! Authors may have every right to assemble all those words on all those pages. But I am sorry, I do think that a really lengthy one from a single author, particularly of an 'academic' variety, which goes through the 300-pages barrier and beyond, gives a hint of authorial arrogance. My apologies if that sounds unfair, but there are plenty of other things to read and do, and so in my view an author does need to show some care for their readers. Perhaps I am being oversensitive but the subtext to me of a tome is that "I have lots of important things to tell you and well your life is rather boring, and you look quite ignorant so you really have nothing better to do than read all of my wonderful book". Personally I would say if you can't get your main messages over in around 300-pages then you probably need to start trimming words to show more care to your potential reader. However, that comes from a complete novice, who has not even written the first chapter of their first book yet! Consequently, I commit to trying very hard to not going on for ages and ages, writing about what could feel like repeatedly making the same point. Although that written the previously mentioned book of Gergen (2009) is about 400-pages and Goldsmith's (1996) is about 500-pages.

Anthropocene assumptions

How we can think about and care for the 'stuff' and matter (i.e. other-than-human) that we are involved in reforming and reproducing is a central concern in writing this book. As considered above we can give significance to certain matter (a book as a symbolising and being a somewhat indelible marker of work undertaken), but doing so has implications in relation to the materials and technologies that have been enrolled into its creation. As well as the potential consequences of how that matter (in this case this book) is part of interrupting and reproducing other 'stuff' and matter.

The Anthropocene, and assumptions about its significance as a descriptor of 'where we are today', is important context for the perceptive I develop. Anthropocene is one of those terms that as I am typing is still quite fashionable, but at the time you are reading these words could be a quite passé. Anthropocene is a word that has been put forward to signal a new epoch in which we can be understood to have left behind the geological period called the Holocene (Zalasiewicz et al., 2010). As others have explained "Anthropocene is a fusion of the Greek anthropos, meaning 'human' and kainos, meaning 'new'" (Clark & Szerszynski, 2021, p. 5). The distinguishing dynamics of the Anthropocene is that humans are understood to be the most significant geological force on a changing planet. Whereas the Holocene is characterised as a geological period encompassing what are understood to be environmentally stable conditions of the previous 10,000 years, following the end of the last Ice Age. However, geological periods are normally identified "by comparing one set of rock strata with another" (Zalasiewicz et al., 2010, p. 2229). If the Anthropocene is to be officially identified as a geological epoch then it would need to be physically identifiable in the sediment layers on the planet which have accumulated in recent years.

The technical specifics of the Anthropocene debate are not within the scope of this book, you may be glad to read, but the questions relating to this concept informs some important assumptions for this writing-learning project. The Anthropocene harnesses narratives of a world based on the accumulations of how humans have 'worked on' the planet, transforming matter to make and build 'stuff'. Doing so with increasing intensity since the eighteenth and early-nineteenth centuries in connection with Industrial Revolutions in Britain and other countries. A key thread of these revolutionary dynamics involves the extracting and burning of fossil hydrocarbons (such as coal, gas and oil) to power human activities. Consequently, the Anthropocene means more than just considering the geological matter of rock strata and earth sediment. The narratives of the Anthropocene involve bringing attention to relationships between human activities over the past two hundred years and systemic changes to chemical and biological processes. These processes include, for example, erosion and nutrient decline of soils due to the use of land for intensive agricultural production. As well as extinctions of animal species who have been displaced from their normal habitat, or have restricted availability of typical sources of food. Or, probably most significantly, in relation to the consequences of human activities, the increasing levels of carbon dioxide and methane in the Earth's atmosphere which are implicated in climatic changes, such as rising global temperatures (e.g. Steffen et al., 2015).

Anthropocene narratives open up questions about how the accumulated consequences of humans can be understood to be transformative to our being-in-the-world. Fundamentally, the recorded environmental stability of the Holocene has been interrupted by human activities so much so that 'thresholds', 'tipping-points' and 'limits' can be appreciated as being able to be exceeded (e.g. Rockström et al., 2009). Which means that Anthropocene narratives stand for ideas of a 'brave new world' (referring to the title of Aldous Huxley's dystopian novel that was originally published in 1932 about a future world), in which the patterns and cycles associated with conceptions of biological and planetary systems are altered to be measurably showing signs of 'abnormality' and 'new' feedbacks. For example, a simplified explanation of a positive feedback (in the sense of reinforcing a pattern) associated with climate change involves the melting of sea ice. Ice reflects sunlight back out to space, when ice melts due to warming temperatures less sunlight is reflected and instead more of the sun's energy is absorbed by the darker-coloured, and so less reflective land or water that is exposed by the melted ice, the increased warmth leads to more ice melting. An assumption associated with the Anthropocene is that there is 'something new under the sun' (referring to the title of McNeill's (2000) book on the environmental history of the twentieth century world), and that we are implicated in the emerging patterns of planetary changes which have consequences for how we can sustain ourselves.

The Anthropocene can be reduced to a currently fashionable global slogan, but brings to our attention a call to action that can be very challenging to comprehend and translate into our immediate surrounds. In this book we will explore how we can try to make sense of our responsibilities and what that could imply for our living and organizing in Anthropocene times. However, I do want to distinguish my Anthropocenic assumptions from aspects of debates that Zylinska has described as:

> "Popularized media versions that the salvation from the Anthropocene's alleged finalism will come from a secularized yet godlike elsewhere: an escape to heavens (i.e., a planetary relocation), or an actual upgrade of humans to the status of Homo deus. In both of these narratives Man arrives in the post-Anthropocene New Jerusalem fully redeemed—and redesigned." (Zylinska, 2018, p. 10)

As we will go on to explore, a perspective that I am seeking to develop in assumed Anthropcene times, is not involving hubristic human responses seeking ever greater godlike control. Rather it is about a modest searching for solidarities of vulnerabilty with the more-than-human.

Sustainability of what?

A topic of primary interest that I have used to identify my previous writing has been 'sustainability', it is a word that I have already 'dropped in' to this opening chapter. Like the Anthropocene sustainability is term that stands for some assumptions that are significant to my learning-writing. Sustainability is an odd term because in many ways what I have previously explored under the label of 'sustainability' is not about sustaining the ways we are living and organizing at all. I have been writing with others, joining expansive debates, about what we can do to think and organize differently to be more sustainable (e.g. O'Reilly et al., 2018).

The sustainability of sustainability is about us not undermining our 'life support systems', by for example not having polluted water and air, or an erratic climate in which we cannot reliably grow food. The general ideas is that we seek to have a "capacity for continuance into the long-term future" (Porritt, 2007, p. 33). As I have indicated through the introduction to ideas of Anthropocene, research in the natural sciences draws our attention to processes, in which humans are thoroughly implicated, that are involved in producing detrimental changes that can reduce the potential for life to flourish (e.g. IPCC, 2018; Steffen et al., 2015). However, like the challenges of a globalised narrative of the Anthropocene, how humans are implicated in activities that result in, for example, more carbon dioxide in the atmosphere, is not evenly spread historically or geographically.

I mentioned how the Anthropocene narrative often begins with industrial revolutions in Britain and other 'western' countries, and it is these places from which the accumulations of the implicated activities are greatest. Additionally, climate change, for example, is very much seen to be 'manmade', rather than 'human-made' because of the general social ascendancy of men over women during the past two hundred years, and beyond, in shaping how societies are organized (Plumwood, 2002a). Consequently, sustainability, like the notion Anthropocene, attempts to communicate to us global realities that we can draw upon as helpful motifs to call for urgent attention and action. However, in many respects these global problems can not be understood as globally made. That is not to say we need to root out the responsible few, although very financially wealthy people do have the highest levels of consumption with connected consequences (e.g. Gore, 2015; Sayer, 2015), but consider the emergence of the more problematic patterns of being and organizing implicated in unsustainabilities. As well as exploring patterns which seem to have the greatest promise for socio-ecological sustainabilities.

I use the term socio-ecological to indicate two assumptions. Firstly, that social values and meanings produce ideas of ecologically 'sustainable' habitats (for example, a 'beautiful landscape' or 'polluted river' are construed through ideas about how they should and should not be sustained). As has been suggested:

> "Ecosystems clearly cannot care whether they lose species, leak nutrients, or have their processes degrade. Such things matter only because people worry about them. [...] Sustainability is a topic of human values. Once this simple point is understood, dilemmas imposed by simple biological or economic conceptions diminish" (Allen, Tainter, & Hoekstra, 2003, p. 23).

It is this valuing and meaning making about how we are being-in-a-world that we will consider in this book. Particularly as to how the more-than-human world can be valued and have meaning in its own right, beyond any interpreting and valuing imposed by human beings. In many senses the terms sustainability and Anthropocene both turn our attention to how we might justify and reproduce our ways of working on the world. They are both terms with connected tendencies of editing out the valuing of others, and interrupting the potential worth of other living things for their own sake. Sustainability narratives tend towards justifying conserving the world which is portrayed as 'resources' or '(ecosystem) services' because of the value that they can bring to human living and organizing. For example, many environmental policy statements on sustainability, such as the United Nations seventeen goals for sustainable development, have been suggested to be underpinned by, and so sustain, anthropocentrism because they involve "setting 'humans' apart from (perhaps even 'above') the 'environment'" (Fox & Alldred, 2020, pp. 123–4).

Secondly, as introduced sustainability is about sustaining ecologies and ecosystems in some desired state as they are understood to be human 'life support systems'. What this means is that the justification or logic for the continuance of ecologies is based on equating the social meaning of their ongoing existence with enabling humans to continue to be alive. This is based on an understanding that ecologies support human life in ways that can not be substituted by human technologies. Consequently, the use of socio-ecological is also to signal that social and ecological life are understood to be materially interdependent (for example, people need to breath air, drink water and eat plants to live). This assumption about material interdependence differs from how we construe what, how and for whom something might be sustained. Related to Anthropocene narratives, sustainability refers to the sustaining of certain forms of 'environment' or 'nature', via meaning making, as in the first assumption, but also in how people and societies physically interact with the nonhuman world. Such 'physical interaction' relates to necessary bodily processes such as breathing, drinking and eating. Dickens (1996, p. 73) helps us to understand these assumptions by considering the existence of a fish:

> "A fish is certainly understood in different ways by different societies. In certain instances, for example, it may assume forms of religious significance which would be unrecognisable in other societies. On the other hand a fish surely has a real physical being, one which can be (and in many instances is being) damaged. It simply ceases to be a fish if it is surrounded by a toxic environment that kills it. … In short, there are real differences between how people construe fishes, but this is a wholly different matter from how a fish is physically constructed."

What we can understand from Dickens is that we value and interpret the meanings of nonhumans, such as a fish, in various ways. Importantly, the ways humans understand and construe the world cannot make a dead fish breath again, unless it was understood to be dead when it was physically alive. Assumptions about the interdependence between different beings and things involves a recognition that organisms have life beyond the human words and the labels that become attributed to them. Such ideas relate to what I wrote earlier in this first chapter about how the partiality and incompleteness of our perspectives on being-in-a-world mean that we cannot claim to speak the whole truth of the "flesh and blood and action" (Bateson, 1979, p. 27). Some material interdependencies may be known of quite comprehensively, such as through research from the natural sciences. However, overall it is assumed, such as in Gaia theory, or in Norgaard's (1994) ideas of 'coevolution', that "life and its physical environment evolve as a single entity" (Lovelock, 2006, p. 35).

Coevolution and emergence are at the core of this book's exploration into understanding responsibility, as a person, and as part of appreciating getting things done together (i.e. organizing) with an attention to addressing socio-ecological unsustainabilities. By drawing on writing about posthuman theory and sociomateriality I hope to write in ways that can extend visibility on our being-in-a-world to help us to make sense of what is now regularly framed as times of 'existential' crisis ('UN Secretary-General's remarks on Climate Change', 2018). Crises which relate to the undermining of humans' potential for existence due to the significance and scale of the changes to the planet that we are implicated in producing.

What next?

Some years ago I was in a meeting of an academic department in which I was working, when the Head of Department suggested that the main aims and interests of colleagues in the department were to do their research, over teaching. One colleague rather brilliantly piped up in response that she disagreed, and understood her main aim as an academic was to 'make a difference'. For me by writing this book making a difference would involve writing that can give pleasure to successfully explain a perspective which can help others to reflect on the potential (un)sustainabilities of our current predicament, and imagine other possibilities. Aims which of course are, in the end, down to you as reader as to if they can be realised. Additionally, I hope that I will work out ways to articulate the technical languages associated with the debates, particularly posthumanism and sociomateriality, so that I can draw these into my university teaching without worrying that they will come over as too advanced, complex or irrelevant.

We are heading into what I see to be exciting and stimulating territories of debate and inquiry. In Part 1 of the book I will continue to introduce and position some of the key ideas and associated assumptions related to sustainability, sociomateriality and posthumanism. This will 'set the stage' for Part 2 in which the dilemmas of the perspective that I am developing – *witnessing-being-witnessed* – will be explored. Part 3 considers some possibilities and potentialities for the perspective offered.

Chapter 2

Sustainability meets sociomateriality and posthumanism

Being human

My main hope for this chapter is that we can navigate through ideas of sociomateriality and posthumanism in ways that we don't get too frustrated and feel tangled up in knots about what they might mean, and their potential implications. To do this I am going to start off with some reflections on, and examples about, ideas of being human, particularly in relation to the concept of sustainability which was introduced in the first chapter. Then we will move into a discussion of some key philosophical underpinnings about the 'relationality' of the perspective that will be developed through this book.

A brief comment before we get going with the chapter is that I have used the term 'being-in-a-world' a few times in Chapter 1, and will use it more. It is a term that is about signalling that we are part of an emerging world, assumptions that we will explore in this chapter. Being-in-a-world has been used by others, like the philosopher Martin Heidegger. However, in case you were wondering I will not be specifically engaging with his work, as we will explore, I have other influences. 'Being-in-a-world' like some other terms, such as 'sense making' (in relation to Karl Weick), I do not understand to be owned and/or patented by certain authors, so can be used variously in uncommodified forms.

When I have read somebody's writing and then subsequently meet them, I sometimes get this sense of regret at encountering them. Their written words offered me new insights and perspectives which made me feel enthusiastic about them. For example, they may have written about alternative ways of organizing that, by challenging social injustices, can be understood as more sustainable. I assume that the writer's prose reflects who they are and how they can be understood as going about being-in-a-world. It might, but their writing more likely reflects their ongoing searching, or personal aspirations for, what they understand to be 'good' ways of being human. It is most probably more straightforward to assemble a text of ideas about progressive ways of being and organizing than to be interpreted as living out those ideas. Indeed, we might assume that the author has a clarity and coherence in relation to the ideas which they have written about, but a more conflicted view about how to, or the worth of, bringing what they have written into close connection with how they live and work. Or, perhaps, since the author typed those words, they became interested in some other ideas which means they no longer attach or maybe even fully remember the words they wrote. Or, maybe the author appreciates that what they write about, and how they attempt to live out their lives, to be separate realms. Or, perhaps they are much more able to be in control of how words appear on a page than in control of the choices that they are able to make on a daily basis. So in many ways the regret or perhaps frustration I feel when I believe that I have seen apparent disconnection between what people might write about and what they do, is likely associated with unrealistic expectations of the human involved.

A useful example of this potential for disconnection could be about climate scientists advocating for decarbonising how we live and work to reduce the potential impacts of climate change, and then flying around the world to conferences and meetings to tell people this message. The writing of a climate scientist could help me to make sense of how the increasing rate of burning fossil hydrocarbons (i.e. gas, coal and oil) to extract, make, move and consume things can create feedbacks to inform changes in planetary climate systems. Then through applying this understanding and using the language of carbon as a way to conceptualise how humans are involved in affecting climate, I could identify air travel as one of the most carbon intensive activities we can personally be involved in. For example, Kalmus (2016), a climate science academic, worked out flying accounted for more than 70% of his overall personally attributable emissions. Consequently, in this hypothetical case the regret that I referred to above about encountering an author 'in the flesh' could be that they are not visibly paying attention to their own advocacy by routinely flying in support of their work.

One way we could look at disconnections between what a person is saying (or writing) and what they are doing might be understood as a 'value-action gap' (e.g. Blake, 1999). Such an approach would relate to assumptions that people are able to fully reflect what they are saying in what they are doing. This would involve an understanding that a person has sufficient autonomy from the people and organizations to which they have relationships in order to carry out the actions that they have articulated as desirable. Hence such an understanding of the world in which value-action gaps could be eliminated would take a view of people as rational. Rational in the sense that they can substantially comprehend their world, are able to express their comprehensive understanding via words, and then successfully implement this understanding within their world via their actions. For example, Kalmus's (2016) account in the magazine article, which I mentioned above, of how he stopped flying and reduced his personal carbon footprint can be understood as a rational account of his actions. Rational accounts place the human being at the centre, as the knowing actor who through a sequential stream of intended and defined actions is able to predictably and comprehensibly command the changes which they want to make. This is a perspective, and as discussed in the introductory chapter all perspectives have their limitations. Such a perspective is distinct from the ideas about sociomateriality and posthumanism which I explore in this book and are explained in this chapter.

A rational perspective would be associated with being 'objective'. Being objective is typically associated with being 'detached' from what is being known about, by not letting, as defined in the online Cambridge Dictionary, your understanding being 'influenced by personal beliefs or feelings'. The origination of an idea of being rational is often traced to the writings of Francis Bacon and Rene Descartes. For example, in writing about sustainability Dresner writes that Descartes "put forward the idea that nature could be understood by the use of Reason. He firmly separated 'man', who possessed rationality, from the rest of the natural world" (2002, p. 9). Objectivist stances are seen to explicitly or implicitly argue that the knower contributes very little to the organizing of experience (Hughes, 1981). Rationality and objectivity are most likely associated with ideals, such that being understood to be rational and objective are 'good' and 'correct'. Additionally the terms are often gendered in their social meanings and interpretations. What I mean by this is that being rational and objective are most likely to be attributed to men, with implicit connections made to women being irrational and subjective. Hence part of recurring sexist narratives about who is most suited to performing different roles in organizations and societies. For example, there is a rich stream of work about the construction of women leaders and managers, and how they are portrayed contrasts with men performing similar jobs (e.g. Marshall, 1995; Stead & Elliott, 2009). The writing in this area challenges patterns of how interpretations of womens' work will more likely be associated with ways of being, such as 'intuitive' and 'emotional', which are construed as at odds with, and so detrimental to, being rational and objective.

Subjective is generally positioned as a poor, or even delinquent, cousin to objective. This is because it does not navigate the 'pitfalls' of beliefs and feelings, which from the perspective of objectivity are understood to be able to be purged from how we understand the world. Objectivity is a dominant ideal in a significant proportion of the area of Management and Organizational Studies which in broad terms my work is associated with. As such it can be seen as *the* philosophical perspective. In this book I am developing a perspective in relation to understanding sustainability in Anthropocene times. It is a perspective that rejects objectivity as a worthwhile and attainable perspective for knowing about being-in-a-world. In this book I am not going to be specifically considering the histories of contrasting philosophies. I am simply recognising objectivity as an idea and ideal which often dominates peoples' understanding about how we can produce the 'right' knowledge about the world. For example, it has been the 'neutrality' of scientific analysis which has been seen to give it authority within societies (Polanyi, 1962). However, as set out in Chapter 1, my two core assumptions relating to socio-ecological sustainability are that how reality is construed is based on the interpreting and valuing imposed by human beings, and that humans' existence is interdependent with nonhumans. Both of these assumptions do not fit within the potential for cognitive and physical detachment which underpin an objectivist viewpoint. Indeed, the very potential for thinking in detached ways, i.e. where humans are able to remove themselves and gain a 'god's eye view' of their world has been argued to be at the 'root' of our socio-ecological unsustainabilities (e.g. Bateson, 1979; Plumwood, 2002). This is because objectivist philosophy suggests that humans can be extracted from the environment which enables their humanity.

Being rational, as discussed, is connected with being objective. Whilst there is inevitable variety in the interpretations and meanings of different terms, such as rational, being rational would be understood to be based on knowing about the world objectively. That is to say that if you have done things properly and managed to cognitively remove yourself from your processes of knowing (i.e. not influenced by your beliefs and feelings), then you have been able to apply this 'neutral knowledge' to inform some ensuing rational action. For example, in the case of the climate scientist Peter Kalmus and his account of analysing his carbon footprint and taking action to stop flying. In many ways his account can be read as a rational and objective process of developing neutral knowledge via carbon accountancy about how his living and working is implicated in carbon accumulating in the atmosphere. I have not spoken with Peter about this process, but he has successfully reduced or eliminated what he self-diagnosed as his value-action gap. However, his actions can be understood to be connected with a construed sense of being-in-a-world which understands feedbacks (e.g. the emissions that come out of an aeroplane in which you are travelling), that are based on an understanding of his interdependency with nonhumans. Consequently, it is these underlying assumptions of embeddedness which we can appreciate as informing knowing about a need to act. The inscribed rationality and objectivity is likely more about communicating and legitimating his actions in ways that attempt to convince others of a need and potential to act on reducing their personal carbon footprint, than fully reflecting how he might know about the world.

Appreciating embeddedness

I am not planning to complete an interrogation of objective philosophy and make claims about why it is the 'wrong idea' or gives a limited view of how living and working unfold. Instead I am acknowledging it as a perspective for making sense of the world. A perspective which is underpinned by assumptions that contrast to those that I want to try to live up to in the perspective that I am offering in this book. Such a perspective is one that engages with human embeddedness and so is attentive to appreciating subjectivities. In so doing it engages with broader ideas about legitimate ways to know about being-in-a-world, ways that would not be allowed from an objectivist viewpoint.

Subjectivity challenges the assumption that there is a singular objective reality to understand and act upon which is accessible to us as long as we can be neutral and disembodied. It achieves this by replacing it with a view of reality which is made sense of in relation to peoples' embodied and pre-existing understanding of being-in-a-world. New encounters are made sense of in relation to our existing patterns of meaning making, ideas are understood to be interconnected rather than discrete. As Polanyi states we are of our 'native roots' with our outlooks informed by our time and place of origin, as well as what has happened to us during our lives (1962, p. 322). Consequently, being human is suggested to be subjective, because we cannot somehow transcend our bodies. Indeed, it is argued that being in our sensory bodies is what makes us alive and so conscious of our existences. This means that subjectivity is not a hurdle to be overcome, or distracting noise to edit out to get to the 'real' truth 'out there', it is about appreciating how our physical and social embeddedness in the world enables us to know about it.

Subjectivity involves appreciating the perspectives through which we make sense of our world and offers us a humbler place from which to understand truths. Particularly if we appreciate that our words are not the flesh and blood of the world, but 'sound patterns' to help us to conceptualise, communicate and remember (Elias, 1991). Such ideas connect back to the suggestions that I made in the opening chapter about the meaning of theory and knowledge, when I quoted Bateson that "we shall never be able to claim final knowledge of anything whatsoever" (1979, p. 27).

What does this all mean in relation to the early paragraphs of this chapter and my suggested frustration with disconnections between what some people write and what they do? Well at a very general level, not taking-for-granted an objective view means that translations between our words and actions can no longer be understood as a straightforward process. One reason for this would be that from a subjective view of the world, whether a person is understood to follow up their written words in their actions is based within the viewpoint of the person making such a judgement. For example, we can go back to the example of academics taking flights to meetings and conferences to pass on messages about the need to reduce carbon emissions due to climate feedbacks. From the academics' perspective perhaps they see themselves as joined up in the sense that they have been able to reduce some flying by rejecting attendance at some other meetings. From the reader's perspective they may understand that the academic flying at all is contradictory, and so at odds to their reading of the academic's writing.

The understanding of reality, of being or not being contradictory, is based on competing beliefs about what contradiction in this situation entails. Subjectivity involves appreciating different interpretations of the situation based on the positions people may be coming from. Additionally, and significantly, if from a subjectivity perspective, we assume that we are socially, physically and culturally embedded, which informs our embodied and pre-existing understanding of being-in-a-world, then we are not isolated and detached beings that can act independently. By understanding ourselves as embedded, and not robotically rational with our words having a perfect and timeless correspondence with an objective reality, understanding actions and the possibilities for action becomes more complex.

By starting to explore this complexity we will through this chapter find our way to, and hopefully into, ideas about sociomateriality and posthumanism, and so justify why these can be helpful theories to consider socio-ecological sustainability. So far in this chapter I have, admittedly quite crudely, contrasted objectivity and subjectivity in an attempt to try to setup our journey towards ideas of sociomateriality and posthumanism. Terms or 'sound patterns' that could well be very offputting due to the technical jargon to which we can image they might be associated. Between, and aside from, objectivity and subjectivity there is much variety which I have chosen to ignore for the purposes of seeking to make a fairly clear and reasonably succinct explanation. Also, I could have chosen to set up ideas of positivism, in which the key idea is "that the social world exists externally, and that its properties should be measured through objective methods" (Easterby-Smith, Thorpe, & Jackson, 2013, p. 57). Against ideas of social constructivism "that 'reality' is not objective and exterior, but is socially constructed and given meaning by people" (Easterby-Smith, Thorpe, & Jackson, 2013, p. 57). I did not, it was just how things unfolded in how I ended up trying to juggled my way, in a few paragraphs, through a few hundred years of debates. Also, just citing an introductory research text book, a couple of sentences back, could well be seen to be limited, but my understandings have emerged in conversation with this text and so I appreciate it for its general definitional qualities. With these distinctions attempted I want to focus in on an area related to social constructivism by setting up how the perspective that I am developing comes out of assumptions about relational ontologies.

Relational realities

Relational ontologies is a key term which needs to be fully articulated, as the associated assumptions relating to understanding the meanings and implications of subjectivity is core to what I am attempting to offer in this book. I have encountered questions about how to make sense of sustainability over the past decade or so with some strong influences from work that is associated with the label Science and Technology Studies (STS). STS is the contemporary title for a multifaceted and multidisciplinary research stream which includes the philosophy of science and sociology of knowledge (Woolgar, Coopmans, & Neyland, 2009). The complex and contested nature of STS includes alternative versions of what the acronym stands for such as 'Science, Technology and Society' (Law, 2004, p. 8). Classic studies associated with STS 'follow scientists around' to consider the practices and processes of their knowledge making. For example, Law (1994) has explored dynamics of how scientists 'do science', organizing through and by the instruments and measurement devices in the laboratory. A core claim associated with STS is that the instruments and experimental arrangements of our actual and metaphorical 'laboratories' for studying the world shape our ability to know it (Rheinberger, 1997). So, if we return to ideas of subjectivity we can understand that as embodied beings with pre-existing understandings how we know about the world is also shaped by the methods and techniques we might use (be they measuring and counting things, or speaking with and observing people). Which means that such methods and techniques do not 'bring in' objectivities, but are themselves subjective by the ways they allows us to count and see world.

Let us take an example in relation to my home discipline of Management and Organizational Studies. You are planning to understand how people are motivated at work by asking them some survey questions about what makes them feel enthusiastic to undertake particular aspect of their job. Firstly, if we are understanding in relation to subjectivity that people bring meaning to their world, then motivation does not exist externally from them. We can appreciate that the term 'motivation' is a construct to help to define the intangible feeling or sensation of enthusiasm to complete some work. Feelings or sensations that we all may well experience differently. Motivation does not exist 'out there' to be discovered, it is a word, a label, a 'sound pattern' that has a meaning, in the language system of English. It has been invented by humans to attempt to make sense of, and grasp a particular felt phenomena. A phenomena which it is assumed is shared, or somewhat similar, between different humans. Consequently, the focus of our attempt to understand how people are motivated becomes defined by how the people participating in the research complete the survey questions. However, it is the participants subjective judgement as to how the words on the survey correspond to their felt feeling of being, or not being, motivated in relation to the different aspects of their work that they are expected to undertake. Tasks which are referred to through the survey questions in generalised ways (e.g. 'completing a report'), so not giving space to take into account the potential for any variety in how doing these tasks at various times might involve any significant differences. These differences could be both related to what is physically involved in the task (e.g. other people, objects or locations), and how a person might feel about them at different moments (e.g. based on the degree of frequency, or how tired they might be feeling at different times of the day or week). Consequently, the ways that survey questions are written, and the potential responses are constructed associated with a conception of 'motivation' will shape how the participants are able to interpret and express a feeling of enthusiasm, or lack of it, in relation to different aspects of their working.

We can appreciate from this brief example how the tools and techniques of our attempted knowledge making, in this case a survey about a concept of motivation, are centrally involved in shaping our capacity to develop knowing about it. Motivation as a framing makes the concept appear 'real', when it is not possible for us to express and collectively agree on what motivation feels like, and be sure when we had the same feeling as others. What this means is how we construe and make connections and relationships between concepts-questions-people determines what can be (in)visible to us. The worlds of natural sciences and social sciences have distinctions in their knowledge making associated with 'instruments and experimental arrangements'. For example, measuring motivation is different from counting atoms, but both need the imagination and commitment that either ideas of motivation or atoms are existing and so can be measurable or countable. Albeit that you can see a thing called an atom through a very powerful microscope, but you cannot see motivation.

As Law puts it, our 'methods' for getting to know about being-in-a-world "help to produce the reality that they understand" (2004, p. 5). For example, we can consider the writing of Sheldrake (2020) about his explorations of the 'entangled lives of fungi'. He explores how his participation in some scientific research about the potential role of psychedelic drugs, by taking LSD, helped him to a "scientific imagination" (Sheldrake, 2020, p. 22). Whereby he wanted to understand fungi, "not by reducing them to ticking, spinning, bleeping mechanisms", but "to imagine the possibilities they [the fungi] face, to let them press against the limits of [his] understanding" (Sheldrake, 2020, p. 24). Just to say, no psychedelic drugs were taken in the production of this book! And, hopefully none will be needed to cope with any potential pain associated with reading it! Jokes aside, this learning-writing project is about attempting to engage in some 'sociological imagining' (Mills, 1959). A project that is trying to be aware of how our ways of getting to know being-in-a-world are 'performative' (more about that term later in this chapter). And so I am understanding that we are compelled to imagine other possibilities that can take us somewhere that does not involve dark futures of ecological collapse. It is an imagination that, as mentioned in Chapter 1, is 'critically speculative', by being "aware and appreciative of the vulnerability of any position" (Puig de la Bellacasa, 2017, p. 7).

To understand more about the meaning of relational ontology we first need to make sense of ontology. In general terms ontology refers to the "philosophical assumptions about the nature of reality" (Easterby-Smith, Thorpe, & Jackson, 2013, p. 18). This is very much the territory that we were in when exploring the contrasting assumptions associated with objective and subjective earlier in this chapter, i.e. if there is a singular external reality, or that realities are socially constructed by being given meanings by the people making sense of them. These are philosophical assumptions which shape how we might get to know of realities. Relational refers to ideas that are associated with a socially constructed view of reality. The main contention of a relational ontology is that "relations between entities are ontologically more fundamental than the entities themselves" (Wildman, 2010, p. 55). So if ontology as explained is about the 'nature of reality' then reality in a relational ontology is assumed to be best understood through an appreciation of the relations between entities. Which means that to understand how we socially construct the world, the focus is on how we relate meanings to physical entities (e.g. a sturdy tree, or some beautiful flowers), and how associations are interpreted, and connections made, between them and ourselves.

In a relational ontology it is understood that every being and thing is only meaningful and/or alive because of its relations with other beings and things. For instance, going back to Dicken's example of a fish in the first chapter, the fish is only construed as being a 'fish' through its connection to that word, a word/sound which has evolved over hundreds of years to become accepted as part of the language known as English to signify a category or type of being. Also, and most significantly for the fish, it is only alive through its ongoing relations with appropriate food to consume, and being in suitably clean water. The impetus behind ideas of relational ontologies is that to think about 'entities' assumes that they can exist independently of other entities, which as with the fish we can appreciate would limit our visibility on realities. As disconnected from the English language, and a river, it is neither a fish nor alive. A stream of ideas that I am drawing upon in this book which are based within assumptions of relational ontologies is sociomateriality.

Making sense of sociomateriality

Sociomateriality is one of those words that appears to be created to frighten you off reading any further. It is a word that kind of oozes "well I am so intelligent I can play around with such terms but you there, you best just put the book down now, you're simply not going to get it..". I have not decided to draw on ideas of sociomateriality to scare off readers, that would be madness. Although by putting it into the book title, alongside the word posthumanism, I may well have already scared off quite a few people! As explored in the opening chapter I am hoping that you are going to stick with me through all the pages that follow. You can run your finger over them right now (if you are not reading the e-book version) there are still quite a few of them, albeit at the moment I am writing this word those pages are yet to be written. If I lost your interest now that would be dreadful, but I don't want to get into pleading too much that could become more than a little pathetic, and maybe quite annoying. So I am best off getting us into sociomateriality, so that we can both feel excited about the potential of these ideas for considering socio-ecological (un)sustainability, and how we might make sense of what to do about it.

Sociomateriality is on these pages as it can help inform a productive perspective on the world. A challenge is writing about sociomateriality so that it can be made sense of. My plan is some careful language selection (i.e. avoiding words that likely appear too technical and specialist by making too many assumptions about what a reader might need to 'know' to make any sense of them), and slow description (i.e. using the 'room' of a book not to make hurried dashes between terms when we could dwell with them for a few moments longer to feel prepared enough for what comes next). Importantly, writing as clearly as possible will probe my abilities for assembling some text that appears to make sense, hopefully helping to convey meanings to you, and helping me learn-write. Also, I am going to 'discipline myself' to include a regular stream of examples, so that I ground the conceptual language in some hopefully graspable daily lived realities.

Sociomateriality is the combination of two words, social and material(ity). Social is related to ideas of society which is about things relating to human action, such as how we communicate, make decisions and work together to organize ourselves. In this sense social can be understood to relate to the 'world of human activity'. Material refers to those things and beings which are not human, i.e. nonhumans. Nonhumans can encompass much variety, as not human would include animals, flora and fauna, buildings, tables, chairs, toothbrushes etc. In Chapter 1 I wrote about how I was using socio-ecological to signify my assumptions of interdependencies in relation to sustainability. We can understand that material is something different and including more than ecological, in particular it incorporates technologies.

The addition of -ity to make material, materiality, is related to giving the concept a more active sense as something which is "an integral part of every organizational process and practice" (Cunliffe & Luhman, 2012, p. 99). So we might imagine material as a solid static lump of something, whereas materiality a fluid evolving body. Anyway as far as I understand sociomateriality, that is the general idea.

Sociomateriality is interesting because by bringing together these two concepts (social and material), it does not merely suggest that reality involves social and material aspects, but that they only become meaningful through their interrelationships. Hence the connection of sociomateriality to relational ontology. Social practices are material, and that material practices are social (Carlile et al., 2013; Orlikowski, 2007). A key claim is that:

> "Without the material stuff of our everyday lives, human action would not be possible. That is, practice necessarily entails materiality. And just as materiality is integral to practice, so is it integral to the knowing enacted in practice. Put more simply, knowing is material". (Orlikowski, 2006, p. 3)

I am not sure that in the above quote 'knowing is material' is putting it simply! It is maybe putting it simply as it is a statement of three words, however making sense of the possible meaning and potential implications seems to me to be a long way from simple. Perhaps a quote from Karen Barad, who is associated with the area of STS that I mentioned earlier in this chapter, can help us to consider this 'simple' statement.

Barad suggests that "we do not obtain knowledge by standing outside of the world; we know because 'we' are of the world" (2003, p. 829). It is a quote that I have used in writing quite a few times before because I like it. I like it because it assertively places our human-being and bodies as embedded within the world. The image that comes to mind is one of those pictures of The Earth from space, such as the one taken from Apollo 8 in 1968 called 'Earthrise'. A photograph of a blue globe with white swirling clouds framed by an eerie darkness of space. Our home and life-support system, 'Spaceship earth' (to refer to the title of Kenneth Boulding's book from 1966) with what some climate scientists describe as having a 'Goldilocks climate' (referring to the fairy tale story) which over millions of years has coevolved with life on Earth to make it 'just-right'. Consequently, knowing is not something that happens detached in a cloud above our heads, like those speech bubbles you see in comic books. Or, distant of our bodies in a galaxy far far away, like some kind of science fiction. What Barad is saying is that we know and feel because of our bodies being-in-a-world. Consequently, that we are materially situated is not incidental, it is fundamental.

Orlikowski (2006) who started us off on trying to understand this simple statement, goes on in the same article to offer us the metaphor of 'scaffolding' as a way to help to consider knowing as material. She refers to scaffolding, which is typically a temporary platform used as part of building works, by suggesting that:

> "It is useful to understanding knowing in practice as scaffolded – both culturally (e.g. through codes, language, norms) and materially (e.g. through physical objects, biological structures, spatial contexts, and technological artifacts)." (Orlikowski, 2006, p. 6)

In her metaphor the scaffolding might be temporary, in the sense of evolution and emergence, rather than in the sense that it can be taken down and removed. Orlikowski is interested in promoting the importance of the materiality of technology to processes of knowing. However, what she is conveying to us through this metaphor is that Barad's 'we are of the world' can be implied to mean that who we are, and how we know, are inevitability intermingled with the 'scaffolding' which makes us. What this implies is that we can understand that 'knowing is material', or that it cannot occur without matter.

A general intent of sociomateriality is to bring attention to how materiality can be entirely overlooked in how sense is made of social action. For instance, Dale and Burrell (2008) suggest that the material form and spaces through which humans act and interact have been ignored in how we understand and study organizations. They suggest that matter has been treated as "fixed and inert structure" which ignores it, consigning it to be a benign and unimportant backdrop to human activities (Dale & Burrell, 2008, p. 213). Or, as Alaimo writes "matter, the vast stuff of the world and of ourselves, has been subdivided into manageable 'bits' or flattened into a 'blank slate' for human inscription" (2010, p. 1). Whereas 'the social' is, in contrast, appreciated as being "active and dynamic" (Dale & Burrell, 2008, p. 213). Similarly, Law (2004) has suggested that within social researching there is a tendency towards understanding 'subjects' as active, knowing and influencing, and 'objects' as passive, knowable and formable. 'Subjects' in this case would refer to the human actor, versus the material 'objects' of their study. What these authors consider is how social and material have been separated, with one understood to be highly significant to understanding reality (social), the other much less significant (material). Consequently, when matter is understood as potentially important in how knowing and action unfolds, the need to focus on the relationship between the social and material emerges. Sociomateriality as a perspective, particularly in relation to 'strong forms' (Jones, 2014), seeks to bring our full attention to the interrelationships.

Challenging dualisms

By drawing attention to a problem, or lack of visibility about how knowing and action occurs, ideas of sociomateriality seek to overcome an imposed dualist separation between social and material. Dualist thinking and the creation of boundaries between things is often suggested to be a problem in relation to, for example, understanding the relationships between humans and ecologies. These language categories maybe functional for appreciating different types of things and phenomena, but delineating 'humans' and 'nature' as separate entities has implications (Bateson, 1979, 2000). For example, in my teaching about sustainability in a Management School I often draw upon some work which sets out three competing conceptualisations of business-society-nature relationships (Marcus, Kurucz, & Colbert, 2010; Stubbs & Cocklin, 2008).

Firstly, what is described as a 'disparate' or 'neoclassical' viewpoint. In this view business, as a process of converting materials and labour into income/profit, is seen to be the primary focus, and society and nature are separate from business and each other. It is assumed that business is "above nature" and "resources are free, plentiful and to be exploited now", with the purpose of business being "sustainable profit growth" with a focus on the "short-term" (Stubbs & Cocklin, 2008, p. 215). The second viewpoint is described as 'intertwined' or 'ecological modernization'. In this view intertwined means that business, society and nature are "partially separable [and] relatively equal in stature" (Marcus, Kurucz, & Colbert, 2010, p. 407). This assumption relates to business purposes being about pursuing social, economic and environmental goals, with connected ideas of nature as a 'stakeholder' with "technological innovation to minimize resource usage" (Stubbs & Cocklin, 2008, p. 215). The third view, 'embedded' or 'ecocentric' sees business as embedded in society, and society in nature. Nature is understood to be a "finite, all-encompassing life-sustaining system" (Marcus, Kurucz, & Colbert, 2010, p. 407), with an assumption of business purpose to be about "increas[ing] quality of life and enhanc[ing] social equity (human and non-human species)", with a long time-frame focus (Stubbs & Cocklin, 2008, p. 215). Consequently, in the discipline of Management and Organization Studies, which is connected to ideas of it having a 'practical focus', we can appreciate that the different ways of drawing boundaries, and creating categories between things (a philosophy) have some clear conceptual consequences.

We can appreciate conceptual consequences to be some of the potential implications to which Bateson refers to above. In this example, we can see how different (dis)connections between ideas of 'business', 'nature' and 'society' relate to, inform, or even produce different purposes for in this case 'business'. And, because of the change in purposes, changes the notion of business to mean something quite different across the three contrasting viewpoints. What this shows, as Bateson cautions us about, is that we need to pay attention to how we delineate in making sense of the potential differences between the aspects of the world that we are in. For example, where society ends and business begins, or where nature ends and society begins. Whilst these categories may seem practical, so that we can communicate with each other about a particular situation or issue, they have performative consequences, because they can inform different relations to, and so potential ethical connections with, the rest of the world. In this case about whether or not we as a member of a 'business' or 'society' have a moral responsibility to sustain or not exploit 'nature'.

To illustrate this point a little further, and show the ways and consequences of how things, people or phenomena may be bounded and separated from other things, people or phenomena, we can consider some of the writing of Val Plumwood. She writes about colonial histories and how the construal of various categories of 'Others' can be understood to produce and sustain patterns of domination (Plumwood, 2002b). Plumwood suggests that these patterns of supremacism and conquest can be understood to be underpinned by conceptions, of not just people from other parts of the world as different, independent and inferior 'Others', but also of nature and animals. These constructions of difference, and associated dualist meanings of inferior-superior, informs understandings of ethical relations between these created categories. She writes:

> "Anthropocentric culture often endorses a view of the human as outside of and apart from a plastic, passive and 'dead' nature, lacking its own agency and meaning. A strong ethical discontinuity is felt at the human species boundary, and an anthropocentric culture will tend to adopt concepts of what makes a good human being, which reinforce this discontinuity by devaluing those qualities of human selves and human cultures it associates with nature and animality. Thus it associates with nature inferiorised social groups and their characteristic activities; women are historically linked to 'nature' as reproductive bodies, and through their supposedly greater emotionality; indigenous people are seen as a primitive, 'earlier stage' of humanity. At the same time, dominant groups associate themselves with the overcoming or mastery of nature, both internal and external. For all those classed as nature, as Other, identification and sympathy are blocked by these structures of Othering." (Plumwood, 2002b, p. 11)

From this quotation we can appreciate Plumwood's argument for how these forms of linguistic boundary making have deleterious consequences for those on the 'lesser-side' of the divide be it gender, race or species. Whereby the perceived worth or value of 'the Other' is produced through its ability to "bear the likeness" or "be assimilated" to be like those colonising (Plumwood, 2002b, p. 20). For example, as we can see within the anguish and anger of the 'Black Lives Matter' movement whilst the physical colonisations of land between 1500 and 1900 in particular by Britain, France, Germany (formerly Prussia), Netherlands, Portugal and Spain are no longer occurring, the associated enduring inscriptions of separateness and difference are palpable for many. So from this example we can appreciate the issues of boundary making and assigning difference are part of a problematic process of (likely by the 'boundary makers') constructing value separations, whereby you can be bound into an ascendant or inferior position. This is because how you are bounded and separated depends on how you are perceived to be similar or dissimilar to those doing the constructing.

The consequences of these processes of Othering, as Plumwood suggests, are mouldings of ethical relationships such that all are very definitely not equal. In this case the performative effects of these colonising binaries means that people can believe themselves to be as the (inferior or superior) group to which they have been ascribed. What this means is that they can come to inhabit the imagined ways and meanings designated to that/their group. For instance, in relation to group dynamics we can think about the 'Blue Eyes, Brown Eyes' experiments of the 1960s by Jane Elliot. These experiments still receive attention today because of the effectiveness at demonstrating how easily prejudice can be learnt based on the imposition by people who have authority (the people doing the boundary construction) of arbitrary distinctions, such as eye colour (Holt, 2020).

By offering these examples in an attempt to ground the potential implications of how language categories create boundaries and differences I am aware that I might inadvertently flatten complex social processes in to mere 'language games'. In particular, in relation to humans and nature. As Dickens, who brought us the fish example that was mention earlier, reminds us:

> "...separations of human beings from nature is not simply the result of people having the wrong ideas about nature. Loss of biodiversity, the thinning of the ozone layer and so on are not occurring simply because we have the wrong ideas. Rather they are results of how human societies have worked on nature and how such work has led to, and been assisted by, wrong ideas..." (Dickens, 1996, p. 107).

Consequently, the power of language and its meanings should not be overplayed. However, we can appreciate it as highly significant in how differences, distinctions and divisions are enabled and persist. Indeed, if we return to the idea of sociomateriality, where we began this discussion, a key aspect of this notion and its conceptual possibilities are related to concerns that language has been granted more power than deserved (Barad, 2003). This is because, as explored, a sociomaterial perspective appreciates language and knowing as interrelated, and interdependent, with the materiality of the situation or circumstance (Carlile & Dionne, 2018). Indeed in relation to the mentioned 'Blue Eyes, Brown Eyes' experiments the action of prejudice is dependent on both the use of language and the social meanings and values ascribed to different words, in this case in respect of eye colour, and the materiality of people 'possessing' irises of different hues. So it is only when the social meanings of colour 'come into contact' with with the matter of peoples' bodies, in this case eyes, that it becomes meaningful for action. In this way, social and material can be understood 'not to exist in and of themselves' (Law & Mol, 1995). The words of colour have little meaning when they are not used in connection to irises of particular peoples' eyes. And, the irises only become appreciated as distinctive through the associations to different categories or types of colour, and in this case their associated value (superior/inferior). However, sociomateriality is something more than just described as it goes beyond notions of social constructivism.

Fluid matter

A key distinction of sociomateriality is that matter is understood to be active and dynamic. As Alaimo suggests "matter is not a passive resource for human manipulation and consumption, nor a deterministic force of biological reductionism, nor a library of codes, objects, and things to be collected and codified" (2010, p. 142). To illustrate the 'mutual enacting' of social and material Dale (2005) uses the metaphor of a river. She suggests that we can consider the social as the river and the material as the riverbanks. Whereby the riverbanks, are being reshaped by the flow of the river, but simultaneously shaping the flow as the "formation of the river itself is created by the shape and configuration of the landscape; as it moves over different forms of structure, over different types of rock, it is also shaped and changed" (Dale, 2005, p. 664). She also expresses how the separation between river and riverbanks can seem an inappropriate distinction as rocks and sediment are gathered into the river flow "held together as a solution, a suspension or emulsion" (Dale, 2005, p. 665). As she explains:

> "The river-and-banks can be seen as the mutual exchange of molecules, of fixity and motion, of solid and liquid, mutually shaping and reshaping. Together, they pass on down the course of the river. The fragments of rock and silt from the river bed themselves create something new out of the river, as the ox-bow lakes and meanderings come out of this mutual enactment of river and banks." (Dale, 2005, p. 655)

Chapter 2

Introducing the river metaphor for understanding sociomateriality: A first photo of the 'flowing' Riverlin Valley a few miles from our house where we walk and jog most weeks

As I set out in the Chapter 1 I am not trying to work out *the* perspective, but develop a perspective that can be productive to extending visibilities on our responsibilities towards sustainability. Consequently, in describing sociomaterial, I, and ideally you, will not be getting too carried away that this is how we must now understand the world. Any perspective will have its strengths and weaknesses, and of course we are going to value some perspectives more than others. Maybe based on their explanatory power, or if we were particularly taken by the person who wrote them, or by somebody else's account of the author or the ideas written. For example, one of the major challenges of sociomateriality is that things can get very muddy when all can only be understood in relation to everything else. As well as language understood to be fundamentally ineffectively, and unhelpfully, separating our world into categories, and bounding things to make them discrete. Of course, it is really hard to circumvent language in our explaining and interpreting. Sociomateriality has been suggested to be in search of that 'goldilocks' situation (to mention that fairy tale again) where we find a 'just right' somewhere between understanding the "physical world as a natural given" and "a strong social constructionism that only recognizes the social and cultural as meaningful" (Dale, 2005, p. 652). However, we need to remember that we are not looking for a 'just right', but a valuable perspective that can develop our understandings about the realities which we encounter.

On to posthumanism

From having tried to navigate us to a reasonable sense of the concept of sociomateriality I am now going to take the bold onwards move of taking us towards grappling with 'posthumanism'! Why? Well as we are starting to work out something about the lavishly named sociomateriality we might as well add posthumanism onto our conceptual bucket list! Some connections between posthumanism and sociomateriality can be appreciated. Particularly, to do with the interests and intents of these areas of debates. Specifically, posthumanism is concerned with reimagining humans and their relations with other inhabitants, and actors of the Earth, in ways that understand boundaries as indistinct between human/nature, subject/object, mind/body, and matter/discourse (e.g. Braidotti, 2013; Hayles, 2008). This means that posthuman theory "questions the relationship between the 'human' and other taken-for-granted categories such as 'nature', 'animals' and 'technology'" (Gourlay, 2015, p. 487). Consequently, a key connection with ideas of sociomateriality is the interest in disrupting and reconceptualising predominant understandings of linguistic-physical boundaries. As such both terms can be understood to have antecedents in poststructuralist debates (briefly mentioned in Chapter 1), which consider the performative implications of language and associated categorises. For example, the earlier discussion related to the work of Plumwood and decolonising. Performativity refers to the idea that the words which make up our descriptions of reality, are not mere descriptions but intervene in it by being involved in producing the phenomena they describe (Orlikowski & Scott, 2008).

Posthumanism is post-human because it is seeks to challenge or destabilise what are regarded as a humanist assumption that human will is the *only* significant ingredient for action and substantial source of control to our existence. A key strand within posthuman debate relates to technology whereby distinctions narrow between the capacity of humans and machines. As Hayles suggests "in the posthuman, there are not essential differences or absolute demarcations between bodily existence and computer simulation, cybernetic mechanisms and biological organism, robot teleology and human goals" (2008, p. 3). Or, as Bennett writes in connection with posthuman theory:

> "In lieu of an environment that surrounds human culture ... picture an ontological field without any unequivocal demarcations between human, animal, vegetable, or mineral. All forces and flows (materialities) are or can become lively, affective, and signalling. And so an affective, speaking human body is not radically different from the affective, signalling nonhumans with which it coexists, hosts, enjoys, serves, consumes, produces, and competes." (Bennett, 2010, pp. 116–117)

Haraway's concept of 'cyborgs', an organism that is both organic and technological is frequently connected with notions of posthuman theory to make the point as to how boundaries "materialize in social interaction among humans and non-humans, including the machines and other instruments that mediate exchanges" (1992, p. 298). For example, we could consider the joining of a satellite navigation device with a car driver as something new in the evolution of human navigation and wayfinding.

Navigation tools such as telescopes, signs and compasses have assisted human navigation over many years. However, satellite navigation has removed the need for human interpretation of the 'data' gleaned via the tool, instead a driver is just needed to point the vehicle in the direction prescribed by the device. Which means that we can understand the driving of the vehicle as a hybrid satellite navigation device-car driver entity (Latour, 1987), where human intention is merely one aspect involved in shaping the possibilities for action and direction of travel that emerges. Or, indeed another conceptualisation might be that the role of the satellite navigation device can be understood to be one of directional force to help to navigate away from, for example, a couple's disagreements on the route ahead. Whereby the pronouncements of the device become a novel focus for a human couple's directional frustrations, as if engaging in relationship guidance as much as offering instructions on how to direct the vehicle. Consequently, we can appreciate that posthumanism is not suggesting that the potential significance of human intention to understanding social action is redundant, but that doing so overlooks the relational ways in which our existence is organized. As Ferrando suggests:

> "Posthumanism is a philosophy which provides a suitable way of departure to think in relational and multi-layered ways, expanding the focus to the non-human realm ... thus allowing one to envision post-human futures which will radically stretch the boundaries of human imagination." (Ferrando, 2013, p. 30)

To try to bring forward some of the potential value of taking a posthuman lens to understanding realities, I am going to explain some analysis I undertook with colleagues about sustainability at an urban regeneration initiative in Britain (Allen, Brigham, & Marshall, 2018). Through involvement at 'Brownfield' we traced and analysed how (in)action emerged on sustainability. We explored how the human intentions related to "visionary, green-inspired organizational actors and leaders" (Allen, Brigham, & Marshall, 2018, p. 30), which are often understood to be *the* ingredient for societal and organizational change for sustainability, could be understood to be marginal in explaining how action unfolded. The approach to analysis involved attempting to pay attention to complex sociomaterial interdependencies associated with human-nonhuman interactions. To achieve this we attempted to map 'mediators' which constituted the network of action (Latour, 2005). Latour describes mediators as entities (which include texts and inscriptions, and technological artefacts) that are active in transforming, translating, distorting and modifying "the meaning of the elements they are supposed to carry" (2005, p. 39). Consequently, understanding mediators involves considering how, in all their variety, nonhumans with humans 'gain form' through interacting and co-becoming.

The categories of mediators that we developed in our analysis included: Measurement devices that monitor and automate spaces of organizations; sustainability discourses and peoples' ability to use language in practice (including spoken visions about sustainable futures); texts (funding frameworks, policies, technical standards, certifications, specifications and contractual terms); and, technological artefacts, or work equipment of varying degrees of sustainability (Allen, Brigham, & Marshall, 2018). We explored how nonhuman mediators were much more significant to how action emerged than the expressions of visions of sustainability by organizational actors and positional leaders. For example, we showed how the most significant aspects in shaping what sustainability became on this flattened piece of land for urban regeneration included: accounting processes, environmental policies, legal contracting processes, 'competitor' benchmarking of waste, energy and water, and, building temperature control systems. A range of nonhuman mediators, associated with other 'locals', which pre-existed the creation of the new space for regeneration. The combined effects of these mediators was to fix and automate what sustainability could become.

Posthumanising sustainability

What we can appreciate from this example of researching and analysing with posthuman attentions, is that visibility can be extended upon the relational dynamics of how things get done by having a preoccupation with considering the potential human-nonhuman interdependencies. As such decentring a humanist assumption that human intention is the most significant aspect for understanding the action that emerges. Consequently, we can understand that a posthuman perspective can bring an expanded awareness to exploring, in this case, the possibilities for progressive organizational changes in relation to sustainabilities.

Significantly posthuman sustainability takes on different hues to more typical conceptions of the meanings of continuities. As Colebrook discusses, in her writing about posthumanism, the assumed "value of continuity" usually associated with sustainability is about a continuation of human life in the same manner (Colebrook, 2014, p. 54). The continuity is mostly about extending "our calculative approach to the future" to make sustainability in human-only terms (Colebrook, 2014, p. 55). Similarly to notions of Anthropocene there is a centrality of 'global' or 'the globe' to the meanings and scope of sustainability. A 'globalism' that can be both potentially productive for imagining our collective and interconnected responsibilities as there is "no escape, no outside, nowhere else to flee now", but also problematic in creating an earth of cultures and beings that are homogenized and on a single timeline (Colebrook, 2014, p. 61). Also, as considered in Chapter 1, in relation to sustainability, such globalising of responsibilities can obscure how human activities (such as putting carbon dioxide in the atmosphere), that are most implicated in activities that feedback to create unsustainabilities for species and ecosystems are not evenly spread historically, geographically or societally. Consequently, Cielemęcka and Daigle attempt to imagine "an inclusive posthuman approach to sustainability [that] decenters the human, re-positions it in its ecosystem and, while remaining attentive to difference, fosters the thriving of all instances of life" (2019, p. 72). Such an understanding, they go on to suggest, means that posthuman sustainability "is about 'upholding' one another, supporting and surviving together rather than positing the human as separate from nonhuman others" (Cielemęcka & Daigle, 2019, p. 80).

By approaching sustainability from a posthuman perspective we seek to entangle ourselves with human and nonhuman 'others'. I use and develop the term entanglement throughout this book as it is a key motif and metaphor associated with sociomateriality and posthumanism, due to its attempts to 'break' with modernist ideals. As Latour describes:

> "Everyday in our newspapers we read about more entanglements of all those things that were once imagined to be separable – science, morality, religion, law, technology, finance, and politics. ... If you envision a future in which there will be less and less of these entanglements thanks to Science, capital S, you are a modernist. ... The dominant, peculiar story of modernity is of humankind's emancipation from Nature. Modernity is the thrusting forward arrow of time – Progress – characterized by its juvenile enthusiasm, risk taking, frontier spirit, optimism, and indifference to the past. The spirit can be summarized in a single sentence: 'Tomorrow, we will be able to separate more accurately what the world is really like from the subjective illusions we used to entertain about it'." (Latour, 2011, p. 21)

Knowing and being as we have been exploring are understood as entangled. In the above quotation, entanglements are about the inseparability of knowledges relating to differently identified subjects (such as 'science', 'morality', 'religion' etc.), with the subjectivities of the knowers. Entanglements mean that a notion of a pure and objective Science, based on the earlier discussions of STS, is not understood to be able to 'cut through' and 'separate things out' to get us to the right answers. What this means is that our interpreting, and the associated valuing that we impose, is inseparably woven within the words, languages, categories and subjects amongst which we have grown. Consequently, they shape our potential to know and communicate our knowingness. As with earlier discussions that is the 'social' aspect, and the 'material' aspect of entanglement is about our bodies physical situatedness in time and space. Both social and material are assumed to be interdependently related, as with the introduced river metaphor. These relational interdependencies mediate our possibilities for knowing and being. It is this notion of entanglement, which will be explored and developed further, that I am seeking to grapple with in assembling words onto these pages.

Posthuman writing

To continue this consideration of entanglement I want to discuss some earlier work in which I have drawn upon a posthuman perspective to explore processes and practices associated with academic writing (Allen, 2019c). I found this to be a particularly interesting and potentially provocative area to consider as if the sovereignty of the 'individual' human is questioned, along with the appropriateness of ideas of 'a separate person' or 'discrete author', how could writing be reconceptualised and reimagined? Also, doing so can challenge and unsettle accepted ways of writing which can imply distinctions and superiorities, that detach academics and their writing from societies and ecosystems.

To consider posthuman writing can be understood as provocative because authors can often like to be seen as independent creative geniuses who conjuror up their work in a vacuum of their own ideas and imaginings. So for writers and academics there can be strong identity attachments to 'my ideas', 'my words' and 'my writing'. Which means that to say to these proud people, well yes, but if we take a posthuman perspective we can see a lot more in these processes of assembling a text than the intentions and 'mind' of the writer. What do I mean by this? That some alien creature comes down and takes over our writing when we are not looking. Well, of course not! However, once we appreciate our selves and bodies as sociomaterial relational accomplishments then we can start to consider and trace the relatings that enable the production of a text. Indeed notions like 'I' and 'self' start to become a lot muddier to make sense of.

Post-structuralist writers (such as Deleuze and Foucault) suggested that the idea of an author needed to become something that is not related to an autonomous and humanist self, but as "the site of a collision between language, culture, class, history, episteme" (Burke, 2008, p. 167). These claims brought attention to how people can be understood as embedded within a socio-cultural world, and hence are produced by, and expressive of, the constellations of influences which they are born into, whenever in time and space. Which might perhaps appear to be an obvious ascertain, but was a radical thought in relation to the objectivist ideals that we considered earlier in this chapter, whereby knowledge can be considered to have a timeless, universal and perfect correspondence to 'an external reality'.

Posthuman theory can be drawn upon to extend post-structuralist suggestions by including materiality (involving technologies and ecologies), along with socio-cultural embeddedness, as active in producing boundaries and realities. In this way posthuman theory is interested in conceptualising 'entanglements', as discussed in the previous section, which means that in this case the 'self' of the writer is appreciated as interwoven within the relations of a sociomaterial world. Ingold offers a helpful example in which he suggests that our skin can be understood "not [as] an impermeable boundary but a permeable zone of intermingling" where "every organism – indeed, every thing – is itself an entanglement" (2008, p. 1806). Connectedly, from a posthuman perspective Bennett suggests that her body "is not fully or exclusively human", giving an example of the crook of her elbow as populated by bacteria, and so understanding her flesh as "populated and constituted by different swarms of foreigners" (2010, p. 112).

To imagine and conceptualise an author from a posthuman perspective I previously offered the idea of the 'unbounded gatherer'. This was suggested to involve:

> "unfolding mediating processes through which written arguments and conceptualisations can gradually and suddenly coalesce. Which means that gatherings is expressive of the wider institutional orderings and networks of practices through which it is performed. This is because the researcher's potential for the flowing of mediatings is becoming amongst the territories of available physical and virtual spaces, taken-for-granted techniques and technologies, as well as accepted institutional and societal discourses and languages. Consequently, gatherings far from being about a heroic researcher's narrative is more likely about the banality of every day movements – like travelling (or not) to the office, or checking citation counts on Google Scholar – which become important and repetitive spaces to relate with. Therefore gatherings helps to shift attention from seeing a lone determined researcher to appreciating research texts as intra-actional accomplishments, expressions of the sociomaterial mediatings through which they are assembled." (Allen, 2019c, p. 67)

Consequently, writing, can be understood to emerge through sociomaterial interactings, as with the earlier mentioned example of the performance of sustainability at the urban regeneration project, decentering ideas of texts as mirrors of writers 'internal' intentions. What this implies it that "images of the researcher as a vulnerable and confused refugee appear much more fitting than something resembling a heroic and knowing discoverer" (Allen, 2019c, p. 74). By returning to Dale's (2005) helpful metaphor of the river discussed above in support of conceptualising sociomateriality, we could extend it to considering writing from a posthuman perspective.

We could position the author as the flowing river being shepherded through the landscape by the evolving shape and contours of the riverbanks. Whereby the river and banks are mutually interacting reciprocally changing and being changed. The author as 'unbounded gatherer' accumulates and deposits the rocks and sediments of the banks, which informs the possibilities for what is physically present and available to become written. Potentially the author is consumed into a gushing channel patterned by well honed concepts, theories and ways of being through which they are reshaped – "flailing in a torrent of sociomaterial mediatings" (Allen, 2019c, p. 73). Or, perhaps their flowing involves moments of perceived calm or poise, to rub against and break apart contours of the riverbank to carry fragments of rock and silt in to different configurations and relations – "opening up possibilities for imagining and bringing ideas together" (p. 73).

From a sociomaterial perspective, in moments of authorial failing and poise, within the flow there is an ongoing sense of unknowability about the mediatings and interacting in which we are engaged, as well as their residual effects. To carry on the metaphor, the river, as author, and its banks are inseparably entangled. For example, without the banks the river can become a puddle heavily exposed to evaporation, and if the banks are no more acted upon by the river flow they become a raised land form continuing to be weathered, eroded and remade by rain, wind, ice and sun.

Hopefully, in the previous paragraphs I have managed to bring in the pretensions of sociomateriality and posthuman in ways that makes some sense. These are expansive concepts and I am not claiming to have distilled and summed-up the multifaceted debates in which they have been included. However, my key aim is to have started to have shown the meanings, implications and potential value of taking a relational perspective to understanding how we are being in the world. In striving to 'cut the crap' in my descriptions. By which I mean not trying to bombard these pages with technical language that sounds impressive but neither I, nor

Considering entanglements: A second photo of the 'flowing' Riverlin Valley a few miles from our house where we walk and jog most weeks

probably you, have any kind of common grasp at its meaning. In attempting to do so I feel like I have learnt quite a lot writing it, so I suppose as a minimum outcome it has been a productive chapter for me!

It is important to write here, before we move on to the next chapter, about how I am seeking to reflect a relational ontology in the text assembling of this book. Perhaps I should have written more about this earlier on, but it needed to come after some initial grounding in key terms such as sociomateriality and posthumanism. In particular related to ideas associated with the 'unbounded gatherer', as we have explored in this chapter, I am assuming my engagement in the world is about being mediated and transformed through my relationality with a becoming world. In trying to take a relational perspective I am endeavouring to experiment and explore how my practical engagement, such as assembling the text for this book, is "'contingent' (could be otherwise – but by no means anything) and 'situated' (reflective of the context in which it was produced)" (West et al., 2020, p. 318).

I am imaging an inability for a comprehensive awareness of my sociomaterial associations, but feel a responsibility to you, as reader, to bring forward what I can of my relational entanglements, when it seems to make sense. Also, the inclusion of some photos within this book is part of attempting to show some of the situatedness and contingency of my relational entanglements. It seems particularly relevant to include the photos because this text was mostly assembled at a times of pandemic, with associated lockdowns. What this has meant is that the physical 'local' of where we dwell has been quite all-encompassing. Hence the places of the river in the photos, which I have include so far, I have been regularly present within as I have been wondering (and wandering) about the possibilities for this book on being responsible from my entangled location in the world. On the topic of responsibility, in the next chapter we will try to draw the array of concepts that we have brought together so far into considering this key aspect of the book.

Chapter 3

Responsibility meets sociomateriality and posthumanism

Multiple responsibilities

This chapter explores responsibility. It is the final chapter in this first part of the book which involves explaining the territory and key ideas of the perspective which will be developed. Responsibly is a key term as it is concerned with how we could respond to our entanglements in unsustainabilities in Anthropocene times. We will first start with some general questions about how we might be responsible. We then move into a discussion of the possible meanings of posthuman responsibility. To illustrate dynamics of responsibility I bring in the term 'affordances', this is to help to explain implications of being responsible from a sociomaterial view. Also, the significance of unknowing is brought into view as it is a central appreciation of the perspective that I am hoping to modestly offer. The chapter is closed in a flurry of excitement, well you will of course be the judge of that, about 'witnessing' which leads us in to the details and dilemmas of the perspective explored in Part 2.

What does it mean to be responsible? Is a question that might be preceded by, 'why might we want to be responsible?'. Do you not think that being irresponsible sounds like more fun and whole lot less stuffy? Irresponsibility maybe has a romantic aura of something like 'that summer of total irresponsibility' probably in your late teens or early 20s. Maybe connected to notions of carefree, even some might say hedonistic. However, there seems to be somewhat of an illusion going on here, as those days of 'not giving a damn', are likely predicated on a sense of detachment from others. That might mean we understood ourselves as a free-floating entity, in some kind of individualist utopia to which we have no attachments to other beings or things. We just did not need to care about the consequences of what we did, because we conceived that there were no consequences. Or, maybe we did have a view of the world that meant we suspected that what we did was done in some concert with other beings. And, well we just didn't care as to what, or who, those might be, and how they might potentially suffer or otherwise from our actions.

Well those challenges to being responsible are perhaps quite, well, challenging. For instance, in Britain connected with a previous Prime Minister, Margaret Thatcher, who in an interview in 1987 with the magazine Woman's Own is quoted as saying "..there's no such thing as society. There are individual men and women and there are families.." which is a mantra that has become fixated upon, and so resurfaces from time-to-time. For example, it came back into view in Britain during the Covid-19 pandemic in 2020, connected with a need to understand ourselves as parts of communities and societies. It was about informing a responsibility to take care in our actions to reduce the possibilities of transmitting the virus, and in doing so avoiding causing harm to other people, in particular the most vulnerable. It was reported that the British Prime Minster, at the time of the pandemic, Boris Johnson, also a leader of the Conservative Party like Thatcher, as one of his last utterances before becoming seriously ill and hospitalised with Covid-19 said "there really is such a thing as society" (PA Media, 2020). Which must have felt like a bit of a victory for those of us who might see themselves as living in, being part of, or studying societies in which we are together with other human beings. We had not gone mad, it was not some completely imaginary and so vacuous descriptor, 'society' could even be publicly recognised by some of its harshest critics as something meaningful and important to life.

I have taught Corporate Social Responsibility for a number of years within Business and Management Schools, and an atomised view of society (or indeed that there is no society) is a hard place to start from in getting students to reflect on what organizational responsibility might mean, and how it could be achieved. For instance, in Chapter 2 we considered how concepts and language make and reproduce boundaries between things, such as business-society-nature (Marcus, Kurucz, & Colbert, 2010; Stubbs & Cocklin, 2008). If we reflect back upon the three viewpoints, even if we are able to consider assumptions underpinning the 'disparate' or 'neoclassical' viewpoint, where nature and society are understood to be separate from business, it is still assumed that there is such a thing as society. So a proclaimed non-existence of society can be understood as a particularly challenging position to approach if you are attempting to explore how we can understand and appreciate the responsibilities of organizations. This is because, as we discussed in Chapter 2, these assumptions reshape our understandings about the purpose of organizations, which means that 'organizing well' or 'doing good business' can have very different connotations. From some possible extremes of, squeezing out the maximum financial profit by ensuring everybody and everything involved in the labour and production process receives the minimum care and reward in the service of solely making sure the short term financial costs are minimised. To one whereby success is predicated on developing harmonious relations with humans and nonhumans, so that a good quality of existence is attained and sustained for the foreseeable future for all involved.

As I explore with the students that I have been involved with teaching in relation to meanings and implications of corporate responsibility, it is these underlying assumptions, that are most likely taken-for-granted and so hidden, around which key disagreements emerge. As we can envisage from the above contrasting extremes of 'organizing well', if we consider, very briefly, some high profile scandals such as the BP oil spill in the Gulf of Mexico in 2010 (for a timeline of events relating to the oil spill see – Guardian Research, 2010), such contrasting viewpoints could inform very different streams of action. From being a public relations inconvenience, due the potential ramifications to the companies 'bottom line' and share price. To an existential crisis of the primary purpose of the business, leading to suggestions that continuing to operate is dichotomous to developing harmonious relations with humans and nonhumans. Consequently, although from a very brief and 'flattened' example, we can appreciate the performative effects of different conceptions of how we are in a world to the responsibilities that we may seek to act upon. As Law writes "words have effects on reality" (2004, p. 162), which as we considered in Chapter 2 in respect of boundaries we are not dealing in highfalutin games of language and philosophy, but fundamental dynamics of our thinking-action, or 'praxis' as it is sometimes called.

To return to the potential position that there is no need for responsibility, which as mentioned is a challenging place to start a chapter (and in many ways a book) about responsibility, because as galling as it is, like the perspective I am developing in this book, it is a perspective. Although one which we might not attribute much authority or value to due to our assessment of the associated assumptions. Assumptions such as that we exist in a social-physical vacuum and anything beyond our own skin has no worth in sustaining. The particular problem with such a perspective of no responsibility, is that it is very simple, and hence has some good potential to become adopted by other people. For example, going back to BP in the Gulf of Mexico, if you come from a disparate view of the world, where all that matters for determining the success of an organization in relation to the consequences of the massive oil spill, is what an accountant signs off as the financial profit number for the company, this can be understood as a narrow and reduced perspective. Or, a position that Schumacher describes as "ruthless simplification", because of what is excluded (1982, p. 137). We can contrast such a view with taking an 'embedded view' (Marcus, Kurucz, & Colbert, 2010), whereby success involves paying attention to the flows and feedbacks associated with all human and nonhuman life implicated within the processes of an organization and the associated oil spill. You can immediately appreciate that one is conceptually more straightforward than the other. As the former may involve members of an organization asking priority questions such as "where can I find a 'good' financial accountant?", and the later "what is an ecosystem, and how do I understand how my organization is acting upon it?".

I am not intending on starting us off in this chapter on some corporate responsibility or ethics course, but am trying to shine some light on the challenges faced in making pleas for being responsible. The challenges include a recognition of some perspectives, potentially quite seductive due to their conceptual simplicity, which suggest that there is no need for responsibility. Although, given that you have got this far with this text, either you are desperate to develop something of a stiff rebuttal to what

I am suggesting based on ideas of responsibility being irrelevant and pointless. Or, you are in some general agreement that we are existing in relation to a world, and that we need to pay attention to what we do as our ways of being and relating have social and material consequences.

Posthuman responsibility

The posthuman perspective that we arrived at in Chapter 2 can be understood to pose some challenging conundrums for appreciating responsibility. In particular, the implications of a perspective that decentres the intention of the human being, i.e. you and me, in the action that emerges. For example, if we remember back to the explanations in Chapter 1 about book writing and intentions etc. we could suggest that they have a humanistic hue. What I mean by this is that I positioned my explanations in what we could suggest to be a 'conventional' way. It was an explanation soaked in a narrative of human intentionality. The general gist was about deciding to write a book, and then well just getting on with writing it. It seems pretty commonsensical really, I decide to write a book and so it gets written. However, as we discussed in Chapter 2 taking a posthuman lens to how things get done can extend our visibility on explanations that place the human at the centre, a directional and controlling being that is unfailingly able to 'sculpt the world as s/he wishes'.

'Common-sense' is one of those terms that is very worrying if we are seeking to take a critical perspective. As written about in Chapter 1 being critical means understanding social and organizational theory as a perspective, model or lens, i.e. not telling us the truth. Common-sense reeks of taken-for-grantedness and hidden assumptions, which if we are trying to be critical some big red flashing lights appear. Of course I am speaking metaphorically, although maybe somebody could have the ingenuity to do that. If they did that could be a fascinating cyborg human-light device assemblage! Anyway, the whole taken-for-granted idea, that a perspective, like the one I am developing through this book, is about shining a light on (not a flashing one this time!) to raise questions to open up new possibilities and visibilities. We can explore those possibilities in relation to writing a book from a posthuman perspective.

Potentially you might be reading this with a quite a strong sense that you are not feeling very excited about the prospect of being post-human. I realise that we have discussed posthumanism in Chapter 2, but I am aware that some people can get a bit worked up and dismissive of different approaches to, and views about, posthumanism. Although, admittedly it does feel a bit oxymoronic to be attempting to clarify my intentions about the use of posthumanism, when I am about to explain more about how posthumanism decentres human intentions in explanations of action. As I suggested at the outset every perspective has it weaknesses. One view of posthumanism is that it is about a project of anti-human despair i.e. that to solve the climate emergency we need to wait for a world that is posthuman i.e. beyond us, as we are all dead. I suppose if there were no humans left to care about biodiversity and climatic changes then in some sense the problems for humans as we understand them would no longer exist. However, this feels, quite literally a dead-end project.

Another view relates to the idea that posthuman is about "find[ing] our next teleological evolutionary stage" (Gane, 2006, p. 140). So that the post-human is after the human in the sense of a new step in some evolutionary process by which we leave how we were before to become something of a new creature-being. With this second view I would agree in many ways that, yes, we do need to do something differently if we are to address the socio-ecological challenges that we understand that we face. However, and proponents of this view may take offence, but I don't see that some posthuman all encompassing 'grand narrative' is going to take humanity to a new stage of evolution, rather that there could be patchwork of fragmented and partial vignettes which could variously inform doing things differently. Consequently, I am most easily connecting myself to a third view whereby the posthumanism perspective in which I am seeking to engage in this book is about "evok[ing] the exhilarating prospect of getting out of some of the oldboxes and opening up new ways of thinking about what being human means" (Hayles, 2008, p. 285). Which means that I see posthumanism to be much more about vignettes than grand narratives, as temping as it can be to feel that in some very board bush strokes we can 'put the world to rights'. Vingettes which, as Haraway (2016) writes in her book 'Staying with the Trouble', a response to the 'spiralling ecological devastation' of the Anthropocene: "make trouble, … stir up potent response[s] to devastating events, as well as ... settle troubled waters and rebuild quiet places" (Haraway, 2016, p. 1). Vingettes that "refuse human exceptionalism" (Haraway, 2016, p. 13) and avoid taking "a position that the game is over, it's too late, there's no sense trying to make anything any better, or at least no sense having any active trust in each other in working and playing for a resurgent world" (p. 3).

More comments on posthuman writing

With those three views put forwarded let us turn back to the posthuman explanation of writing this book which I have promised. In Chapter 2 I wrote about the idea of 'Unbounded Gatherer' in relation to conceptualising posthuman writing (Allen, 2019c). In doing so I developed these ideas with Dale's sociomaterial metaphor of a river, which we can draw on here to position what a posthuman perspective on writing this book can be appreciated to involve. To do this, as with some of my previous writing I will draw on Latour and his notion of 'mediators' to help to describe sociomaterial entanglements. Mediators is a word that

I did already dropped-in to Chapter 2 with little explanation, sorry, I will try to do that now. Gourlay has also drawn upon Latour's (2005) notion of mediators in debating posthuman writing – to explore how the entanglements of persons, devices and other artefacts produce writing and meanings – which she described as "changing and transforming texts as they interact with them" (Gourlay, 2015, p. 496).

In Chapter 2 I described some of the mediators which could be understood to be involved in 'displacing' human intentionality for visions of sustainability at an urban regeneration project (Allen, Brigham, & Marshall, 2018). To develop the metaphor of the Unbounded Gatherer, some examples of potential mediators from the analysis in the article, included a category of 'Discourses and associated performances of academia':

> "a research stream called 'Science and Technology Studies' can be appreciated as a potentially significant mediator. This subject area assemblage which can be associated with certain academic practices and identities, theories, conference arrangements, texts etc. can be understood as setting possible trajectories for unbounded gathering. This is because the emerging text becomes enrolled into and modified through the patternings of intra-actings that produce 'Science and Technology Studies' as brought together within the ordering of a particular conference and associated academic department." (Allen, 2019c, p. 72)

Consequently, from this example mediator we can appreciate the enrolment of the flow of the author, as in the sociomaterial image of river and riverbanks, into a space of academic debate. 'Science and Technology Studies', the description of the area of debate, can be appreciated as shaping the potential for flowing, and the rock and sediment (say, concepts and theories) that might be able to be brought into solution and so 'in conversation' with the emerging text. Another example mediator from the category, used in the article, is 'Texts and inscriptions' :

> "'transcripts of the interviews', documents created to translate the spoken words of the managers interviewed into searchable texts. These documents in electronic and printed format are generated by the author to capture the words and utterances of the managers. However, taken-for-granted practices and conventions of creating and forming these documents, for instance tidying up sounds into a coherent patterns of language, to enable the enactment of accepted qualitative analysis techniques modify the intra-actings they stand for. The resulting materials and the possibilities for searching and gathering within and across the transcripts transforms the potential ways meanings can be ascribed and supported in analysis." (Allen, 2019c, p. 72)

In the example analysed in the article, as suggested from the quotation, interviews took place as part of the process of qualitative research. In this case accepted ideas of 'a transcript' shape how the utterances of interviewees are encountered and materialised into words, and then the presence of documents with these words of the interviewees rendering them searchable. For example, by being searchable via key words and themes as search terms, the assignment of meanings to what was spoken about in a range of disparate interview contexts is made possible. In this case the flow of the author-researcher deposits these 'pebbles' of interview transcription, as social realities, on to the river bed which in doing do mutually reshape the potential for flowing of the river. The third category of mediator is 'Technological artefacts and writing devices', of which an example mediator is:

> "The 'voice recorder' can be understood as capturing 'verbatim' the spoken word which can be translated into text. The presence of the voice recorder is transformative to the research process, beyond note taking, by allowing the sounds of the managers' [the interviewees] voices to travel between locations and be replayed. Also, the sensitivity and clarity of voice and background sound patterns recorded enable and produce an organization of text into transcripts that extend the boundaries of the researcher's sensory awareness of the interviewing." (Allen, 2019c, p. 73)

In this example we can appreciate how the presence of the device produces an interviewer-recorder entity. Whereby the content of interview conversations are able to be transformed into a digital file that can be mediated in to text via processes of transcription, which will stand as the interview conversation. Indeed the interviewer-recorder entity, rather than an interviewer (i.e. without voice recorder), can potentially reshape what might be spoken about, due to interviewees understanding that utterances in this conversational context will be able to be translated into a textual format that can be variously reviewed and circulated. In the metaphor of the river the recording device could be appreciated as a stone which is able to gather more sediment (words spoken) into the river flow, to be transported to another part of the river, but also repel sediment (words not spoken) so that they are excluded from the flow. The fourth category is 'Academic publishing systems', of which an example mediator is:

> "'Google Scholar' is fleetingly mentioned [in the example given in the article] for the associations it brings to texts via the calculations of citations in other academic texts, in doing so implying and modifying the legitimacies and authorities of certain texts based on the speed and frequency at which they have been referred to in subsequently published texts.

> Hence, the ongoing algorithmic accounting preferences bring visibility to some texts over others, distorting intertextual meanings to reconfigure writing-reading." (Allen, 2019c, p. 73)

From this example mediator, we can appreciate how the measurement, calculation and display of the citation counts from an author's writing become performative to how writing becomes understood and value attributed. Consequently, a text becomes 'marked' through the search software algorithmic calculating that have been used to discover it, which reconfigures its potential for significance by either hiding it from view, to be rendered insignificant. Or, brought prominently into view with associated citation calculations marking it out as of greater significance. In the metaphor of river this aspect of academic publishing systems could be conceived of as a some kind of underwater plant, growing from the river-banks bringing with it prominently into the flow some tendrils (highly cited texts) exposed to be drawn into the flow whilst hiding others (those scoring low on algorithmic calculations) in the murky depths out of reach from being gathered into the strongest currents and eddies. The final category is 'Physical and virtual spaces of intra-acting', of which an example mediator is:

> "the 'Management School' to which the award of a possible PhD is attached for the researcher, stands for particular subject discipline identities which informs inclusions and exclusions of people and technologies into the associated spaces in buildings within which the author is provided a desk with computer. Like the spaces of interviewing the Management School edifice modifies the possible sociomaterial flows of gatherings." (Allen, 2019c, p. 73)

In this example, the mediators relate to spaces in which interacting occurs, particularly here the buildings of the academic department within a university of a 'Management School'. This is the space which the author's body regularly moves through to complete processes of undertaking research, in this case the completion of a PhD. Here the metaphor of river-and-banks can give us the sense of the banks as the spaces for the flowing of authorship being the banks, guiding the possibilities for movement and interacting. There is a fixivity of where the buildings are, with how they are constructed channelling possible movement through them, they are not like a tent that can be quickly re-pitched elsewhere. However, the positioning and placing of people and things within the buildings can be relatively dynamic, and hence can be understood as a space that is evolving via the sociomaterial confluences which occur within. The banks (spaces of the buildings) being reshaped by the human flowings, but in many ways holding their shape to sustain various patterns of movement and being.

About the use of 'I' and 'we'

By exploring these ideas of posthuman authorship, using ideas of mediators, I am hoping that we can make some observations about the implications of such a perspective for conceptualising writing, in particular how it departs from humanist notions. As we have considered the human 'I' in writing can be appreciated as being produced and mediated by a web of sociomaterial relations. We could suggest that a humanist view of 'I' would be the image of the author as 'boat navigator', in connection with our river metaphor, using their independent powers of propulsion to move through the water in whatever intended direction, when and however wished. Consequently, if we are to understand their journey, the author undertaking some writing, along the river we merely need to gain a clear explanation of their intention for the trip. In this way the 'I' is something of a free-floating self which can be understood as a discrete bounded being. As was mentioned in Chapter 1 a view that was described by Gergen as associated with an "individualistic tradition" which "portrays the author as one whose mind is fully coherent, confident and conflict free" (2009, p. xxv).

In a posthuman perspective the 'I' of the author is an entangled 'I'. No longer are we imagining the 'boat navigator' wilfully sailing across the river in ways of their choosing, but we return to our metaphor of the author as the river. As Barad suggests in her 'agential realist' account, "'humans' do not simply assemble different apparatuses for satisfying particular knowledge projects but are themselves specific local parts of the world's ongoing reconfiguring" (2003, p. 829). What this means is that the flowing 'I' is in mutual exchange and entanglement, conjoined with the evolving 'landscape' within which it is moving through. This relates to Barad's assertion that there is "no 'I' separate from the intra-active becoming" (2007, p. 379).

The mutual inter-actings of social 'I' in material 'world' involves considering the potential array of entanglements through which the 'I' is produced, such as we discussed above in relation to some example mediators. These mutual processes of exchange which enable living, being and meaning, understood from a posthuman perspective, give a diffused sense of 'I' in a text. As Butler describes the 'I' becomes dispossessed in the "crucible of social relations" which enable its telling (2005, p. 132). Consequently, the 'I' can be read not as one of control, coherence and completion – a "heroic discoverer", but more as something of inevitable and perpetual struggle for moments of clarity and orientation – "a vulnerable and confused refugee" (Allen, 2019c, p. 74). As described in relation to the riverbanks metaphor the flow is mediated in ways that the mutual affects can be unknowable and untraceable. The intentions of the 'I' can be understood as constellations of multifarious mediatings which enable the assembling of text. It is from this posthuman perspective that the 'I' is written on these pages.

I (if I may) also want to notice that I have been pretty handy with the 'we'. Which I assume if you have got this far has not been so irritating that you felt compelled to stop reading. Sorry if it was getting you annoyed. I suppose the 'we' is a bit trite and naff, and is not something that has appeared in writing that I have been involved with before. Except when I have been writing as a 'we' of co-authors. I first noticed the approach in some writing by a former colleague, which I have tried to track down, but failed. That 'stone' seems to have been swept away amidst the torrent of living. Clearly I am in need of being better mediated!

I noticed the 'we' in the mentioned article as it was a single-authored piece i.e. not referring to a plurality of authors speaking. Instead it was about talking to the reader whereby, "we have covered such and such..". At the time I remember not feeling overly enamoured with it, indeed in many academic settings with a positivist bent, as I mentioned in Chapter 1, the 'I' in text can be the subject of much scorn and scoffing with mumblings of being 'unprofessional' or 'unscientific' (of the detached variety). So the inclusion of a chummy 'we' goodness knows what some might think! Anyway, I have adopted this approach in this book, part experiment, part that as I set out early on I am trying to keep the reader (you) with me on this exploration of text assembling in writing-learning. So anyway that is my explanation of how it got there and some justification, if you are reading this then 'we' are somehow together with the text (albeit likely not in the same space or time), but 'we' are interacting via these words, paragraphs, pages and chapters and so it is something of an acknowledgement of that. Hopefully it is not too jarring if it is not your 'cup-of-tea'.

Affordances

We have been exploring the meanings of posthuman responsibility and authorship. However, if we reflect on the mediators which I suggested and explained so far, there appears to me to be an important dimension that needs to be noticed. This is that the mediators that are identified can be considered to be of a more human-created, than nature-created, orientation. Whilst we have been repeatedly coming back to how we are seeking to overcome, transcend, circumvent, or simply 'just get rid of' dualist divides, much of the work on sociomateriality I notice has a limited attention in its range of nonhumans. There can be much variety in a category of nonhuman including what could be regarded as 'human technologies' such as a table, to 'animals and ecologies' such as a bumble bee or a forest. Given a major stream of work developing ideas of sociomateriality is connected with studies of technology (for example, Orlikowski, 2007, 2010; Orlikowski & Scott, 2008) the attentions to machines, computers and other devices is not unexpected. However, there is a need for care when taking a sociomaterial perspective to not inadvertently overlook socio-cultural 'nature'.

There are significant potential consequences related to the mediatings of nonhumans as to what action and organizing emerges that is associated with 'animals and ecologies'. As suggested in earlier writing an example is "human settlements [which] can often be understood to be substantially organized by the physical landscape, such as growing from proximity to rivers for water and transportation" (Allen & Marshall, 2019, p. 103). The substantial consequences would be that when/if the river dries up due to changing climates there is limited potential for the settlement to continue. Hence the 'lost cities' of ancient worlds (Zalasiewicz et al., 2010). Which means that to develop a sociomaterial perspective requires us to consider how our possible entanglements include fundamental bodily exchanges with "the ground that we walk on, the air that we breath, and the water we drink" (Allen & Marshall, 2019, p. 104).

A concept that can help to enrich our conceptualisations of being within a sociomaterial world by bringing attentions to socio-cultural 'nature', as much as technologies, is the idea of 'affordances'. The concept of affordances attempts to bridge dualist ideas of the subject–object dichotomy, which we discussed in Chapter 2, by suggesting that agency resides in both subjects and objects (Gibson, 1977). I am slightly reticent about drawing in yet another concept into the mix that I am bringing onto these pages. However, in developing sociomaterial appreciations, particularly in relation to the metaphor of the river that we have been exploring, hopefully affordances should add some explanatory potential and clarity in considering a posthuman perspective, more so than it might overly muddy the water, so to speak!

The notion of affordance can add texture to bringing sociomaterial appreciations to an understanding of what actions do and do not emerge, because it is a concept that has been developed with particular attention to 'ecologies'. Affordances refer to how "specific action unfolds in that unique moment and situation, whom and what it enrolls, and how it affects the world" (Faraj & Azad, 2012, p. 255). The word speaks to what can be afforded, i.e. what is possible or achievable within the web of sociomaterial arrangements enabling a given moment of being and doing. For example, Hutchby explains how the dynamics enabling and constraining action differ between beings and contexts, e.g. "water surfaces do not have the affordance of walk-on-ability for a lion or a crocodile, but they do for an insect waterboatman" (2001, p. 448).

In relation to affordances the idea of agency, i.e. the capacity to act, like in other areas of theorising, such as actor-network approaches (Latour, 2005), becomes something that is not purely connected with a human being. Consequently, agency is understood as an interactional accomplishment achieved through the conjoined relatings of social and material. Much of the writing so far in this chapter has involved developing attentions to decentering humans (intentionality) in understanding how action emerges. Affordances can be a complementary concept to further develop explanations and implications of posthumanist understandings of being-in-a-world.

Like every concept there are contested definitions and conceptualisations of the meanings of 'affordances'. My interest here is in the work about affordances that takes a 'relational' approach – connected with assumptions of relational ontology considered in Chapter 2 – whereby any affordances are relationally "bound with specific, historically variable, ways of life" (Bloomfield, Latham, & Vurdubakis, 2010, p. 428). This approach means that affordances are not understood as "simply functional interactions, such as the possibilities for using materials in different ways ..., but inescapably relational and situated within historical socio-cultural evolutions" (Allen & Marshall, 2019, p. 106). As Bloomfield et al. express "the body comes to grant particular affordances to the (made) world and conversely, the world comes to be 'mirrored' in the ... action capabilities of the body" (2010, p. 429).

> "In affordance terms the (natural-artificial) physical environment affords different peoples' bodies differing action possibilities or capabilities, such as .. water afford[ing] different possibilities for different types of animals. This could be about peoples' skills or strengths, such as being challenged by their bodies' mobility, and how the ways the physical environment is constituted and construed shapes movement and the meanings of (non)movement, as well as how those movements relate to others' bodies, and the varying social

> values and identities placed on the ways people move themselves and objects." (Allen & Marshall, 2019, p. 106)

What the notion of affordances brings to a posthuman perspective is being able to offer further purchase on how our beings are socially and materially embedded within a world and it is that embeddedness that gives us life and shapes our possibilities for action. This is because "affordances brings a dynamic orientation to action possibilities which can heighten attention to noticing how materials can shape and be shaped through social interacting" (Allen & Marshall, 2019, p. 106). Or, as Hutchby suggests, "certain objects, environments or artefacts have affordances which enable the particular activity while others do not" (2001, p. 448).

To bring affordances into the posthuman perspective that we have been exploring we could do with considering how this concept relates to mediators. However, in attempting to do so I am concerned about ineptly pushing these differently grounded concepts together. Whereby mediators are most obviously associated with actor-network approaches and sociologies of translation, where as affordances are associated with ecological psychology. Although, Bloomfield et al. (2010) do notice a potential 'actor-network compatible' definition of affordances by Akrich and Latour which suggests it to mean "what a device allows or forbids from the actors – humans and nonhuman" (1992, p. 259). Even though the vocabulary of actor-networks is more than a little slippery the definition sounds enticing as it can be nice to link things together. I do admit to feeling regular needs for some neatness to feel sane, but my main reservation here is the move to the language of 'device' in the definition. My reservation is that 'device' takes me, and potentially us, back to (human) technology and diverts our attention from the more-than-human, and more-than-human-technology. As I suggested at the outset my interest in this fairly brief this movement onto affordances is that it is a concept that brings with it a resolute attention to the more-than-human beyond technologies.

With the river metaphor affordances could be understood as referring to the landscape and riverbanks in which the river has emerged. The landscape creating and affording the possibilities for the flow of mediatings of the river. The riverbanks afford possibilities for flow and are acted upon and reshaped by the mediatings within the flow. So the mediations are the processes of the sociomaterial co-mingling of flow-river-bank, and the affordances are the moments of possibility for the co-mingling flow. Although beyond this suggestion, based in metaphor, an attempt to bring together ideas of mediators and affordances could well be choppy water and is not something I have particularly envisaged attempting in this text. It may well be far too easy to inadvertently mix some established 'academic tribes and territories' who will become annoyed by my naive dabbling in their decades long debates. However, the main point as suggested that I hoped to make here is that whilst, as already explored, in Anthropocene times our technologies have propelled us to being considered the most significant geological force on the planet. Our potential to be such a force is based through our entanglements with non-human beings and species. Crucially we need to take care to not inadvertently exclude 'nature' from possible 'mediating' interactions by reducing the nonhuman to devices and technologies as 'tools' for human use. Or, becoming overly fixated by some algorithms that have been 'let out of the box' to become significant in how we understand ourselves and become organized. Importantly, by bringing attentions to socio-cultural 'nature', as much as potentially unruly technologies, posthumanism involves challenging and decentering human intentions as the expression of the action and organizing that emerges.

Responsibility and unknowing

From these discussions about our relational being, drawing on ideas of posthumanism and sociomateriality, we can understand that complexities emerge for how we might make sense of being responsible. This is because we can appreciate that our knowing about being-in-a-world is maybe not all we thought it was cracked up to be. What do I mean by this? Well, as mentioned earlier, the movement away from the humanist 'I' of the "heroic and knowing discoverer" to a posthumanist 'I' of the "vulnerable and confused refugee" (Allen, 2019c, p. 74). Because of the sociomaterial entanglements associated with a posthuman perspective our preoccupation can become about appreciating the dimensions of our unknowing, as opposed to some kind of resolute insistence on knowing. This is unknowing as opposed to not-knowing. Where unknowing is the "realisation of inadequacy to anything approaching full and comprehensive understanding" (Zembylas, 2005, p. 142). With not-knowing being understood as "a momentary state of, or temporary ignorance, that can be overcome to achieve a full understanding of the situation or issue in focus" (Allen, 2017, p. 126). This turn to unknowing is reflective of our river metaphor, whereby we can see ourselves as "flailing in a torrent of sociomaterial mediatings" (Allen, 2019c, p. 73). To be enlightened in this case is not about feeling some firm grasp of knowing about reality, but that we need the 'lighter touch' of unknowing to bring appreciations and respect for the agency of others in how we are produced.

Unknowing is a departure from ideas of knowing and truth, words which are likely connected with ideas of Modernism and dualist divides (i.e. knowing-subject, inert-object). Dualisms which allow imagined boundaries to construct distance between a human-subject to be able to know a nonhuman-object. However, as we have explored challenging these linguistic and performative divisions with a perspective of sociomaterial entanglement means we need different languages and appreciations for being-in-a-world. Ideals of full and comprehensive understanding can become replaced by multiple perspective taking to gain critical awareness of the assumptions that are guiding how sense is being made of situations and phenomena. As mentioned earlier in this chapter my reasons for engaging with a posthuman perspective and associated imaginings is about "getting out of some of the oldboxes and opening up new ways of thinking about what being human means" (Hayles, 2008, p. 285). Consequently, this is not an unknowing of anti-human despair as part of some attempt to wipe away notions of an Enlightenment. It is about seeking to find ways forward within our entangled predicament in a world of socio-ecological unsustainabilities. Ways forward that can productively work within the soup of Anthropocene narratives which, as explored in Chapter 1, bring attention to how the combined consequences of humans (as the most significant geological force on the planet), can be transformative to being-in-a-world. As well as appreciating the unknowability of how we are entangled in the sociomaterial reconfigurings of 'Spaceship Earth'.

In many ways, what I am suggesting, is that being responsible, is about engaging with unknowing. It is about developing critical awareness of perspectives and assumptions. To refer back to the Corporate Social Responsibility teaching that was discussed at the beginning of this chapter. In this teaching we also discuss notions of ethics to explore personal and corporate responsibility. Some of these theories of ethics include considering the consequences of the act (utilitarian ethics), the act itself (deontological ethics), and the virtues of the agent (virtue ethics). These theories tend towards a humanist bent, whereby they assume a person has some comprehensive understanding of the situation, and can trace the implications of their actions, and so is completely 'in control'.

They can certainly be helpful as part of taking different perspectives on the situations we may encounter to explore meanings of being ethical. However, they are not overly compatible with the relational view of the world that we have been exploring as part of the developing a perspective informed by posthuman and sociomaterial thinking. In searching for ways of conceptualising our ethical responsibilities in this perspective, theories about an 'ethics of care' appear helpful. Now I am not about to launch onto some discussion of ethics, it is not something with which I am claiming much theoretical agility so you will be spared, but I just want to notice the kind of ideas in this space that we are coming into connection with. As writing a chapter that is seeking to consider ideas of responsibility ignoring ethics could likely be seen to be remiss.

An ethics of care takes a view of 'interdependent actors within a social web' whereby ethics, and being morally right, involves avoiding harm through the 'maintenance of relationships' (Crane & Matten, 2010). Ethics of care is underpinned by logics of 'cooperation, compromise' (Crane & Matten, 2010). Consequently, the focus becomes less about 'getting it right', where there is an understanding that it is possible to figure it out, and more about being together in the most respectful and commensurate ways. For example, Puig de la Bellacasa (2011, 2017), in her posthuman informed 'critically speculative' approach to ethics and care, develops notions of 'matters of care' in relation to more-than-human others which involves engaging with their becoming. It is this focus on the ethics of the processes of being and relating together to which ideas of unknowing could most readily connect. This is because unknowing is about appreciating an 'unresolvable unknowability' that emerges from our sociomaterial entanglement (Allen, 2017). As mentioned earlier the posthumanist 'I' is one which is standing for 'constellations of multifarious mediatings' a sense of, or desire for, comprehensive knowing is incongruent with a relational ontology. Hence my repeated insistence on the assembled words in this book being about a perspective, one that is inevitably partial and limited, but is hoped to offer some useful prompts to understanding being responsible in Anthropocene times.

A(n) (dis)association

One thing that I do want to try to 'put to bed' now, maybe I should have mentioned this earlier on these pages, is my dis-attachments to Critical Realism. Sorry if this section jumps out unexpectedly, but having presented some of the ideas that we are exploring in this book, I have found it quite bemusing and a bit annoying when a few people afterwards have given me a nudge saying 'you should look into Critical Realism'. Or, 'what you are talking about sounds like Critical Realism'. So in seeking to address questions of that ilk, and help to avoid any more of those well meaning encounters I want to clearly address potential relations with this text and Critical Realism. In some ways, which I will now explain, I understand Critical Realism to be part of something of a counter-narrative to the perspective that I develop in this book. This is mainly because Critical Realism seeks to 'work it all out', avoiding and neatly tidy away entanglements.

I know, another damned technical term which has entered the academic vocabulary that has now been drawn into this writing! Firstly, if you have some attachments to Critical Realism that is great, I am delighted that you have found it a helpful stream of ideas, but I am not attaching myself to it. I have to say seeking to distance myself from Critical Realism feels much more an emotional response to the label and how I have found that the territory has been de-marked, than some substantial analytical engagement that I have had with associated writings. Critical Realism is a stream of ideas about a way of understanding reality which is generally traced back to the work of Bhaskar (1979). There are competing descriptions of what Critical Realism is, however in times of need I do like to turn to John Law's helpful glossary in 'After Method', one of the books that I mentioned at the start of Chapter 1 as one of my three favourites. He writes that it is:

> "a contemporary and politically radical version of realism. Building on the realist suggestion that empirical and experimental investigation is unintelligible in the absence of an external world, and human capacity to intervene in that world and monitor the results of their action, it argues that the world is composed of objects, structures and causal or other powers, and that it is the job of the scholar to offer revisable theories and hypotheses about these." (Law, 2004, p. 158)

Whilst this is complex theoretical territory and I am not seeking to develop some full blown critique based on this quotation, theoretically I have a problem with the notions of 'external world'. In particular its echoes of positivism (as mentioned in Chapter 1 – "that the social world exists externally, and that its properties should be measured through objective methods" (Easterby-Smith, Thorpe, & Jackson, 2013, p. 57)). I am not sure about Critical Realist claims to objectivity and I imagine they are variable and multifaceted. However, from taking a sociomaterial and posthuman informed approach to developing the perspective offered through these pages I am associating with being entangled, i.e. seeking to challenge and collapse linguistic boundaries, and in doing so find the notion of 'external' part of a very different vocabulary. Also, I have a problem with 'causal' as this suggests to me dualist distinctions of a subject (a person) causing something to happen with an object, with connotations of 'laws' and 'rules' of which understanding is evolving, but in many ways is generalisable. As has been suggested in writings about Critical Realism, sociomateriality is not easily reconciled into its ways of seeing the world (Mutch, 2013).

All that written, I do want to be clear here, I am not being dismissive of Critical Realism as there are many people who write and associate with this term whose ideas and writing has far more clout than words I have assembled. However, Critical Realism is a perspective and my biggest concern with it is not the assumptions that I understand it to encompass, but that it can often be rolled out in the Management and Business School setting as *the* perspective. Whilst I am sure I have much to learn from Critical Realist scholarship it is my reading of an associated insistence in being *the* set of ideas that are going to help all those naive positivists / social constructionist / etc. finally get it right. As per the Goldilocks fairy tale story mentioned a few times before, Critical Realism can come with a smugness that it got it 'just right'. For example, in Chapter 1 I wrote about reading Malm's (2018) book and to me that is what comes through most strongly. A sense of 'well Barad, Haraway .. you really have not got it right, what you need is Critical Realism which will give you the right way of thinking'. Also, reading Mutch's (2013) writing about Critical Realism I get a similar impression. Although as I mentioned sociomateriality might also be associated with similar claims about getting things 'just right'.

Admittedly, I have not ever spoken with either of them, Malm or Mutch, and so this arms length criticism is probably more than a little unfair. However, I am very happy that they are contributing to debates to try to develop our understanding about how to rethink our relationship with realities of our socio-ecologically degrading world. It is just the posture of 'going hard' on a viewpoint in pursuit of some right way, right answer etc. My view is that we need, to pick up on one of Norgaard's metaphors, a "patchwork quilt of coevolving" perspectives (1994, p. 177). We cannot comprehensively know and that is the point! By understanding being entangled in a relational world implies that it necessarily exceeds our capacity to fully know about it. That is how we are able take some fun and joy from this creative process of writing-learning. For example, in doing an apprenticeship for academia, a doctoral degree, there can be a pressure to conform and use the right labels. Critical Realism is one such label that can be grabbed for so that you think you sound legitimate. The problem with grasping and holding tight other people labels is that they can become an excuse to stop exploring, stop inquiring and stop questioning. Where is the joy in that? When going back to that quotation from Hayles we want engage in a processes of "evok[ing] the exhilarating prospect of getting out of some of the oldboxes and opening up new ways of thinking about what being human means" (2008, p. 285). In my PhD thesis I wrote about 'academic labels':

> "My seeking to break with conventions, acting without an authoritative theoretical label to attach, did appear to bring with it a greater burden to fully explain what you did to help deflect any assertions in an attempt to avoid being hocus-pocus. This is a consistent theme throughout my work. I have endeavoured to articulate my sense-making richly and to resist lazily grasping theoretical terminology and forcing it instrumentally upon my research." (Allen, 2012, p. 20)

I suppose I am portraying my writing as being rather heroic here 'break[ing with conventions', how daring! What a guy! However, what I am seeing here as important is two fold. One, is a need to think differently, not be stifled by what is allowable or legitimate to imagine. Doing so in the service of finding our way to positive and harmonious planetary futures, and emerging from our plethora of Anthropocenic slow moving car crashes. Oh goodness I am such a hopeless romantic! Two, is the need to be modest, we are but limited entangled beings and whilst there are many wonderful things we can achieve we are of course more than a bit vulnerable, and quite puny, within a world. By envisaging that there are definitive answers to find, is I am afraid, of a decidedly anthropomorphic bent, i.e. us human beings at the centre and able to know all of our world. We need to 'get real' (to steal the name of an advertising agency I once came across) and for me that means modesty and humility. We need to develop our perspectives, warts and all, in what has be regarded as feminine ways "that nurtures growth and acknowledges pain" in contrast with a "dominant masculine position that aims to impregnate" the right ideas in to passive minds (Fotaki, Metcalfe, & Harding, 2014, p. 1257). In relation to developing a theoretical perspective, that is how I would understand responsibility.

Enter witnessing

What is it that I am setting out as a perspective in this book? Up to here I have been attempting to explain something about the 'ground' from which I am seeking to 'stand'. By this I mean the key assumptions and theoretical resources that I will draw upon in order to develop this story about the perspective that I am offering in this word-assembling-book-writing-endeavour. As we will go on to explore the perspective for considering responsibility in Anthropocene times will be orientated around the notion of 'witnessing'. As I will attempt to explain (fingers crossed as in learning-writing when I am first typing these words I have very little idea where all this is headed, and whether it will turn out to be substantial enough to fill out the expected pages of a book!), how witnessing can offer us possibilities for appreciating responsible-being, because it relates to tentative, nuanced and embodied ways of unknowing. It is a concept that can be understood as emanating, and so is congruent with, ideas of sociomateriality and posthumanism. Also, when I write about developing a perspective I am not going to be offering something fully formed and free of any blemishes. As I have repeatedly insisted upon, probably to your annoyance by now, but I am not judging the quality of what I am seeking to offer on its potential to resolve all those unfortunate issues with those 'poor misguided other perspectives' (something that as I have just asserted ideas of Critical Realism could be accused of). Instead on the imagination and modesty associated with how witnessing could help us to grapple with slippery sociomaterial dynamics, in substantial part because it offers us an alternative metaphor to knowing.

Donna Haraway, whose work (1997, 2008, 2016) is associated with STS (which has now got a mention a few times since we began, as a stream of multifaceted and multidisciplinary researching which includes the philosophy of science and sociology of knowledge) was likely the first to prominently use this term in respect of ideas about 'modest witness' when she suggested:

> "Witnessing is seeing, attesting; standing publicly, accountable for, and physically vulnerable to, one's visions and representations. Witnessing is a collective limited practice that depends on the constructed and never finished credibility of those who do it, all of whom are mortal, fallible, and fraught with the consequences of unconscious and disowned desires and fears." (Haraway, 1997, p. 267)

From this quotation witnessing is given meanings about being present and responsible in relation to some aspects of being in a world, but with the awareness of an inability to fully appreciate what you are being present and responsible towards. As we will go on to consider a core aspect of witnessing, or as some describe 'bearing witness', is the assumption of some burden associated with the witnessing. For example, as David Hill offers, “when we see the suffering of others ... we are called to take on the burden of responsibility, to respond to what we see: to do something” (2019, p. 28). He goes to explain that witnessing “is more than just seeing: it is also a moral response, that is, to perform our responsibility” (Hill, 2019, p. 28). As Kelly Oliver describes “witnessing has both the juridical connotations of seeing with one’s own eyes and the religious connotations of testifying to that which cannot be seen” (2000, p. 31). She suggests that witnessing is “a powerful alternative to recognition in formulating identity and ethical relations” (Oliver, 2000, p. 31). This is because:

> “Acknowledging the realness of another’s life is not judging its worth or conferring respecting, or understanding or recognising it, but responding in a way that affirms response-ability or addressability. We are obligated to respond to what is beyond our comprehension, beyond recognition” (Oliver, 2000, p. 41).

Janet Borgerson suggests of Haraway’s notion of witnessing that “modesty here raises issues of deferral; or recognising that final judgements or completed essences, in fact, invoke constant questioning in the face of fallibility” (2010, p. 84), which offers the potential to consider interaction and co-creation at the heart of intersubjectivity. Intersubjectivity, in general, meaning the combined or interacting subjectivity (as discussed in Chapter 1) of different beings. In taking a relational ontology as described in Chapter 2, we understand subjectivity to be unavoidable. As Michal Givoni (2014) proposes, witnessing is not about construing something that one is (i.e. being a witness), but rather as an appreciation of our being as ‘mediator’ (Bruno Latour’s term already referred to); transforming, translating, distorting, and modifying within sociomaterial entanglement. Ideas of witnessing have also been suggested to have de-colonising potential i.e. challenge potential colonial binaries such as the discussion of Plumwood's writing in Chapter 2 (Gaertner, 2014). This is because of the potential for 'other' ways of knowing to be included.

Sorry, I realise I am going quickly here, call it excitement, or call it trying to stay around 9'000 words per chapter, that made my proposed book an 'acceptable length', according to one publisher. However, in closing this chapter I am hoping to have 'wet your appetite' that we are off into to exciting territory as witnessing will hopefully challenge us to pause and think again about being and doing, and wonder what might be possible. From Part 1, comprising of the first three chapters, we are now flowing onwards, when I first type these words, towards a yet to unfold Part 2. Part 2 will involve considering and developing witnessing which will be organized around three dilemmas as to the possibilities it may offer for responsible-being in Anthropocene times.

PART TWO:
Three Dilemmas

Chapter 4

Dilemma One: Centrality?

How many words?

We will begin this first chapter in Part 2 by attempting to bring forward some more glimpses of the situatedness and contingency of assembling this book. Doing so, as mentioned from the start, is key to developing and expressing the perspective of witnessing. The glimpses explored relate to writing-publishing processes and associated mediatings. Before we move onto exploring the first dilemma – centrality – we consider why being critical in offering a perspective involves close engagement with key associated dilemmas. The dilemma of centrality relates to issues of humans being the source of all valuing, as well as our bodily being 'the centre'. By considering ideas of mutual witnessing we will explore how we might understand valuing of and by 'others'.

We hurried a little to get to the end of the last chapter when I was bringing in 'witnessing', and suggesting that this notion is core to the perspective that I am trying to offer in this book. In retrospect I am not so sure why we made that quick dash at the end there, as when I was discussing with some potential publishers about books they were keen that I 'pumped up' the suggested word length, rather than tried to keep it down. As I mentioned early on, this is my first foray in to book writing after a heavy focus for text creation on the more accepted currency, at least in my part of academia, of journal articles. In publisher discussions when I was exploring possibilities for book writing I was told that 80'000 words is a 'sweet spot' in relation to 'depth', and something was mentioned about the physical binding working better if it is at least 200-pages. Although looking at my notes I can't really make sense of that point. However, it is interesting how the binding process, when there is much reading of e-books, is helping to organize the amount of appropriate text. New to this exciting world of book writing, I was trying to note down all the advice offered even if it seems quite nonsensical now.

As we discussed early on in Chapter 1 based on my reading of 'academic' books about 300-pages seemed a pretty good target so that I do not waste too much of anybodies time. Consequently, I have this 80'000 words figure circling around as to what would be involved in a 'good' outcome from this writing effort. By calculating what has happened so far on first drafting I am heading a little shy of this target. My current plan is for seven chapters each coming in at around nine thousand words, which is more or less what the first three in Part 1 were on first drafting them. I wonder if the mentioned 80'000 word figure included references?! What this means is I can likely chill out a bit, and that rush at the end of the last chapter was not necessary. Probably, it was more about the end of the day/week approaching and a felt need to have my first go at Chapter 3 assembled so that I can make some claims to tangible progress on what is quite a marathon endeavour.

I do not want to get all fixated on fitting this book into the appropriate 'box' in terms of length and organization. Particularly as the more expansive canvas that this book offers is about opening up space for creativity and imagination, along with making room for the hoped for benefits and richness of slower explanation. However, I am of course learning here, as I explained at the start of this book, a, or the, key purpose for embarking on this writing is about learning-to-write something that we can be regard as somehow worthwhile and of value. If we are here together via these words then Part 1 is behind us. Either that, or you just happened to scroll down an electronic version of this text on your screen, or from thumbing through the pages of a physical book to be here. Maybe you are looking for something in particular, or you have arrived by just having a bit of a 'sniff around' to see if reading some of the pages could be worth your effort. Well, if that is the case, you have missed so much!

What I can tell you at this point, when I am first drafting this text, is yes this book writing it still a daunting undertaking, and the question of whether it will ever get fully written and to the publisher still looms, but I am enjoying it. It does feel freer than having to compress and contort ideas into a journal article in order to squash your writing into some blemish free perfectly honed acceptable formula. You can of course try to have some fun in attempting to produce different journal article formats, for example some of the writing I have published with Judi Marshall (e.g. Allen & Marshall, 2015, 2019). Although the number of allowable words in a journal article does bring with it inevitable constraints. Of course it does mean for those reading who are confronted by a world of masses of texts in circulation being a 'scavenger', skim reading to get as quickly as possible to the key statements that are relevant to cite in your own writing, an 8'000-words journal article is a lot less to 'get your arms around' than an 80'000-words book.

Book matters

The potential for peoples' equitable access to writing has become discussed more and more in recent years. The movement for open-access is about making sure that academic writing is not made exclusive behind a paywall, where only the wealthiest universities are able to afford the subscriptions to give their staff and students access. In the discussions that I had with potential publishers a key area of concern that arose for me was the question of the price of the book. In this category of academic books a 'monograph', which is most frequently classified as writing about a single subject by a single author, are not likely to be seen to be items that fly-off of the shelves at your local book shop. Particularly if you are new to the book writing scene and are trying to get your first book written, even if you have stream of journal articles in your name. What this means is that something like this book, addressing themes about 'posthumanism' and 'sociomateriality', are instantly regarded as specialist. With this classification the assumed economics of it all are seen to add up to making sure that the price tag that becomes attached to the book is large. By large I was told that it would have to be about £80 for the hardback copy and that a paperback at best, based on some reasonable sales performance, might be available at a less eye-watering price about 18 months after the first publication. The logic here, as far as I understand it, is that the publisher is mainly expecting university libraries to be the eventual book purchasers, and so the best bet is to try to squeeze them for £80 a pop to maximise revenue, before having a paperback in circulation at say a more 'affordable' £25. These were discussions with various not-for-profit university presses, I did not get very far into a dialogue with what we can regard as the more commercial for-profit publishers.

The conversations with potential publishers left me with a significant dilemma about book writing. Why would you want to write a book which even if somebody who wants to read it could not sensibly afford it, and would only have access to it if they were a member of a wealthy university whose library had purchased it? Although even the most wealthy libraries are likely to be increasingly careful with their diminished budgets related to the continuing ruptures from the Covid-19 pandemic. Indeed there are mounting tensions between university libraries and publishers with the rapidly expanding price tags of e-books, particularly during a pandemic when physical copies are out of reach in closed libraries, which may well hasten any unravellings of these undesirable arrangements (e.g. Hotten, 2020). Consequently, by taking on writing a book with these publishers you are being enrolled into a relationship that would make your assembled words highly exclusive. Exclusive to the point of nearly every member of the human population not having access to them.

I thoroughly support the ideals of open-access, as goodness knows, often very few people will ever read any of those journal articles that I and others have spent so many hours toiling away over. So what would be the rationale to put all the time in to writing a book that virtually nobody would be able to read because only the world's wealthiest can get their hands on it? All apart from a handful of 'academic books' will raise enough from their sales for their authors to buy much more than a rubber dingy, let alone a yacht if that were something you might be hankering after, perhaps a rowing boat if you had some good fortune! I have these recurring images about the occasions in academic seminars at which the presenter would proudly wave around shiny covered newly published book, accompanied by some embarrassed mumblings that it was rather expensive, but they did have a piece of paper that would give you a 10% discount. On wandering up to the front of the seminar room later on to have a look at the book I remember having to manage my shock at a price tag in the £80 territory, as was quoted to me. It took some stern focus to avoid blurting out 'that's ridiculous', which was going around in my head.

These orderings of book writing-publishing are good enough to put you off. Not only are books not seen to be such a great idea in many parts of academia over writing journal articles or trotting out funding proposals, with the likelihood of a colleague being noticeably shocked that you have even contemplated, let alone attempted it (as considered in Chapter 1). But, you also have the unattractive prospect of hawking your ideas around at an academic seminar post publication worried that the slightly peaky looking academic in the front row may keel over in shock at the price tag. Not to mention the projection of a subtext that your ideas are so good, and so significant, that if others want to read about them, and share in your genius then they will of course need to pay an appropriately excessive sum. My imaginings are that this would be a very deflating scenario, because after putting in all the work to get a book together, that you are happy to have your name on the front cover of, you are thwarted by your inability to share your text due to the numbers which follow the currency symbol on the back cover. What to do?

Well fortunately there is 'an alternative' the open access publisher which I am delighted has supported me in developing this book. The publishing model is very different although the 'end product' of a book in physical and electronic forms is the same. We don't need to go into the details but in this arrangement a file (of the electronic variety) becomes available on the publisher's website which is open-access i.e. free to anybody to download who wants it. If in the case a to-be-reader would like it as a physical copy then they can get hold of a copy via any online of physical bookshop which is selling it on a print-to-order basis. Or, potentially buy it directly from the author at a physical in-person research seminar if those things ever come back into fashion after a pandemic.

Entangled authorship

What I am trying to consider with this reflection on publishing arrangements, which came out of noticing a compulsion to adhere to expected chapter word counts with this book when closing the previous chapter, relates to what we have been discussing in Part 1. Notions of entangled person-authors mean that attempting to trace and notice these orderings are not because they are somehow 'behind' the text, but that it is through these sociomaterial orderings which the text is produced. A story of the freedom of choices available to the author can cover up how the potential for a flowing together of author-words-book-publisher are contoured, so that the way things may unfold is given meanings and materialise in particular ways, at particular moments.

The idea of a book comes with social meanings that have evolved to be so over many years (e.g. in Britain of it being a rectangular shape, having a cover, title and contents pages, the order of the text goes from the front to back, the text on the pages read from left-to-right etc.) with connected processes and associated technologies for producing, distributing and selling. Hence, when we bring our bodily engagement to book writing we become enrolled into, and so entangle ourselves in these established flows of sociomaterial relations. What this means is that noticing, what are likely quite banal details (e.g. 'yes of course a book is not shaped like a banana!'), because they are taken-forgranted, takes some destabilisation and effort. Going back to our river metaphor, its like trying to grab hold of an eroding bank in an attempt to find or launch ourselves into a different current or confluence. However, that is not to say this 'other' flow removes us from an understanding of being part of problematic ethical relations, transplanting us onto some serene pedestal of ethical righteousness and ascendency.

For example, the situation I have just outlined of becoming contracted as a writer to an 'alternative' publishing model. In the typical book publishing model, I explained about issues associated with pricing. The alternative model which enables open-access, which I have sought to participate within through this book writing, opens up other questions. Such as, how the selling of physical copies of the books happen and what materials are used (inks and papers) to print and assemble the book. The likelihood is that online purchase might be most freely be available via Amazon, whose labour arrangements and treatment of warehouse staff has gained much criticism due to intensive surveillance and being dehumanising (e.g. Sainato, 2020). Also, the materials, because the printing of books via the publisher is typically 'on-demand', likely are not closely tied into ways that are centred around being as responsible as possible with the inks, papers and binding adhesives that are used. Although the specifics of what is involved in how any given book comes to be physically in front of you, in relation to the possible ethical dimensions, is very likely unknowable. Unless you were able to be with the physical piecing together of the book from its inception, to see the addition of every material and the ways in which peoples' labour is engaged through production, distribution and selling.

The point that I want to make is that because 'more complex activities' (such as making and distributing a book) which require a medley of different processes of organizing we are inevitably becoming enrolled into a web of (un)ethical relations. We can of course, as in this example, make choices, but to some degree we have to accept that many of our entanglements are hidden well 'out of view'. As well as specific situational and contextual moments reshaping their envisaged ethicality. For instance, I can be sniffy about a focus to make money out of writing books. However, when I last checked I am still a full-time salaried academic who is certainly not flush with cash, but is not in imminent need of having to visit the nearest foodbank for my next meal. Some people will write books with the aims of excessive personal profit, which we can certainly see to be undesirable (although that potentially depends on what they might do with the cash, perhaps they use it to support their local foodbank), but other authors probably just need to pay the rent, trying to find ways of earning money so that they can give up a job at their local supermarket.

This is the wonder, and dare I write 'fun', of writing books, you can take moment to ponder a little without some intense pressure to not 'waste words' and get to the point! We could agree that I have started this chapter by going for a bit of an unexpected wander with words, to pick over what we might be getting ourselves into when writing a book, extending some of the discussion from the early chapters. I suppose if it feels like just a bit of a distraction before getting on with the business of the theory stuff then that might be feeling annoying. Although we cannot just 'go hard' on explaining theory for the whole book, we would likely both be completely worn out! My view is that we need these spaces of relative calm, like the start of this chapter which opens Part 2 of the book, that can give us room for a 'bit of a chill out' with a slower pace of explanation and more meandering feel. In contrast with the quick-fire closing of Chapter 3. However, not in a rather pointless 'I am just going to aimlessly tap away at my keyboard until I clock up a few thousand words to get this chapter going' kind of a way.

Perspective taking and making

By starting this chapter, in the way that it has unfolded, it is about attempting to review, draw connections and add to that which has come before, as well as trying to do as much 'showing' as 'telling'.

What I mean by this is bringing forward some of the sensibilities that I am attaching to the key concepts that we have explored so far of posthumanism and sociomateriality. These sensibilities include a perspective of the 'I' entangled, and often befuddled, in trying to notice and make sense of entanglements, their consequences, and whether something might need to, or could, be done about them. A wondering about what we might be seeing, and what we might be missing, as well as pondering if we have any possibility for agency to challenge and reshape relations in which we appear to be tightly bound. In many ways these are concerns at the heart of this book about understanding responsibility in Anthropocene times. In this first chapter of Part 2 I have promised that we are going to get into the perspective that I am offering in this book by considering the dilemmas and tensions which can be understood to be connected with the view that I am offering.

There are three chapters in Part 2 of the book, which each take in turn a dilemma as a way to 'modestly' explain a perspective. This chapter is about the questions and dilemmas of human 'centrality' in relation to ideas of witnessing. Now, as I first type those words, it appears to be quite an ambitious undertaking. Probably a very ambitious undertaking. However, as I have repeatedly tried to convey I am not professing to offer answers here, or heading off on some heroic mission to 'figure it all out' as if like magic before your very eyes. In taking a critical approach there is an acknowledgement that all perspectives have underlying assumptions, and are a view from somewhere, and hence can, and need to be, questioned and challenged. Although admitedly, I am not offering the ideas of witnessing that I will develop as just another perspective, as to me I am investing in it as a valuable and productive way to approach issues of socio-ecological unsustainability in Anthropocene times.

From a critical viewpoint we may well recognise and seek to appreciate a range of perspectives. But, those we most closely associate, hold tightest, or peer through longest (as in the metaphor of a lens) we hope to become more aware of the assumptions we are connecting with, as well as those of other perspectives that we are rejecting. Whilst in some respects there is a critical sense of looking at the world by taking different perspectives, such as the business-society-nature relationships that we considered in Chapter 2 (Marcus, Kurucz, & Colbert, 2010; Stubbs & Cocklin, 2008). It is not with the aim of being dispassionate and distanced from them all in some objectivist move, but about engaging with the commitments and assumptions of our viewpoints to explore, with zeal and passion, our subjectivity. As Judi Marshall wrote about her personal processes of researching "I work from a particular position; I appreciate other positions, and I feel that each has its own integrity" (1981, p. 399). At the very least the positions and perspectives that we may reject, or wish to disassociate with, can help us learn about those that we feel a need to cling to. Although, it would be challenging, and deeply unrealistic, to see ourselves as perfect beings, as it can be very hard not to dismiss different viewpoints out of hand that cut across ideas that we hold. Hopefully we can strive to explore, not from a belief that we might be convinced otherwise (as some views can of course be disturbing for their irresponsibility and immorality), but that we might learn something about the integrity of our own position. By attempting to view the world through different perspectives we can not transcend our felt and embodied being-in-a-world. But, trying to do so gives us the opportunity to learn and be confronted with other possibilities.

I am aware in a chapter about advancing witnessing as a perspective, and associated more careful and tentative knowing and being, that these suggestions about critical appreciations could sound like we are in 'total control', and able to comprehend and move between perspectives at will. Something of a process of the human "find[ing] our next teleological evolutionary stage" which we previously considered in respect of three views on posthumanism, and dismissed it as not how I am seeking to draw upon these ideas (Gane, 2006, p. 140). Instead I located the intent, quoting Hayles, of "getting out of some of the oldboxes and opening up new ways of thinking about what being human means" (2008, p. 285). So in this sense what I think we are doing involves a perspective making and taking of intrigue and inquiry, based on an awareness that there are always other perspectives, and knowing more about the limitations of what we call our own perspective enhances our understanding and doing. Perspectives are appreciated as evolving, through drawing-ins and repellings of emerging concepts and ideas. As well as performative, a notion considered in Chapter 2, our perspectives both help us interpret and describe being-in-a-world, along with producing the world that we see.

In a posthuman sense, perspectives may likely take us, as much as we can understand ourselves as taking them. For example, I co-authored an article, as mentioned in Chapter 2, that took an actor-network approach to making sense of the realities that had been encountered in researching how sustainability became translated and enacted at an urban regeneration project (Allen, Brigham, & Marshall, 2018). However, in the process of reflecting on how the perspective helped to extend visibility on mediators and sociomaterial entanglements there is a lurking, and inevitable, sense of how the attentions and vocabularies of the actor-network approach can help to produce our potential (in)visibility. A perspective can become more a self-fulfilling 'guiding logic', than 'conceptual device' that helps to sensitise our attentions in particular ways to make sense of different realities. When we start looking for mediators, a slippery and malleable concept, we might well notice some. Consequently, there is a need to take care of how we can appreciate our potential to comprehend the realities which we seek to know.

Back to witnessing

As suggested at the end of Chapter 3 given the attentions to posthumanism and sociomateriality, that I am attempting to reflect in developing a perspective on responsibility, the concept of witnessing offers possibilities. This is because witnessing is about being present and responsible in relation to some aspects of being in a world (such as challenges of socio-ecological sustainability), but with an awareness of an inability to fully appreciate what you are being present and responsible towards. In many ways, as we will go on to explore through considering different dilemmas associated with a witnessing perspective, the notion of 'knowing' as core to being responsible is subverted. This is not to suggest some awareness via telepathy or a mythical creature, but witnessing as a bodily-being-aware which resolutely engages in fallibility and vulnerability (Haraway, 1997, 2008, 2016). The idea, as we discussed in Chapter 1, is that paying attention to the challenges of the Anthropocene necessitates an engagement with an anthropocentrism which understands the human at the centre of all things. Witnessing could loosen 'our grasp' on the world, but how might it help us with these problems of understanding the human as the centre of the universe?

Various authors have considered possibilities for decentring the human in our understandings of being in a sociomaterial world. For example, by considering ethics in relation to materiality Lucas Introna explores the problematic of human centrality. He writes that "in our entanglement with the material world it is the human being that is always more significant, more worthy, of consideration" (2014, p. 2). Introna suggests that there appears to be an unavoidable bifurcation of matter between the human (as active, knowing and influencing) and nonhuman (as passive, knowable and formable) through which the human being is privileged as "the unquestionable value from which all other values derive their meaning" (2014, p. 8). He argues that "the appropriation of the non-human other, it seems, is always in our own terms" which promotes and reproduces anthropocentric bias which, as I have explained, can be understood to be a central issue in reproducing and sustaining socioecological unsustainabilities (Introna, 2014, p. 3). Introna goes onto argue for an ethics, or ethos, of 'letting-be-of-things' which involves "giving up of our incessant desire to know and to order beings" (2014, p. 16). We will go on to explore Introna's arguments in a moment as it was some writing that when I was copying out key sentences and paragraphs to quote in later writing, I found that I had copied down a large proportion of the paper i.e. it is rich in prompting pause for thought and reflection.

As I already mentioned we are in some ambitious territory. We are seeking a philosophy which undermines its own contingency. What I mean by this is that philosophy is about 'big' questions like: 'how do we understand existence?'; and, 'what is knowledge?'. These are human questions about the meaning of human existence and how we go about knowing about that existence. The starting point of these questions is to place the human at the centre of any inquiry as the intelligent being to whom the world needs to be made intelligible, meaningful, relevant etc. Hence the human is the starting point and so at the centre and the locus of an inquiry into being-in-a-world. This is the notion from Introna (2014) of the world 'on our terms' that we are interested in subverting and reimagining in pursuit of responsible-being. However, we can not overcome our bodies. Crucial assumptions underpin the perspective I am seeking to develop, these are about our embeddedness in the world and appreciating our subjectivities, it is our being entangled in the world that enables our living and existing. Which means that our questions can, and will inevitably, emanate from our human-being, but upon their asking they need to circulate in ways that as Introna (2014) suggests do not produce, what we can regard as, irresponsible bifurcations i.e. the division of things into two parts. As we have discussed, with ideas of entanglement we are resolutely attempting to avoid dualist divides. Particularly, as the giving of meaning and value to categories of human and nonhuman is overwhelmingly a human-centred project.

What this means is that crucially for a perspective to properly embrace posthuman and sociomaterial appreciations, and so be responsible on terms I have set out earlier, there is a need for the allowing of the inscription of nonhuman meaning and valuing. Not merely a recognition of, and appreciation for, difference and some naff momentary 'ah, isn't that lamb cute!', but as with Introna's (2009) metaphor, it enables 'the speaking of things'. So we are thinking about a philosophy in which the voice of the human is entangled amongst 'the voices' of more-than-human others. A move that could be starkly contrasted with a recalcitrant anthropomorphism, in which us humans are shouting so loudly that nothing else can be heard. Rapt in our own continued existence that all we can hear of is the necessity to keep on marching in the same direction, 'as normal', which as we considered in the early chapters, is towards some challenging times.

Potential disaster

When we consider these images, as I have just done, of marching in the same direction, we do need to be careful about the linearity of our thinking in our forecasting of climate meltdowns, with connected social collapse. This is an important consideration for the perspective of witnessing that I am developing. The science of climate and biodiversity makes grim reading, and climatic changes are already having significant implications to the lives of many beings. Islands becoming engulfed by rising sea levels is an example (e.g. Gallagher & Jong, 2019). The historical analysis by people like Jared Diamond has given us many accounts of how ecological degradation can be connected with archaeological evidence of the collapse of civilisations (Diamond, 2006). However, we need to be aware of imposing ideas of 'Social Darwinism' onto how people behave in times of crisis (e.g. Raymond, 2000). Such a position draws on the thesis of 'survival of the fittest'. By using this thesis as the lens, humans are assumed to be competitive and aggressive, just out for their own interests, and hence any situation of 'stress', in particular to life giving ecosystems such as rivers and fertile soil, means war! Indeed a recent BBC World Service radio series was named 'Climate Wars'. It was certainly worth listening to, in particular hearing some first hand accounts from across the planet of where people and other species are facing significant challenges and hardship due to changing climates. However, just from the title you quickly get the idea, that when things get tough in relation to the so called 'nexus' of food, water and energy, they get bloody.

A 'survival of the fitness' framing is of course a very simplistic tale, and one which Rebecca Solnit challenges in her book 'A Paradise Built in Hell: The Extraordinary Communities that Arise in Disaster'. She explores through an array of historical examples, how in times of crisis and disaster people 'rise to the occasion' in support each other and their communities (Solnit, 2010). Solnit does not claim a universal narrative about the 'human condition' in times of crisis, but she does show in her analysis how the primordial thesis of Social Darwinism is very limited in its potential to explain and explore what emerges when people are required to respond to disasters and crises. She suggests that ideas of inevitable wars from emergency situations are more easily understood as associated with an 'elite panic' (a concept associated with Kathleen Tierney a 'disaster sociologist'), than the realities of what most people do in crisis circumstances. 'Elite panic' is reported as explained in a talk by Tierney as "fear of social disorder; fear of [the] poor, minorities and immigrants; obsession with looting and property crime; willingness to resort to deadly force; and actions taken on the basis of rumour" (Solnit, 2010, p. 127).

In this 'by-the-way' moment, just when we were starting to get into witnessing, I am not trying to suggest that climate breakdown could be understood to usher in a new era of human caring and mutual aid. Which means that we should all wait for the extinction of many species and emergence of inhabitability for all living beings in many parts of the world, then we will be able to properly able to 'bliss out' with each other. That would be pretty mad, and of course as we have explored in developing critical appreciations of theories, and their inevitable assumptions, Solnit's story is one of a patchwork of possibilities. However, determinism can be a bit of trip wire for what be might see as the 'environmental movement'. This is because in order to push for action now, there is a need to make tomorrow sound so horrible that we can do nothing but change our ways. It is of course a strategy, and one which in some ways has been quite effective at raising attention, it probably got me to sit up and notice, and in the words of the poet and rapper Kae Tempest, break from the anthropocentric spell of a 'tunnel vision' of ecological ignorance. However, and I promise I am going to get back to the human centrality discussion soon, after this paragraph, by fixating on some inevitable Mad Max future (those dystopian thrillers of the 1970s and 80s) where we are firmly in the grip of some crazy 'wild west', is a very partial view. A view of humans which rather undermines the potential, and worth for, a project of posthuman responsibility, as with the general idea of this book.

As we have explored before these ideas and theories about how things are, can be worryingly performative i.e. they produce, not just describe, realities. For example, we had those headlines about the mad rush for toilet rolls when we were heading into the first lock-downs due to the Covid-19 pandemic (e.g. Mao, 2020). The narrative is that you are going to need to fight dirty down at your local supermarket if you want a clean bum when things really 'hit the fan'. It is the amplification and tight holding of certain views of the world that is so problematic, and likely quite damaging to ourselves and others. Like when one person dumps their old sofa in the local woods out of a population of millions, and suddenly we can all be regarded as callous dumpers in some 'dog-eat-dog' world. We could imagine, going back to that mention of 'elite panic', that such ideas play well into those stories of a 'survival of the fittest' society that can be preferred and perpetuated by elites. Elites who are so, because of their accumulations of capital and associated influence from the ownership of institutions, such as media outlets including television channels and newspapers. Consequently, dog-eat-dog narratives may well be attractive to those who may profess that there-is-no-alternative, no worth in trying to make anything any better, as they do not want to lose their imagined 'ascendency'.

Valuing the other

We can bring my little sojourn on linearity and determinism, back to our dilemma on human centrality in a few ways. Firstly, it reminds us that the future is inevitably not something we can comprehensively understand, and so grasping dystopian images and holding them tightly has its own forms of violence. It is violent because other voices are silenced, as well as possibilities for others to have a voice. We moved toward the potential for witnessing because it opens up opportunities to bring into focus the unknowability associated with being entangled. As mentioned in Chapter 3 we can not escape our bodies into some alternative "teleological evolutionary stage" (Gane, 2006, p. 140), this is not the posthuman 'wagon' that we are on. It might be helpful to categorise the world and divide it up to get to know it, or make sense of differences, as we considered in Chapter 2. But, addressing human centrality requires an entangled 'lens' that opens up other possibilities by drawing in voiceless others, and somehow assimilating the valuing that they do. Witnessing subverts ideas of knowing, because comprehensively knowing things is understood to be of a different realm. A realm of anthropocentrism. In a relational view, which we discussed in Chapter 3, being in a sociomaterial world means that our relations necessarily exceeds our capacity to fully know about them. The subversion of human philosophical ideals to know, opens an opportunity to 'do witnessing', instead of 'doing knowing'. Because as introduced, witnessing is about being present and responsible in relation to some aspects of being in a world, but with the awareness of an inability to fully appreciate what you are being present and responsible towards (Oliver, 2000; Haraway, 1997).

Significantly, in considering human centrality, whereas knowing seems to be indelibly human, witnessing can be understood as a more-than-human way of being. What this means is that it opens up the potential for a mutuality of witnessing. Mutuality involves the other 'staring back', witnessing us. Given the variety that we can associate with the category of nonhuman, encompassing 'human technologies' such as a table, to 'animals and ecologies' such as a bumble bee or a forest. There is not one form of witnessing, no singular way for all to witness others. For instance, we could not imagine that a table or a bumble bee may witness us in the same ways. So this is a perspective of imagination, as much as it might be one of a natural or physical science of things and their potential for awareness. We cannot ask them, the 'thing', the 'other', what they witness as they do not 'speak' a human language. However, witnessing brings a different sort of awareness and appreciation, because whilst we are still 'contained' to a human imagination, being witness involves being witnessed.

Perhaps this all sounds a bit fanciful, but remember I am not attempting *the* perspective, but a perspective. This is the modest project that I have set out from the start, which I suppose can come across as the ultimate 'cop-out'. However, what this means is that it is not an approach at rocking human centrality, which for example, is necessarily anti-Science – to use a Latour (2011) big 'S'. Although *witnessing-being-witnessed* would be anti-Science as the route to enduring and universal truths about being-in-a-world. As Feyerabend wrote about science, when it is run according to fixed and universal rules of understanding, it is "less adaptable and more dogmatic: every methodological rule is associated with cosmological assumptions, so that using the rule we take it for granted that the assumptions are correct" (1978, p. 295). Do not worry, we are not about to embark on some brief look across the history and philosophy of science, which I have to confess I do not feel thoroughly acquainted with. The point I want to make again in taking a critical approach, is that any theoretical perspective rests on assumptions. For example in Part 1, I spent time setting out the assumptions of the perspective that I am developing in this book, trying to 'walk the talk'. By being aware of these assumptions we create opportunities to critically engage with different perspectives, which in combination enhance our understanding. A posthumanist impulse requires us to reimagine the possibilities for our assumptions, as these shape our ability to understand and take action.

By being attentive to underlying assumptions we can give rise to possibilities to develop a perspective further, because assumptions can be questioned and evolve. For example, if we consider the work of Bateson (1979, 2000), which I mentioned in Chapter 2 in relation to questioning language categories and the boundaries which they produce. Bateson's celebrated ideas attempt to overcome dualist divides by conceiving of the living physical world (human and nonhuman) as one vast interconnected mind. Bateson's approach has been described as "monistic", which is a term that involves much variety, but that 'the world' can be conceived of as a whole which is made up of interconnected parts (Charlton, 2008, p. 42). This conceptualisation of systemic interconnectivity helps offer new imagination to what could be regarded as atomised views of science, i.e. where things are studied as separate entities. Connectedly, Kimmerer (2013) in her exploration of indigenous wisdom and scientific knowledge, expresses how language can limit our potential to consider our interconnected lives with the more-than-human. She explores issues related to 'animacy' and the reflection of animate and inanimate binaries through agreed language patterns and 'grammatical rules', which are significant because they deny nonhumans life and "the right to be persons" (Kimmerer, 2013, p. 57). She writes:

> "English doesn't give us many tools for incorporating respect for animacy. In English, you are either a human or a thing. Our grammar boxes us in by the choice of reducing a nonhuman being to an it, or it must be gendered, inappropriately, as a he or a she. Where are our words for the simple existence of another living being?" (Kimmerer, 2013, p. 56)

The potential for our discovery is shaped by the languages we use and the assumptions that we hold i.e. the lenses and blinkers through which we see the world. For example, if we look at some recent studies about plants, we can consider how our perspectives shape the questions we ask and what we can 'see'. Please try not to get too picky here, I am just trying to illustrate a point, and I am not claiming substantial botanical expertise. Recent studies on 'green leaf volatiles' suggests how plants are able to communicate with others plants in the same area to 'warn' them of predators, such as caterpillars, so that they can initiate their chemical responses (e.g. Ameye et al., 2018). Which in terms of Bateson's 'mind', and ideas of species interconnectivities, is apposite. However, recent work reported by Simon Gilroy a Botanist at the University of Wisconsin has even suggested, that predators of caterpillars, like the parasitic wasp are also able to 'read' these stress signals from the plants producing 'green leaf volatiles'. These readings enable the wasps to locate the caterpillars, and eat them, thus responding to the plants 'cries for help'. Which as suggested by the naturalist and presenter, Chris Packham on a 2020 BBC series of Autumn Watch can give us an image of 'plants talking to animals'. Bateson would have likely suggested that this is some kind of 'animism', involving "extending the notion of personality or mind to mountains, rivers, forests, and such things" (2000, p. 492).

New imaginings?

From the breif example about green leaf volatiles I am not suggesting that Bateson was right, now we have the answers, although his ideas have been compelling for many over the past forty or so years. However, to develop research to ask questions about being-in-a-world that has the opportunity to consider that plants 'talk' to plants, and even animals, requires some sensibilities for that to be a possibility. As Karl Polanyi once insisted "we must now recognise belief once more as the source of all knowledge" (1962, p. 266). What I am taking from this writing of Polanyi is that belief in something else, the possibility of a different way of understanding is needed to take us 'further'. In this case beyond seeing an atomised world of discrete plants 'doing their own thing', to one in which flows of interconnectivity can be conceptualised and appreciations of them developed.

There are of course potential issues with the assumptions of some kind of monistic connectivity, such as that within Bateson's writing. For example, if we consider the writing of Rene Descartes whose ideas have been suggested by Ravetz, referring to ecological unsustainability, to be "the roots of our problem" (2006, p. 275). The story is that Descartes work is particularly important to informing ways of thinking and researching that placed things in dualist opposition (i.e. mind/body, human/nature etc.). Ironically, the work of Descartes in the 1600s can be understood to be about attempting to overcome the 'philosophical challenges' associated with different monistic views which were connected with some of the worlds major religions such as Hinduism, Buddhism and Sikhism. Descartes writing suggested that scientific progression required these 'primative' ideas of monism or animism to be understood as something of the past, in need of being moved beyond. Interestingly, instead of a some image of building blocks of objective knowledge, one 'set of ideas' on top of the others which construct an ever higher wall, which atop we can stand 'enlightened', these reflections can help us to notice the likely circularity of human ideas amongst a flowing of subjective influences. Such as appreciating how the recent work on green leaf volatiles is based within assumptions of relationality and interconnectivity, rather than separation and oppositions.

Academia, like many other areas of contemporary societies is predicated on a need for, and celebration of 'newness'. Like this book, a key question for potential publishers is: What is new about it? For if it is not 'new' what could be its worth? Writer-academics are of course entangled within the situation in terms of wanting to get our ideas noticed and 'out there', so that an email might appear in our inbox saying 'oh, your work is so interesting, how about you come and talk to us about it'. We may well want to feel like we are 'at the cutting edge', and construing ourselves as so is often important for careers and justifying why we are worthy recipients of research funding. However, the 'modesty' that I wrote about in Chapter 3 means that we need to take care in being too proud of our ideas as unique, as better, as more advanced, cleverer etc. For example, as Hunt (2021) considers, appreciations that human sustainability rests on a respect for our interconnected relations with nonhumans is old news for indigenous peoples.

Criticality invites us to appreciate a circularity ideas and how we are subsumed in a flow of thinking-writing that is much bigger than us. An anthropomorphic project would see us at the centre, with the 'godly' potential to reverse the river of words and move it elsewhere. In the Anthropocene we, collectively understood as the most significant Geological force on the planet, may well be prone to 'game changing' fanciful imaginaries by continuing to show our potential, along with the deleterious effects. For example, the river metaphor we have been developing, meets the megalith of a massive concrete dam, which can go very wrong. Such as, the Fundão dam which collapsed in Brazil leading to burying a town, contaminating the water supply and impacting biodiversity (Franco & Wentzel, 2019). Perspectives that attempt to decentre humans, tempering assertions about the possibility for comprehensive knowing, involve awareness about the purposes and assumptions of the perspective as well as how these ideas are conveyed. To convey the partiality of a perspective could include closely engaging with dilemmas and linguistic conditionality, as I am seeking to do in this learning-writing. Doing so refers to, as mentioned in Chapter 3, what can be regarded as about developing an approach that "nurtures growth and acknowledges pain" (Fotaki, Metcalfe, & Harding, 2014, p. 1257).

Being in-body

A core challenge for the centrality dilemma is that we are each 'at our centre'. We are inevitably the bodily centre of our world. We have explored in relation to sociomateriality, how the notion of 'I' becomes diffuse through appreciating its entanglement in meaning and matter. As Barad wrote there is "no 'I' separate from the intra-active becoming of the world" (2007, p. 394). However, there is still an inevitable physical located-ness to our being-in-a-world. When I first type these words my body is sat here in our spare bedroom in Walkley in Sheffield in Britain, it is 2:19pm on November 27th 2020. We could argue about notions of time (we already did a bit of that in this chapter in relation to linearity and circularity of idea development), but fundamentally (unless I am very much mistaken!) my body is here in this moment – now. Some writers have interestingly attempted to tackle questions such as 'where is my body?'. For example, Annemarie Mol, an STS researcher (the area of study that I mentioned in Chapter 2) stated at a seminar I attended some years back that she was exploring such a question. It was something that she had considered in an inaugural lecture called 'This is my body: Material Semiotic Investigations' in Amsterdam on December 15th 2011. She explained how in this lecture she explored how her bodies protective devices could be reconceptualised to be stretching out globally by considering the practice of workers washing bananas in a Costa Rican plantation. Bananas that she imagined would make it to her fruit-bowl and then be eaten by her. This is a nice example to help to ponder how to conceptualise a broadened or unbounded 'I'.

Witnessing offers a different approach to the de-centring conundrum. It is not so much about a relocating or reconceptualisation of body. Although, as with the appreciations from sociomateriality and posthumanism, entanglement does unsettle notions of enclosed separate bodies, due to acknowledging the complete agential involvement of things (Latour & Venn, 2002). But, as mentioned already in this chapter, witnessing requires a different sort of awareness and appreciation, that is more tentative and potentially less violent than 'knowing'. If we return to the plants we discussed with their 'green leaf volatiles' we can prompt imaginings about Introna's (2009) 'speaking of things' in the mutualities of *witnessing-being-witnessed.* For example, I may be witnessing the trees as I jog through some local woodland, they are witnessing me. Not only is the configuration of the pathway been shaped by their physicality, and undulations produced by their roots, but also we can have an attention to what we are to them. This is delicate territory I am maybe running close the wind on being accused of some speculative superstition. I can hear "woohoo the trees are speaking, this person must be a crack pot!". However, as I have taken care to explain this is not a 'this is it' perspective, but more of a 'what if..' perspective. Where does allowing the possibility to be entangled amongst 'the voices' of others take us? As Ted Hughes writes in his classic poem 'Wodwo':

> "..for the moment if I sit still how everything stops to watch
> me I suppose I am the exact centre but there's all this what
> is it roots.."

What is it to watch-being-watched by 'others'? For example, Ingold writes about 'wayfinding' of the movements of the person-traveller as "the unfolding of a field of relations established through the immersion of the actor-perceiver within a given environmental context" (2002, p. 220). Ideas akin to the notions of affordances, that we considered in Chapter 3, whereby the landscape creates and affords the possibilities for the flow of mediatings of the river. The riverbanks afford possibilities for flow, and are acted upon and reshaped by the mediatings within the flow. In an immersion in the relations of a context, Ingold describes 'wayfinding' as about the person-travellers "feeling his[/her] way", "continually adjusting his[/her] movements in response to an ongoing perceptual monitoring of his[/her] surroundings" (2002, p. 220). Witnessing appreciates the skilful embodied sense of 'wayfinding' because it as much about 'the environmental context' creating a way for the traveller, as the traveller finding a way. The traveller can not be in-and-with the environment without being noticed and 'spoken to', and potentially enrolled as a valued constituent. Indeed, as I mentioned in Chapter 2 our wayfinding may also involve the potentially heavy-handed mediatings of a satellite navigation device. Although, if such a device helps us towards food when we are desperately lost due to unskilled map reading, then we may well find greater affection for being resolutely mediated by it.

Are you sitting comfortably?

In Chapter 3 we explored how much of the writing in relation to sociomateriality can be connected with interests in conceptualising humans and (information) technologies. As I mentioned in Chapter 3, by drawing in the notion of 'affordances', there is a need to understand sociomateriality as about entanglements in ecologies, as well as technologies. Doing so offers us opportunities for developing posthuman appreciations, by decentring humans, and the connected dominance of our stories about our intentions largely equating to action. So far we have been most attentive to ecologies. Indeed 'critical animal studies' is a substantial stream of work in itself which I have so far carelessly 'lumped together' with ecologies. However, this is an area of debate which I am yet to have any substantial engagement with. Which means that I am wary of making a precursory search, just so that I can weave in a few references to say it is covered, ignorantly ticking it off some imagined intellectual 'bucket-list'. Consequently, I am simply noticing that there is this as a potential 'hole', and that maybe it will be a source of inspiration for another book! Yes, nearing around half-way in this debut book writing effort and I am not feeling drained of enthusiasm for 'having another go', assuming this text is successfully assembled into a book. But, I digress, what imaginings can witnessing bring to human technologies?

We previously explored the meanings of a sociomaterial lens and considered the notion of mediators, how through ideas of mutual agency technologies transform and are transformed by humans. For example, in the study of an urban regeneration project and attempts for it to be sustainable (as mentioned in Chapter 2), we considered how sustainability was translated into a quantitative measure associated with energy use, the regulation of building temperature 'delegated' to, and performed by, a computer system. The computer system as part of a web of mediators (including, contracting arrangements for 'building management' and formalised energy reduction targets), setting 'how things are done' informed by algorithmic computing of seasonal temperature averages, transforming the warmth of human bodies within the spaces that they work. The humans involved, if they so wished, could not simply switch-off the computer system to 'take back control', they would need to navigate the policy and connected legal texts which hold things in place. Witnessing can add to this understanding of mutual entanglement of human and nonhuman, in this case technology, by extending considerations of mutuality. This is because, in witnessing all things are transforming (and being transformed), translating (and being translated), distorting (and being distorted), and modifying (and being modified). Not that all things are alive and breathing, but that all things can be active, in their ways, by witnessing our being despite them being dead.

For example, the table at which I am currently organized is witnessing me, modifying my bodies positioning through a history of expectations of encounters with it, and being transformed by the location it has been put and the accompanying narratives. Such as, perhaps being read as woodenness and of trees, instead of standing for its oily plastic make up in our hydrocarbon age. The table is doing so in connection with the chair at which I am currently sat. The chair perhaps being more impactful on my bodily shape at this moment. This now substantially taken-for-granted technology, a chair, was historically rare or non-existent, becoming popular in the 18th and 19th centuries during the Industrial Revolution (Cregan-Reid, 2018). Prior to their more general use, chairs were items typically associated with being powerful and in-charge, as in a monarch (Cregan-Reid, 2018). Indeed Cregan-Reid's in his analysis of the chair – the general use of which ushered in sedentary leisure activities such as cinema, radio and TV – he suggests that can now be seen as the symbol of Anthropocene times and bodily inactivity. His analysis can even be read as the chair mediating the duration of our living, with deaths of 'modern' humans most commonly associated with metabolic disorders that are often relatable to persistently inactive bodies. Consequently, the witnessing of mutuality is about what these things, be they trees or chairs, afford of us, and we can afford of them.

The responsibility dimensions of the witnessing of technologies is perhaps more complex than other more-than-human others. This is because assuming living things have a right to exist beyond humans can bring them value in their own right. However, technologies are substantially tools for human-being. Removing ourselves from centre stage to witness and be witnessed by things of which human hands were involved in their creation, could feel a bit like letting Frankenstein's monster freely wander-off out the door. As in the example above of the table and chair. Witnessing, along with how technologies mediate and afford our bodies (non) movement possibilities, can be about the 'make-up' of things. Such as what wood or oil was used to make that table? Where did that wood or oil come from? What fossil energy was used in its production? What were the labour conditions of those who were contracted to make it? As we explored with the making of this book at the start of this chapter, being fully aware of these ethical dimensions is unknowable. Unless as mentioned before, we go back to the very beginning of the things inception and trace the processes step-by-step to observe the coming into being of our table. This could be very interesting, and eye-opening, although likely time consuming and expensive due to the need to travel to be and stay with the emerging parts of the becoming-table. Indeed, in STS 'following things around' is a celebrated research strategy (e.g. Law, 1994).

The tables right-to-be can be mainly appreciated as a derivation of an assumed responsibility to an imagined tree that we don't want cut down to make its replacement. Or, some oil that we want to 'let be' and leave in the ground. So with us no more at 'the centre', the 'gazing back' of a table or chair, is more about a general respect for the "rights of matter" (Allen & Marshall, 2019, p. 104). This of course gets complicated if, for example, that matter is radioactive or toxic and its presence causes harm to human and nonhuman beings. However, the 'rights of matter' is about a mutuality that challenges "matter being used flagrantly and hurriedly in the service of efficiency and convenience in human-only terms" (Allen & Marshall, 2019, p. 104). By witnessing we would likely become disturbed by departing a post-meeting scene, being glared at by a cluster of one-use cups and plastic lids, which following intimate bodily contact, we are consigning to many years of painfully slow decomposition.

Witnessing-being-witnessed, and giving rights to matter, is attempting not to be seen as anthropomorphizing, whereby other species, beings and objects are treated as if human in appearance and behaviour. Although writing about the 'gazing back' or 'speaking of things' is undeniably overlaying human sensory awareness onto nonhuman others. Which in the case animals, that I have mentioned is a space in which I do not plan to naively consider, we may more easily associate because of their own sensory arrays. However, as we have attempted to expand our imagination by drawing on Introna's ethos of 'letting-be-of-things' which involves "giving up of our incessant desire to know and to order beings" (2014, p. 16), our lexicon of witnessing is about bringing to the fore the entanglement of human-nonhuman voices. Doing so is about attempting to bring into greater focus the core sociomaterial challenge to dualist thinking, because it variously inscribes unwavering inertness onto nonhuman others.

In this chapter about the dilemma of human centrality, in our searching for a posthuman appreciation of responsible-human-being, we have considered how our physical locus is inevitably our vulnerable bodies. Bodies which are defined by and kept alive through their sociomaterial entanglements. Consequently, *witnessing-being-witnessed* is searching for a mutuality of valuing-being-valued which feels, to my imagining, that our explanations are unavoidably encased within our human languages. As Bateson suggests such relational engagement with the world involves an expansion of the notion of self, including an appreciation for "unconscious process[es]" (2000, p. 467). However, this is of course somewhat challenging to put into words, as with my struggles here to explain and give life to witnessing with an anti-anthropocentric hue. In the next two chapters in Part 2, by exploring two more key dilemmas, we continue to develop notions of *witnessing-being-witnessed.*

Letting-be-of-things? A photo of a shed being 'propped-up' to continue its life on an allotment site in the Riverlin Valley that we regularly walk past which is a few miles from our house

Chapter 5

Dilemma Two: Proximity?

Considering activism

This chapter is about the second dilemma associated with *witnessing-being-witnessed* – proximity. We will go onto explore that there are some connections to the first dilemma of centrality, as proximity refers to the potential for witnessing when we are, and are not, in close contact with more-than-human others. To achieve this we will consider notions of affect, relating to sensory contact and touch, as part of seeking to approach some of the limitations of language mentioned in Chapter 4. The examples we will use to consider the dilemma of proximity mainly relate to repairing things, in particular windows. We will also reflect upon the potential implications for *witnessing-being-witnessed* when others are within easy reach versus far away.

From closing the last chapter, which explored the first of the three dilemmas that we are considering in Part 2 of this book, I am a bit concerned that *witnessing-being-witnessed* is not closely engaged enough in horrors of the Anthropocene. What I mean by this is that I may be accused of inferring that our unsustainable predicaments could be appropriately responded to with a jolly and playful project of reimagining what it is to be human. Bluntly, species are becoming extinct in substantial part because of our ham-fisted taking of centre stage to produce these Anthropocene times, flexing our muscles so much that we can be understood to have interrupted the relative Earthly stability of the Holocene over the past 10'000 years.

I remember some years ago being at a seminar at which John Foster was speaking about his latest book 'The sustainability mirage: illusion and reality in the coming war on climate change'. He was reflecting on us being generally in denial about climate change, noticing that writing the book was likely a symptom of his own denial. I suppose he was considering his book writing as some kind of a self-indulgent distraction from being politically engaged and active by 'hitting the streets'. In many ways this could be a fair point, learning-writing could well be understood as a rather egocentric endeavour. Although, in a relational world it is certainly complex to trace the reverberations of some humans actions in relation to changing and influencing our flowing world. The idea that marching around town holding a placard about an issue of concern is doing activism, and assembling words into a book about an issue of concern, to learn about it and hopefully share some of the learning with others, can not be involved in activism, is an interesting one. Clearly, there is a place for both forms of acting, and 'being activist', the consequences of either of them, the placard waving or the book writing, is dependent on the broad field of acting within which they are taking place. As well as how they may, or may not, translate into what might be regarded as 'productive' or 'positive' ways forward.

I was recently listening to a recorded webinar about

'Decolonizing ecological relations' where one of the contributors was Daniel Ribeiro who worked for civil society non-profit organization in Mozambique. There are a couple of aspects that I want to notice about Daniel's great contributions to the event. Firstly, he was described as 'an activist' which was set up alongside, or even perhaps in opposition, to the main speaker 'an academic'. So he could be identified as somebody who was 'on the ground' and 'at the coal face' so to speak. As such 'activism' was framed as being something that is clearly different and distinctive to being an 'academic'. Perhaps these are just the ruminations of a 'navel gazing' academic, worried about justifying the meaning and value of academic work, including writing this book!

In Chapter 1 I considered how the category of 'academic' is often socially understood to mean not having 'practical effects in real life', as per the definition that was included from the online Cambridge Dictionary. I am not trying to mount some resolute defence of all academic work, as some of it I would not be that keen on defending, but notice that this separation (activist and academic) is intriguing. This is because it suggests that we know what activism, 'direct and noticeable action' (going back to the online Cambridge Dictionary) is, and how to do it so as to have an effect and change things for whatever we might see as 'the better'. I do not think we do. I would observe that it seems to be a constellation of actings, some of which might be meticulously planned by communities of people, others entirely accidental that can appear to accumulate into some lumpy processes of change. Changes that can be substantially imperceptible, but might become manifest by coherent narratives being generated about it. For example, going back to Daniel, from his brief biography for the webinar we can read the coherent narrative that "together with other citizens of the grassroots movement, he has opposed and successfully ended a Danish funded toxic waste incinerator project in Mozambique".

The second observation, or inspiration, from Daniel's contribution to the webinar was his frank comments about the delusion of our potential to change the world alone. A thought which signals something else that is important to consider about activism from a posthuman perspective. Some of my teaching is about leadership, in which we explore how ideas of 'heroic' individual person-leaders single handedly creating change is just one view on the subject, and one which can be understood as romanticising the potential for an individual in a field of actions (e.g. Collinson et al., 2018). We can understand this romanticising, anthropocentric imaginings of 'superhero' human beings, also in connection within ideas about activism. For example, I am a fan of Greta Thunberg the young Swede who, described as an 'environmental activist', has become very prominent in relation to telling governments about their underachievement, and the need for urgent and radical action on the climate emergency. However, to historicise her single act of sitting alone outside the Swedish parliament on strike as a 'trigger moment' which created a global (youth) movement in support of action on climate change is a significant flattening of realities. A flattening which can undermine all the other moments of action and activism which enabled the connecting of many bodies together (metaphorically more than physically!), through the school climate strikes, in which young people have signalled their collective dissatisfaction with affairs.

When I am involved in teaching ideas about leadership we explore how people can be observed to often have some collective predisposition to making hero leaders. Both in terms of making people 'over there' in charge so we can have some sense of comfort that somebody is going to fix it on our behalf, and can get on with watching our favourite television programme. As well as, part of a politics of activism, whereby crafting a story of action in relation to an imagined superhero person is neatly understandable, bringing confidence that we can be, and are, part of making whatever positive change we might be seeking. For example, Greta pictured scowling so wonderfully at Donald Trump as he arrived at the 2019 UN climate summit in New York, giving a sense that 'our hero' is scowling for us, helping us to stare-down 'our adversaries'. Although, as Daniel reminds us we need a modesty about what we can do, which is key to considering how our meshing into a web of sociomaterial relations can potentially help us to make sense of the unknowable possibilities and achievements. We will revisit and further explore some of these themes in Part 3.

Before we continue on to the main focus of this chapter by exploring the dilemma of 'proximity', what I want to take out of this opening is to remind us of the metaphor of the 'I' as "a vulnerable and confused refugee" which we considered in Chapter 3 (Allen, 2019c, p. 74). In this earlier chapter, when writing-about-writing I suggested that the 'I' can be understood as constellations of multifarious mediatings which enable the assembling of text. In a posthuman view we are compelled to accept that it is not congruent with notions of individual all-seeing and all-conquering human heroes, be they 'writers', 'leaders' or 'activists'. As was explored with the first dilemma of centrality in Chapter 4, decentering the human requires an acceptance that we are *witnessing-being-witnessed*, thrashing about within that flowing river of sociomaterial relatings. In doing so, we have thoroughly renounced that humanistic 'I' which can offer us a mirage of clear-mindedly sailing atop, aloof of the river of the other-than-human beneath.

The last few paragraphs are not some convoluted extricating of myself from any possibilities of delusion, in this book writing endeavour, whilst 'the world burns'. Well I suppose they might be, something to keep me busy, distracted from grim realities. As Kae Tempest writes in this brief excerpt of her song-poem 'Tunnel Vision':

> "..You can't face the past, the past's a dark place
> Can't sleep, can't wake, sitting in our boxes
> Notching up our victories as other people's losses
> Another day, another chance to turn your face away from pain
> Let's get a takeaway
> And meet me in the pub a little later, we'll say the same things as ever
> Life's a waiting game
> When we gonna see that life is happening?
> And that every single body bleeding on its knees is an abomination
> And every natural being is making communication
> And we're just sparks, tiny parts of a bigger constellation
> We're miniscule molecules that make up one body.."

The last two lines were spoken to me by our radio alarm clock one morning a few years back when Kae Tempest's song was being played, its Bateson-like tone drew it from background 'wake-up' noise into a foregrounded chorus. Talk about the speaking-of-things! I can only wonder about the potential tapestry of sociomaterial ricochets that brought these words to me as I woke up, Tempest's work does not seem often to appear in 'mainstream' channels of communications.

Being affect-ed

To consider the dilemma of proximity I want to return back to the writing of Introna which was quite prominent in the previous chapter. One key strand to the ideas that Introna (2014) develops, who is coming into this mostly from an (information) technology orientation, is that his suggestions about developing the ethical appreciations of things requires bringing in the notion of 'affect', or 'affective'. So after dragging you through sociomateriality, posthumanism, mediators and affordances, I am now going to bring in another term! This one is core to considering the proximity dilemma which I am associating with developing a witnessing perspective, so I do not see any way to avoid it.

Affect is one of those terms that I have noticed which has been 'doing the rounds' on various 'academic circuits'. As I mentioned before with the need for, and valuing of, 'newness' these words become fashionable, its kind of like name dropping at a party to gain legitimacy, but in this case it is with certain words and concepts when giving a presentation or writing an article. This name dropping is about being able to be 'academically hip' and 'down with the lingo'. Okay so that is being a bit naff, I notice myself of being guilty of it, but it is always nice to 'fit in' by appearing like you know what you are on about. Although, the idea of 'affect' is one that I have generally steered clear of, as despite my efforts I am not sure that I 'get it'. The problem with these words 'of the moment' is that we can begin to assume that we and other people know what they are talking about, or indeed that we are all talking within the same understanding of a term. Whereas we might all be as confused as each other and there is no 'getting it', but at least we found a way to briefly drop it into our conference presentation. However, with witnessing as we will go on to consider notions of 'affect' can help us to approach the second dilemma of witnessing in relation to 'proximity'.

In her writing about witnessing Clough suggests that because witnessing "does not use language to speak, but to touch" it is necessarily affective (2009, p. 150). By referring to the work of Sue Grand, she describes enactive witnessing as "sensory, prelinguistic and devoid of agency" (Clough, 2009, p. 153), "below meaning" (p. 151). Affect like many, or even all concepts that have gained attention across a range of areas of research and associated writing, and can be understood to be connected with a technicoloured variety of meanings. A range that I am not about to claim any substantial coverage of in this chapter. However, as with the statements of Clough, a general idea about affect is that it is a human reaction or feeling, often associated with ideas of emotion, which is somehow beyond the linguistic inscription of a particular word with associated meanings. As we considered in Chapter 2 attaching words to particular things, to categorise them as distinct and different to other things, seems a pragmatic and practical way to go. But, as we also discussed doing so can make us naive or ambivalent to the performative consequences of these inscribings, which can reverberate beyond the 'surface-level' description. An example of the implications for such delineations, that we have already considered was for 'business' and 'society', and the dis-embedding of one from the other, by making them as different realms. A general inference of 'affective' is that it is about grasping for ways of being which circumvent language. Whereby human language is seen to be something which can be problematically cast like a net to overlay all others, and so drawing the world inescapably together, only able to be understood within its threads. So, if with witnessing we are seeking to decentre human-being and valuing, appreciating 'affective' contact with others can offer possibilities. This is because, as informed by Haraway (1997, 2008, 2016), witnessing is given meanings of being present and responsible in relation to some aspects of being in a world, but with the awareness of an inability to fully appreciate what you are being present and responsible towards. Remember the version of posthumanism that we are pursuing is one of getting out of those 'old boxes' to make sense differently for the benefit of others. As Abram (1996) writes about the meaning of making sense in his book exploring 'perception and language in a more-than-human world':

> "A story that makes sense is one that stirs the senses from their slumber, one that opens the eyes and ears to the real surroundings, tuning the tongue to the actual tastes in the

> air and sending chills of recognition along the surface of the skin. To make sense is to release the body from the constraints imposed by outworn ways of speaking, and hence to renew and rejuvenate one's felt awareness of the world. It is to make the senses wake up where they are." (Abram, 1996, p. 265)

In connection with these ideas of a being in a world through a bodily awareness related to something of a 'broader sensory array', a significant part of Introna's argument, whose writing we considered in Chapter 4, involves appreciating contact with the other as affective, which he describes as "in the flesh" with nothing in mind (2014, p. 14). He suggests that this an important idea because contact can involve a "radical openness to the mystery of the otherness of the other" which "resists the force of human consciousness" (Introna, 2014, p. 17). A human consciouness that as explored in relation to the human centrality dilemma, can usher in a hierarchy of beings based on human valuing. In Introna's writing the emotion of affect is not suggested to be a humanistic sense of conscious emotion in the 'mind', but of bodily being, of the flesh. The way in which Introna seeks to explore affect is orientated around the human sense of touch, this is because as he describes:

> "Touch, unlike other senses, such as vision and hearing, creates immediate proximity—yet it has no specific organ, it requires only flesh. In touching there is no distance, no intermediary. In the moment of touch there is simply no 'gap' in which the incessant and insistent intentionality of consciousness can insert itself, unless of course we allow it to do so in due course." (Introna, 2014, p. 19)

Introna poetically writes towards the end of his chapter that "the ethos of letting be is impossible – and so it should be" (2014, p.

26). In many ways signalling that there seems to be something of an inevitable impossibility in this searching for responsible-being. If we grasp at posthuman 'alternatives' too definitely and confidently, they will slip away from us. We by definition cannot know the unknowable. Although, in the service of helping to develop the perspective of witnessing I remain enthusiastic for the imagining that this work can prompt us towards. In particular, a sense of the need for affective contact to overcome humans as the supreme source of all valuing of the usefulness of others.

To imagine the possibilities for *witnessing-being-witnessed*, and the mutual speaking between things we are moved towards a conception of unknowingness that is so, because it is pre-knowing. Going back to the ideas of Bateson about respecting the significance of the unconsciousness of our interdependencies, notions of affect can help to extend our visibility. However, although these ideas can seem attractive as part of circumventing the naming and construing of boundaries around things, witnessing beyond language may well feel out of reach, because as soon as we may notice it to be so, it becomes lost to us. Also, if affect, understood as being a physical emotional process rather than a cognitive one, is about contact and our ability to feel through our flesh, does witnessing become restrictive to things touchable that are proximal and willing? Would this mean that our bodily potential to make contact becomes a new ordering of things, i.e. those out of reach can only matter less? Or, if our bodily potential to move to be in contact is compromised, is our potential to relate with many aspects of a world is somehow disabled?

It is with this notion of touch and contact that we find ourselves opening up questions associated with the dilemma of proximity. What I mean by this is that if affect is about touch and the flesh, if appreciated as physically more than a metaphor, then our body would need to be in some close physical proximity to whatever 'other'. For example, like the writing of Valtonen and Pullen (2021) who explore 'being touched by rocks'. This is an interesting path as by taking being in this way, of being in-touch aside of the mediations of language, implies that we can start to consider different ways of being-our-entanglement. As well as consider possible meanings of being 'close enough' to witness being gazed at by an-other, remember those disposable cups mentioned in Chapter 4. However, if we reflect back on the dilemma of centrality, considered in Chapter 4, being-in-touch puts us in 'the centre' of the action.

Witnessing-being-witnessed attempts to draw us back from any compulsions to make claims to knowing the other, to a more tentative way of feeling our whereabouts within the flows of being. Touching, as Introna (2014) suggests, potentially opens up a different kind of sense, it also gives an impression that we have to bring and gather things towards our bodies as the locus of any 'letting-be'. What this means is attempting to negate an anthropocentrism of knowing all in relation to us, could be understood to become an anthropocentrism of proximity to our bodies. This is because, that which is out-of-reach to a human body cannot bring about affective responses, and so be 'let-be'. In this learning-writing let me be clear I am not trying to launch some critique towards Introna and others, we are exploring the possibilities which their assembled texts appear to offer in the pursuit of developing ideas of witnessing. The connecting with others' words in this writing-learning process drawing in other texts, via referencing, is about transforming the visibilities and possibilities for what might be possible in our posthuman imagining.

Staring through windows

Let us try to explore where we might be with this proximity dilemma by working through an example. In the summer of 2020

I painted the frames of the front windows of the house that we moved into when we relocated to Sheffield, a city in the north of Britain. Glass in its various forms has been suggested to be made by humans for many thousands of years. Although it was in the 'early industrial age' (beginning c.1760) that glass became a product "to enclose windows from the elements and admit light while preserving a view outside" (Eskilson, 2018, p. 1). If I walk around our local area, windows with glass in them are ubiquitous, apart from perhaps a few uninhabited, partially derelict or derelict buildings. By reflecting on a human history glass windows we can understand that they have not been involved for very much of it. Like the technologies of chairs mentioned in Chapter 4. However, where I am, in space and time, they are an accepted, and likely taken-for-granted, part of how we 'do buildings'.

Windows are a pretty handy technology at doing the work of keeping inclement weather out whilst allowing light in, and enabling us to look through them to the outside. Features which are particularly relevant if you are living in a cooler part of the planet, so nearer to either pole than the equator. Also, as Eskilson (2018) considers particularly emerging in the early 19th century the notion of light and 'enlightenment' connected with progress, versus some prior ages of 'darkness', is a narrative that has became closely interwoven with what windows 'stand for' and how there are understood. Of course there are many different types of windows, many different frames and glass, and different ways of glazing enable varying heat retention in the building. I am sure that the variations can get more than a little bamboozling, and I do not have any particular awareness of these. My awareness of glass stretches to sand being a key component, and that achieving its transparency requires substantial heating and rapid cooling.

Attending to our front windows does not seem a very remarkable moment, which is mainly because it was not. Although as briefly

Being-in-proximity? A photo of the repaired front window frames of our house of which I was in close contact

just discussed it is a technology that is transformative to how we construct buildings, and also our being within them. If the window to my left was not allowing me light and holding the winter cold outside, it would be challenging, or impossible, to be typing these words towards assembling the hoped for outcome of a book. As well as the electrical circuitry of the computer which is allowing my typing not standing up to well to being regularly precipitated upon. Without the window my writing by necessity would become much more seasonally orientated than it is currently. A dry and windy day as a 'washing day', due to being more able to dry washed clothes on a line outside, might also become a 'writing day', as wearing gloves to keep your hands warm that may intervene in the potential to type would not be needed.

The metaphor of 'enlightenment' can be extended into making connections with the previously mentioned dualisms, such as associated with writings by people such as Descartes. This is because glass can be appreciated as a hard but transparent a boundary, between the inside and the outside. Often framed in angular pure white, plastic or wood. Such that we are enclosed, particularly for example behind the windscreen of a car, from 'the outside'. We tend not to find nicely glazed windows on barns on farms so that the cows, or whatever animals they contain, may be able to see out whilst they are keeping out of cold and damp fields during winter months. So we can understand them to be a boundary for humans, physically separating us from 'nature' i.e. very fitting for those imposed dualisms. Also, allowing and enticing us to be safely behind them as we are able to peer upon that 'nature' which is 'outside'. Although, for many of us living in urban spaces there may well be more concrete to gaze at through our windows than living things. Or, alternatively looking in from the street through a shop window at the shiny objects for sale inside which are 'starring out' at us. The window can be a very tangible reminder of how we have bred ideas of our implausible detachment from others. Indeed during times of pandemic windows have become a protective layer for our bodies, as we stay at home behind them attempting to keep safe from contracting or transmitting the virus. Ironically, during these times if we are inside with others enclosed by windows we could well be at greater risk of passing the virus between ourselves, as we understand that we become safer in the open air where droplets of the virus can disperse more quickly and widely.

Painting windows

The concern that I had developed for our windows, more particularly their wooden frames, is that they themselves should be protected from the weather which they protect us from. In this example, related to exploring the dilemma of proximity, which we will consider over the coming paragraph, this is where we get into tricky territory for how I might understand myself to be responsible-being by witnessing our windows. If I reflect on this situation of window painting and repair I can not suggest that I left much potential for mutual witnessing. I did touch the window frames, I felt the flaking of paint in some places and the slight cracking open of parts of the wood. The next step to preserve the window seems obvious, that 'they need' to be covered in more of the white coloured paint to preserve them as protective layer to the outside. It is a reflex for how to exist along with these windows, which as explored, have become pieces of everyday banality.

The flaking surfaces of the windows needed to be 'rubbed down' to allow more paint to take hold. Doing so involves stroking the surfaces of the wooden frames as you go to make sure they are smooth enough to receive their treatment and 'revival'. From the stroking I felt an unfortunate squidgy sense of wood, which made me realise that in one part the window frame lacked the hardness of wood that my fingers would expect of this solid boundary maker. Consequently, I needed to pick out the unfortunate 'deadness' of this wood which had become exposed and rotten, it went deep in one place, I grabbed a screw driver to score-out the dampened wood. It was not an inconsiderable wound. I was not expecting that there had been such an attack on this able defender of weather. I remember cursing the neglect of previous humans who dwelt in this place, the window is not that old, maybe seven years or so, but to have 'allowed' such harm. My fingers went deep into the wound that I exposed and hollowed out. I continued to scrape at its edges with the screw driver until, to my touch, there was a minimal sense of dampness. It was then time to fill the hole that I had created with wood-filler. It is certainly not a filler-of-wood, it is a filler-for-wood. It did not smell of wood, but instead reeked of adhesive, so prominent even outside, one of those smells that feels so alien that you become desperate to 'stop smelling' so that you do not catch even a faint trace of if. The filler came with a small piece of flat plastic to use as a spatula, this pungent and gelatinous substance can be harmful if it comes into contact with hands. I tried to quickly smear it into the hole that I had made by scoring-out the rotting wood from the frame, this was not a substance that I want to be in close contact with for long.

I returned back to the windows after half-an-hour or so, as this is the time the tin which holds the filler instructs me will be enough for it to dry hard and be ready to be rubbed back. There was now no hole in the frame just the browny-yellowy colour of the hardened filler. To create a smooth finish, to fully cover up the puncture, which the window has endured through my removal of the damp bits of wood, I brought back the sand-paper which I earlier used to rub down the flaking of the previous layers of paint. This time the cloud of dust particles that I produced from my rubbing was worse than before, because the particles of dust I create by rubbing the hardened filler are smaller more numerous, and they waft down on to the soil and towards the small nearby pond in our front garden. With the slight movement of breeze around me it was impossible to keep the filler-dust-particles under control so that they can all be swept up into the bag in which I tried to collect the detritus from this window work. I swept up and wiped down the patched-up frames with an old cloth, a part of an old t-shirt, so that they were prepared for their surfaces to be coated in the white paint. I ran my fingers over the surface to feel for any missed knobbly parts which the sand paper has not eradicated. Following this physical inspection I checked the tips of my fingers to see if they had picked up any dust, this would show me that my wiping to clean the surface was not entirely successful. The flesh on my fingers was not obviously covered in any grime, and I did not perceive knobbliness, so the window frames appeared ready for being painted.

At this stage before the paint might be applied. To preserve the maximum see-through-ability of the glass it is necessary to try to prevent it from becoming involved in being painted. I pulled masking tape from its reel to stick it where glass meets wood to form a temporary barrier. Also, as part of this protection of things from the paint I placed a bed cover, now rejected from covering beds, over the ground below, to be there to receive any drips and splashes that my painting might produce. An old table spoon allowed me into the paint pot, and also enables me to stir the liquid, once again this is a substance which tells me that I should avoid getting it onto my skin. And, absolutely avoid swigging it as if it could 'refresh me', as I hoped that it will do to our understanding of the appearance of the windows on the front of our house. By clutching the wooden handle of the brush I began the painting, covering over the filled wound so that no other being will be aware from a glance at the window of the surgery that I performed on that rotten part the frame. It was a warm summer evening, outside painting is ideally a seasonal activity for avoiding becoming too cold a human body. Also, as the windows need to be in an open position for painting, to get paint into all the required places, if it is cold outside it will make human bodies inside cold. Small flying insects became inexplicably attracted to the fresh layers of the frame, inspite of my occasional wafting and protestations they kept coming, some stuck by becoming enveloped in paint, they are now also window. I repeated three cycles of applying paint across a couple of days, as I am keen that the frame does not suffer another rotting lesion. They were done, white, again, able to appear 'looked after' to anybody who wanders by, and with a thicker 'skin' to repel whatever weather may come.

Stories of proximity

There are at least two stories of being-responsible in relation to my close window contact. They are very much contrasting stories, which can help us to explore the dilemmas of proximity that we are considering in this chapter. The first story is of a romantic orientation. Whereby the main narrative is one of human care and being-in-touch with a window which is part of a home. From a witnessing perspective my family and I have become with-house, bound together with this building in the flow of contracting within arrangements of private ownership, enrolled into this binding through our embeddedness within regimes of capital accumulation. With-house we become tied to dwelling within this place, moving and being within its walls. We are more than in proximity to it, it becomes are locus, particularly in locked-down pandemic times! The home-owning entangles us into being in care of a heterogeneity of matter which constitutes it, as well as the array of contractual obligations which are tied to sustain it as a recognised dwelling, such as the provision of water, sewerage and electricity.

Our house has stood for over one hundred years, in some ways a very permanent presence, but one that has been with us for a mere snapshot of human, let alone planetary, evolution. However, it is here, and although its interior will have changed, its walls were here before all of us. Being-responsible witness likely draws us towards ideas of respect and associated preservation. To not tear down, or rip out its interiors, but to be-in-contact and maintain its integrity, whereby we can be understood to be at its centre, not it at ours. A posthuman explanation may well draw our attention to how our house organizes us, and our lives, often much more so than we organize it. The house making us as human inside, rather than placing us as feral creature outside. In such an approach the window repairing which I have written about seems fitting. A process of touching, smoothing and patching up – feeling, listening and smelling those things in proximity. Ways of connecting potentially beyond the logic of wanting to engage in home maintenance. Such a reading could place us a valued-witness if we were to engage with windows in the ways that I have explained. As well as, by preserving a window, 'saving' and being in solidarity with an other, perhaps a distant tree, that would otherwise be taken, dragged and carved up to become its replacement.

In another story we might find ourselves written as being the midst of a more violent turn. In which by inhabiting this building, we are keeping out all 'others', which through its dereliction, and associated reconfigurings to be rubble those 'others', perhaps the badgers currently residing in a garden space that has become 'wild' further down the road that our house is on, could become permissible entrants. It is a story of keeping us at the centre and enclosed from others. By keeping our windows we keep our humanity, and associated distinctions and superiorities. As mentioned earlier that window technology which has become normal over the past 250 years, a suggested part of 'an enlightenment of our lives', keeps us away from the outside, but allows us to see it, whilst not physically being with and 'in it'. A repair can be retold as a defence of this distance and bolstering of a protective screen, of keeping us at the centre. By cutting out wood to flagrantly apply 'other worldly' chemical formulas – I can not forget the stench of wood-filler – this barrier is shored up. By spewing particles previously unknown to the life-giving soil or water in the pond, as if an array of incendiaries which may well become toxic inside other species, I perhaps becoming implicated in their death. By insects beings becoming encased as part of the window I can be understood to have killed them by trapping them in the sticky paint surface.

The sharp distinctions between these two narratives, is not one of competing intentions, because as we have explored a posthuman sensibility displaces humanist intentions at the centre of any explanations, with that of entanglement within often turbulent flows of mediatings. Remember, from our key metaphor, we are immersed within the river, not being a-top enclosed within our boat. In this view the windows we have considered have agency from their sociomateriality. This is because they are involved in organizing us behind them, in this case helping to negate 'outdoor cold-ness' for 'indoor write-ability', by affording our bodies a protecting and illuminating layer. This protective layer as an 'extension' of the body. But, unlike Mol's previous example in Chapter 4, that involved workers washing bananas in a Costa Rican plantation as an extension of bodily protection, the window is in much closer physical proximity. These paragraphs were first put together whilst snow was falling outside the window, a first floor window this time of our house. A plastic framed one with double glazing that we arranged to be installed last winter, but I think we have maybe indulged sufficiently on the downstairs window example. So let us not 'go there' in contemplation of the different histories of the upstairs window! The window is *witnessing-being-witnessed*, transforming the potential for this text assembly to be 'all-weather'. However, the responsibility towards its wood-glass composition, as these two narratives suggest, is not one that can be simply understood. Indeed my proximity, having spent some time touching and being-with-it does not easily connect to some sense of affective involvement, becoming 'moved' through the time spent together. As has been suggested the sustaining of this window through my mending and protecting, is to maintain the exclusion of other beings, such as the nearby badgers, from the human homespace that it is part of encasing. A contractual 'owning' of the house with its walls and windows, as well as its physical and legal connections into networks of water, electricity and gas distribution, enrol a necessity to maintain it as enclosed from many 'others'. Witnessing is not a perspective that is meant to 'tell us' what to do with our windows or any-thing else, but explore the possibilities for meanings of responsible mutual interacting.

Being benign?

When we consider responsibility for sustainability, we can be drawn to what we might describe as an eco-narrative. There is an accompanied sense of a need for 'treading softly' by changing those things that we see as useful for human activity into the most 'ecologically benign' formulation possible. Of course there is substantial merit in being aware of the materials you might employ and their potential consequences to others. For example, I wrote about books, this book specifically, at the beginning of Chapter 4, and tracing the potential constellation of sociomaterial relations which can be entangled in putting books together. However, by using things we do likely enter into a minefield of potentially competing ethics. Here I am referring to an 'ethics of care', which we briefly considered in Chapter 3, that is about avoiding being involved in relations that harm interdependent beings.

An instance of matters of care would be the use of the wood filler that I mentioned in relation to the windows. It was from a nearby local independent painting and decorating shop that I walked to, and when I asked for wood filler for the window that was 'the thing for the job'. A relation of minimal energy used to gather the material from the shop and 'support' the organization as something of the 'local' area. However, with all its chemical infusions that produced the stench that I encountered whilst applying it, and the tiny dust particles it dispersed when being rubbed down, its use feels highly problematic for potential harm to other creatures. Significantly, the filler-ing was likely the most affect-ing part of my window maintaining, emanating an odour that was repelling me, and with a need for my skin not to come in to contact with it.

The eco-narrative would tend to signal to us to do-things to a minimum, or not at all, typically from some firm sense of knowing what is situationally and momentarily best. Such a perspective is a very valuable view for the attentions and moments of reflection it brings. Although it does likely centre a knowing autonomous human who is 'in control' and able to choose the 'right-thing' or 'right-way-of-doing' to consciously make their own destiny in their world. Perhaps witnessing could come across to some as rather wishy-washy and not militant enough in times of climate emergency, but the eco-narrative can unfortunately, and somewhat paradoxically, render our nonexistence more sustainable i.e. that many species sustainabilities are eminently more attainable without humans. That potential literal 'dead-end' of some versions of posthumanism that was mentioned in Chapter 3.

In this chapter we are considering the dilemma of proximity based on the suggestions that being-in-contact with others allows some affective connection, which offers us opportunities to somehow circumvent a net of language which we cast upon the world. A net of sound patterns, words, and associated categories which produce boundaries and differences between things, rendering them more knowable and available for human use. We have tried to explore how witnessing with its underpinning assumptions of sociomateriality, that 'social' and 'material' aspects only become meaningful through their interrelationships, can involve us appreciating ourselves as becoming affect-ed when our bodies are physically connected to 'others'. As Introna writes about ideas of 'letting-be' - "dwelling in the midst of the radically other without succumbing to the desire to turn it into something knowable, that is, into something in our image" (Introna, 2014, p. 16). However, ironically, in relation to ideas of affect, we might need to physically draw things towards us, for them to have value in their own right from us touching each-other. There is also the challenge of things that affect us, can do so, in ways that are not so much about the close contact, but more the memories we associate with them. This is because of the meanings we give to them, that can connect to feelings of emotion towards them. Such feelings can be hard to be understood as bodily emotions, in the flesh as with Introna (2014), but more towards an inscribing of meaning to them through their associations with others.

On repairing

There is a television series on BBC 'The Repair Shop' in which crafts people use tools to repair the old, or 'antique', items which are selected to be brought in for repair. To make it as entertaining as possible a story is given to explain how the objects (for example, a clock, a teddy bear, a child's toy etc.) which are selected for repair have particular significance to the people who possess them. Typically, it is an object that has close association to a deceased relative or friend. In this situation, the touching and care of the object is given over to the crafts people, and their accumulated skills of repairing, in ways that 'retain the integrity' of the object being old i.e. they generally replace any parts with those that are appropriate to the time and place of the object's creation. As the viewer of this television programme you are taken through the journey of each objects repair with the craft persons' commentary about how and what they are going to do.

The culmination of the repair is its return to the person who brought it to 'The Repair Shop'. This encountering of the now transformed object by its possessor is often one that elicits emotions, most visibly by the person, or people, crying or becoming dumbfounded. Of course if we are thinking about 'affect' we cannot understand what is going on here. However, there is an intriguing sense that those, the crafts people, who have done all the touching and caring of the object, perhaps completely dismantling and rebuilding it over many days, seem often little affected by it, as far as can be determined by the snapshots of entertainment you as viewer are presented with. When there might be a noticeable sense of the repairer being affected by the object being repaired, this tends to be associated with a story of how they give meaning to it, via a sense of similarity, to people, events and things in their own lives.

Whilst we can not 'boil down' emotion to tears, and with it affect, how we can understand ourselves to encounter and relate to others, as we have considered in a few examples, is complex. From this Repair Shop example we could suggest that it is the long-term proximity to having an object, and touching it, looking after it, that has been involved in developing this outward emotion of tears when re-encountering it, following the object being 'operated upon' and 'resuscitated' by the skilled crafts person. The object has touched the possessor over time in an affective relationship "in the flesh", beyond words (Introna, 2014, p. 14). Although in that moment of the object being returned to them it could be read as a 'conscious emotion' of the mind, rather than based within this history of contact. However, it is the history of meaning associated with the object, who they knew had it, what they did with it, how it came to be with them etc. that is what constitutes the spoken explanation. This is a socially credible explanation, for likely inexplicable sensations of being in connection with an-other. An explanation which constitutes a post-hoc rationalisation of how we came to express an emotion, which is based on attributing meaning to the object through a constructed narrative of the humans who have kept it. It is an anthropocentric narrative whereby it becomes impossible for the object to have value in itself, as it is always a derivative of human involvement and use. Thereby making sense of 'affect' seems to be predicated upon the bifurcation of human and nonhuman, which crucially witnessing is attempting to evade.

Witnessing-being-witnessed, if this is a perspective of possibilities, would need to be elusively beyond our explanations. This is the point, unless perhaps our explanations are expressed in other than words, maybe some form of artistic creation. If we are to engage in unknowingness, which as we considered in Chapter 3 can be appreciated as 'going with the territory' of understanding within a relational view, it becomes hard to engage in expressing unknowing, beyond a shrug of the shoulders and a mystified uttering of "I have no idea". As above, our makings of what is going on rests on a legitimacy of making a clear enough 'cut', to refer to Barad (2007), between us and them/it for an explanation to fit within the accepted web of sound patterns which allow our explaining. To go back to Orlikowski who was quoted in Chapter 2 about the claim that "knowing is material" (2006, p. 3) – based on ideas that it is through our bodies materially being-in-a-world that we are able to appreciate any-thing – in relation to this consideration of witnessing and the dilemma of proximity, we could extend this appreciation to our awareness of things being material. What I mean by this is that with the questions of 'affect' it is something which can be understood to be physical, through being and doing with others.

Animal proximity

In Chapter 3 I was keen to make sure that the perspective of witnessing involves an attention to the more-than-human that is more-than-human-technology. In particular other creatures, species and organisms. I have already written, in Chapter 4, that nonhuman creatures or animals is 'a space' in which I want to be very careful to 'enter into', as it is not an area of debate in which I am claiming any particular specialist understanding. However, more-than-human-technology is crucial to bring into developing a witnessing perspective. This is because of how the possible futures of living beings are becoming transformed by changing climates, and the degrading of life giving processes within ecosystems e.g. increasing acidification of oceans. Creatures encompass huge variety with a heterogeneity of sensory arrays. For example, Barad's 'brittlestar' discussion, "an animal without a brain" with an "intertwined skeletal and diffuse nervous system" (2007, p. 374). Also, in Chapter 4 we considered the example of how a stream of research into 'green leaf volatiles' suggests how plants are able to communicate with other plants in proximity to 'warn' them of predators. Consequently, to contemplate witnessing in relation to a plethora of 'other-forms-of-life' which are more-than-human-technology is decidedly complicated. In this critical exploration, we need to remember, once more, that we are seeking to develop a perspective, and to not get overly lost in the potential for it to be *the* perspective.

In relation to living beings, although this includes massive variety, a sense of *witnessing-being-witnessed* feels perhaps more graspable. As mentioned these beings are understood to have different forms of sensory array in which they, in various ways, may be able to feel the presence of 'others', and to 'speak'. In many ways because we can understand these beings as beyond language they seem like obvious partners to be-with in mutual witnessing. Albeit we might find that it is more appealing, or possible, to be *witnessing-being-witnessed* with the robin singing in a garden in Britain, than a western diamondback rattle snake hissing at us somewhere in North America. Although as I have been shown by sitting through many hours of the BBC television series 'Deadly 60' with my daughter, snakes with venom that can be deadly to humans, are unlikely to bite unless provoked or mistakenly trodden on. One demarcation of animals is whether they are 'domesticated' or 'wild'. However, in Anthropocene times, in which, as we explored in Chapter 1, as we are understanding ourselves to be implicated in transforming global climate, notions of 'wild' can become a complex and potentially distracting labelling (McKibben, 1990). For example, if that rattle snake is hissing at us from behind the glass boundaries of a vivarium.

When we started to consider the dilemma of proximity in relation to other-forms-of-life, as we did so with technologies, we turned our attention to that which we touch, or is touchable. However, with animals touching them, as in a 'petting zoo' or at a pet shop is most easily associated with ideas of subornation or control, that of domestication. The potential to be able to touch them means that they are not 'out-there' moving through the settings in which they have evolved. They are 'in-here', in the case of a pet shop, literally valued for the pleasure they may bring to a human, in their possession, as a pet. I have to admit I am really not a big fan of pets largely based on the images just conveyed.

To take an example to explore witnessing let us consider a domestic cat. An animal which, going back to the windows example, that we can understand as a barrier to the feral, is allowed into a house. Indeed more than allowed, the house is mutually construed by owner and cat as 'at home', a relationship of domestication that has been suggested to go back thousands of years to ancient Egypt. Indeed the domestic cat 'Felis catus' was been declared a distinct species in 2003 by the International Commission on Zoological Nomenclature. There is mixing of the alive more-than-human in this de-marked human domain, a house.

We are clearly in-touch with the cat through stroking it when it is sat on our lap, it may purr back at us during this time together. We could argue that the cat is 'free' to go out, it might have its own flap in the back door of the house so that it may come and go unassisted. Perhaps a digital collar device worn by the cat allows only this/our feline in through the flap in the back door, repelling others. The cat then goes out-side into its 'wild', possibly the streets of a city, it will likely prey on the local bird population. If you are in some parts of London the local bird population will include 'feral' parakeets which have taken up residence by some escaping their capture in cages in London houses, having been kept for their 'exotic' look (Hunt, 2019). The cat returns to its home to eat the 'cat food' which comes out of a tin, probably containing some 'factory farmed' and processed animal, such as cow, chicken, pig or fish – assumed as 'good cat nutrition'. This presents us with something of a complex tapestry of Anthropocene domestic-wild 'naturalness'. This is because feeling these nonhuman others, creatures and other species, 'in the flesh' by bringing them into close proximity with our bodies we can appear to take-away their otherness.

The rights that these creatures have, like the cat, are centred around our claimed rights to caring for them. The two dilemmas that we have been exploring so far, in this and the previous chapter, of centrality and proximity, can be understood to create their own tensions. This is because, by being-in-touch, in respect of understandings of being affect-ed in the body, requires at a minimum a drawing toward to be in physical proximity, it may even require the capture and domestication of another animal-being. In doing so we are making ourselves at the centre. Although, how we came to be with cat could be various, perhaps we 'saved it' from being a stray, it came to us. Also, the cat may bring order to us, control our movements and doings, as much as we might be implicated in shaping and constraining the cat. For example, our associations to the cat, and its expressed needs, may not afford us possibilities to be away from home for many days. Or, due to breathing difficulties from a body coming into contact with cat fur, for that body 'a friend' the house may be transformed into a space that they are no longer able to enter. Consequently, we can see the potentialities for *witnessing-being-witnessed* are far from straight forward, and as already written were never envisaged to be so.

A closing thought on distance

In this exploration of proximity, the last aspect that I want to discuss is the potential of mutual witnessing from 'a distance' i.e. when beings are not within the same physical space. This is because a strand of the writing about witnessing involves ideas of being affected through mediated experiences, such as via television news reporting (e.g. Hill, 2019). In this situation of 'the news' being reported to us, we are 'turned away' from the possibility feeling affect in the flesh, moved towards wording and categorising, because these inform the images and messages being communicated to us. Although, it is possible to suppose that the mediators of messages and images about these distance things or events could be something of 'art', beyond words. Such as for Ruskin with the poetry of Wordsworth and the paintings of JMW Turner, imagining them as "a way of perceiving eternal moral realities in nature" (Szerszynski, 1996, p. 125).

The opportunity of witnessing at distance seems important. This is because as we have explored in relation to the unknowability of things, which was first considered in Chapter 3, that which comes into proximity with us, in particular technologies – books, chairs, wood-filler etc. – much of what 'that stuff is made of' is beyond view. Hidden in chains-of-supply, with the mediatings of our relational entanglements not often of the proximate 'local'. Being able to witness beyond what we can touch may well then seem an important aspect of responsible-being. However, as mentioned there is a potential problem of how, because the distance is bridged through a language, the valuing human holds its place at its centre. Also, *witnessing-being-witnessed* is about a mutuality, a hoped for ethical equity, which in the case of creatures, for example an image of a polar bear on a melting ice-flow, we are well beyond their sensory array sat in-front of the screen which we are viewing them on. Indeed if we were within their sensory array they may well make us aware of their dissatisfaction about that arrangement! Although, of course it is also a mutuality in metaphor, in the case of a table that does not care if we are near or far to imagine its witnessing, which means that potentially the 'gaze' could be from afar.

By being 'on screen' the other, in this case the polar bear, becomes something of entertainment, human-entertainment. It is here however that our more-than-humans collide. We may be holding our screen, a device assembled by connections between extracted materials and minerals from the Earth, upon which the polar bear is shown, placing us somehow in-touch. Could the in-the-flesh become something that is mediated via a piece of electronic technology? The polar bear placing itself 'in the frame' being brought to us via a device with a screen that has taken hold of us, as in the satellite navigation from Chapter 2 becoming our directional force. The algorithmic throbbing of devices entangled in our living may feel to be inseparable from our bodies. This is the posthuman imagining that we can do with *witnessing-being-witnessed*. It is not a perspective of prescription, but of unsettling. *Witnessing-being-witnessed* can not be one thing, it is potentially momentary and ongoing. It may well be about the nearby but also perhaps of others afar. We would need to work at it, but not think at it, not with any humanist tendencies anyhow.

Chapter 6

Dilemma Three: Freedom?

Freedom from..

In Part 2 we have been exploring core dilemmas associated with possibilities for *witnessing-being-witnessed*. In this chapter, the final one in Part 2, we will consider meanings of, and implications for, the third dilemma – freedom. In particular we will consider key notions of 'freedom from' and 'freedom to', and potential interconnections between different forms and perceptions of freedom. As we will explore these are expansive debates which can be a struggle to enter. We will engage with some challenging critiques about human freedom in relation to ideas of posthumanism and sociomateriality. A key example used in exploring dilemmas of freedom, and responding to critiques, is about flying, in particular academics flying. Freedom and hierarchy in organizations, is also considered, a theme which will be expanded upon in Part 3. This chapter closes by bringing together dilemmas of freedom through considerations of being 'passively-active'. In the final part of the book, which follows this chapter, by drawing upon the learning-writing in Part 2, we will explore implications for *witnessing-being-witnessed* in respect of 'being' and 'organizing'.

At the beginning of Chapter 3, when we began to consider ideas of responsibility, I mentioned some competing ideas, or ideals, about people and organizations. I described a 'neoclassical' viewpoint as rooted in assumptions of separation and disconnection (Stubbs & Cocklin, 2008). I also explained that such a viewpoint, because it does not allow for any appreciations of interdependence, makes understanding any responsibility for sustainability, challenging. In a neoclassical view, the attainment of ideas of 'freedom' is based upon the preservation of what we could understand as a fantasy of separation. In this fantasy, freedom can be understood to be about doing what the hell you want, when you want, because there is an assumption of no consequences. Assumptions of separation and disconnection mean that there is somehow no feedback from what you do to other beings or things. It is a view point that is reliant on there being no dependencies on any-thing, or any-body, for action.

It is fair to say that I am not a fan of a 'neoclassical' perspective. It is a perspective in which I see little truth or value. Indeed we have spent many pages together now, if you have kept going with the words on these pages from the beginning, developing a sociomaterial perspective in a rather different direction! However, freedom in this 'neoclassical' view is perhaps quite straightforward, highly disagreeable, but quite straightforward. This is because you are free of any responsibility to anything at all. As we have explored, such views of human detachment are often noticed to be problematically at the heart of stories which propel the unsustainability of 'spaceship earth'. This is because socio-ecological sustainability assumes feedbacks and systemic connections that are denied from a neoclassical viewpoint.

When we consider a posthuman perspective which assumes sociomaterial entanglements, doing so raises questions such as: what are the implications and meanings of freedom within this perspective? This is the third of our three dilemmas for *witnessing-being-witnessed*. Remember, we are exploring dilemmas in this way as imagining we might be developing *the* perspective, *the* one-right-way of making sense, would be a massive mistake. Before exploring this dilemma we likely need to consider why we might care about freedom as something that needs to be part of, or somehow reflected in, a perspective that we might develop.

In some sense freedom could feel like a bit of a human-ist obsession, even perhaps self-obsession! Based on some idea that there is a need to 'self-actualise' and doing so involves being independent and in control. For example, if we could just accumulate enough money we would not need to care about anything else, we would be 'free'. Or, in the current context I write this, dare I type the letters, Brexit, oh damn it is even in this book now! A political imaginary that has harnessed support that is based within narratives of detachment, independence and a chest thumping 'taking back control!'. If we can only severe ties then we will be fine, our problems are because of 'them', those 'others' etc. That is all I can manage on it (the B-word), I am not even going to type those letters a second time, but it is an example of the significance of detachment for gaining political traction. It evidently can be highly palatable to blame some 'others' for all your ills, severing ties to cure your 'sickness'. Becoming 'free', without limitation. A set of ideas that, to use the words of Schumacher (again) in respect of his criticism of organizations whose entire locus is financial gain, are a "ruthless simplification" (1982, p. 137).

Enslavement

Historically we might well locate notions of, and needs for freedom, with slavery. Which included European colonisers forceably 'taking ownership' of Africans, estimated to be 12 million people, as free labour for a range of activities including working on sugar plantations. The history of this 'trade' is horrendous, rationalised at the time within assumptions of the superiorities of some humans, typically 'white-skinned', over others 'black-skinned'. For example, Carl Linnaeus a renowned scientist 'taxonomist' from the 1700s classified and characterised humans of different race including 'Africanus' as lazy, cunning, without shame and governed by caprice; which he contrasted with 'Europeanus' as gentle, acute and governed by laws (Eshun, 2021)! We briefly considered in Chapter 2 coloniser-colonised 'boundary making' and its sociomaterial consequences.

The key point that I want to make as we begin this chapter, is that notions of 'freedom' have powerful associations with becoming 'unshackled' and no longer in somebodies possession. The possibility to be able to make choices about how you live without having to defer to, or be beaten-up by some other human being. So one key aspect of freedom that we can understand is about being able to move through physical space, without being somehow caged and your potential for movement restricted. In this extreme case, relating to the scars of histories of slavery, which disastrously are still very much with us as 'modern slavery'. For example, the Global Slavery Index in 2016 suggesting that globally over 40 million people are victims of modern slavery. Consequently, being 'free' can be appreciated to be about liberation from the total domination of other people by them being physically imprisoning others. The door is locked, or the wall is too high, your body is not free to go beyond.

Once we move beyond an understanding of freedom as about a physical constraint, it is concept which 'seeps out' in a multiplicity of directions. Our potential to have freedom from, or be free from, opens up an endless list e.g. illness, harm, injustice, prejudice, etc. All words that are associated with expansive territories of possible meanings, as well as contrasting interpretations about the situations we may find ourselves as to whether they, or we, are indeed free from what is claimed. For example, in Chapter 2 I mentioned the Black Lives Matter movement, which protests about, and seeks change in relation to violence inflicted on Black communities. From this social movement there is a clear sense that many Black communities do not understand themselves to be free from prejudice, which is seen to be most palpable from recently recorded acts of police brutality upon the bodies of Black people. Consequently, the closing of Martin Luther King Jr.'s famous and rousing 'I have a dream speech' on August 28th in 1963 at the Lincoln Memorial in Washington D.C. in the US – "Free at last! Free at last! Thank God Almighty, we are free at last!" – freedom still feels more hope than reality for many.

In contrast others, who would likely oppose such protesting from Black Lives Matter, might claim that Black communities are free from prejudice, justifying it by suggesting that, for example in the case of Britain, that Black people have the 'same' right to vote as people identifying with other communities of race. So we can understand differing 'degrees' and interpretations of the meanings and implications of prejudice. Slavery, which I mentioned above, as well encompassing horrific histories, is a very extreme form of prejudice with accompanying appalling forms of physical violence and segregation. Indeed the disturbing reverberations of such histories are still indelibly intertwined within the felt prejudices that people experience today. However, racial discrimination can be rationalised away, particularly by those who do not see or feel a sense of prejudice towards their subjective bodies and being. This is more than an example as it refers to some major 'fault lines' within human communities. I feel that I have now taken on more than I had planned with making this point, to open up this chapter, but what I am trying to show here is that 'freedom from' when we move from physical constraints, is most likely a felt sense not one that is so easily 'pinned down'. Whereas if you are having a medical scan (e.g. MRI) to check for an illness the readings from the scan may well show you that you are free from the illness scanned for. There are no medical scans, with some fairly definitive picture or reading, that will tell you if you are free from injustice or prejudice.

Freedom to..

With 'freedom from' there is also a connected 'freedom to'. 'Freedom to' can be associated with 'rights' which are involved in political and legal debates. Perhaps 'freedom to' has the potential to be more 'clear-cut'. Such as having the freedom to get married, get divorced, buy a house, sell a house etc. It seems very much about the right-to, through some 'contract', formalise some attachment or non-attachment to other people or objects. This does sound potentially more clear-cut, although the social meanings and associated rituals of such things as marriage and divorce will vary, but freedom becomes associated with a documented list of rules and legal processes, which the majority may or may not conform to. So freedom to do things can appear to be about a legal prescription that supports you to do it, which does not sound overly 'free', other than being free to follow the rules as they have been set out for you. Although, as with the recently mentioned B-word, disagreements can involve who has, or should have, the right to set rules. However, we are moving into spaces of political and legal debate that I am not feeling any great need or competence to 'enter'.

What I am attempting as we start to explore this third dilemma related to *witnessing-being-witnessed* is to offer some general discussion of this sprawling and slippery concept of freedom, and as we can see I am struggling with it! I am starting to realise how it came to be that in some previous writing about developing a posthuman perspective I wrote "an expanded and entangled idea of self opens up difficult questions about researcher freedom ..., which are beyond the scope of this article" (Allen, 2019c, p. 74). It is good news that we have the room, or could I say freedom(?), of this chapter to try and make some sense of this 'difficult question'! Instead, of continuing to try to consider a general scope of meanings that can be associated with freedom, let us go to a key point that is the main impetus for how this dilemma became one the three dilemmas about *witnessing-being-witnessed*. As we have explored the need to notice and engage in dilemmas associated with any perspective is fundamental to taking care with the work we are doing to make a perspective rather than *the* perspective.

Straw persons

When I searched around for some reading on posthumanism and freedom to help me consider this dilemma one of the texts that came up is a piece by Chandler (2013). By referring to Chandler's (2013) article we will try to better get our 'teeth into' the issues. He describes how freedom is often central to what can be understood as "liberal modernist conceptions" of the world and societies (Chandler, 2013, p. 517). As Chandler explains such liberal modernist conceptions can be set up as some kind of 'straw-man'. When I first heard that term 'straw-man' I had no idea what it meant, I was in America at the time and just assumed that it was some kind of other worldly idiom. Also, I am now noticing how it is an interestingly gendered term. Anyway the idea of this 'straw-person' is that it is about an imagined human figure that is made of straw i.e. appearing in outline to be a human body, but because it is composed of straw it is fairly easy to knock-down and/or destroy. What this means is that the image of a 'straw-person' has connotations of a 'scare crow', that is placed in a field to keep birds away from eating recently sown seeds or tender crops.

We can make some assumptions about the intriguing, and likely problematic, gendering of the term, i.e. how could the 'tender' and 'delicate' bodies of women perform such a scaring role! Remember we did have the discussion at the start of Chapter 2 about issues associated with essentialising gender (i.e. bringing some universal and enduring categorises to things being innately male or female), such as to make divisions of associated meanings, and connected valuing, between things being objective or subjective. Interestingly, I was made aware from watching a television programme, ironically a comedy panel show, about a not much spoken about story of the suffragettes who campaigned for women's rights in Britain in the early 1900s. Many of the women in the movement are remembered as having learnt the Japanese martial art of Jujutsu to defend themselves during their protests from any physical attack by the police (e.g. Williams, 2012). These bodies could not be easily be regarded as 'tender' and 'delicate'.

Back to the straw-person. Chandler writes about a straw-person, 'liberal modernism', assembled by explaining:

> "This radicalised, more agential, materialism [associated with posthumanism] derives traction from its critique of liberal modernist conceptions of a binary world in which agency is seen to lie solely in the human subject, invested with 'free will' and subjectivity. Outside and external to this constructed world of the subject lay 'nature', the external or non-human world. This was conceived as a world of purely passive objects, mechanically destined to merely exist as causal intermediaries, with no agency of their own. This external world was contrasted to the world of human 'freedom' as a world of necessity, bound by law, regularity and repetition, waiting for the human subject to appropriate it as its object. In this binary understanding of Enlightenment or modernist frameworks, humans constituted themselves as ends and everything else – nature – as merely a means." (Chandler, 2013, p. 517)

As we can read from this quote these are complex arguments, both conceptually and linguistically. However, the movement from what we previously described, in particular in Chapter 3, as a 'dualist divide', such as between knowing-subject and inert-object, to one of a relational ontology can be appreciated as significantly reconfiguring conceptions of freedom. This is because as per the quotation from Chandler, freedom, in a dualist or binary world, can be mostly positioned to be about knowing the 'laws' of an external nature. The knowledge of these laws of nature is connected with an ability to 'harness it' and 'transform it', becoming 'enlightened' and with it freed from a pressing necessity to just survive, to one of 'becoming free'. We previously mentioned the association of this narrative with names such as Descartes.

In writing this book I can see that I may well be accused of being involved and complicit in assembling this straw-person of a humanist and anthropomorphic 'modernity'. When I read back over the text so far there is often a tendency to explain through binary accounts, where it was not one thing (e.g. objectivist), but something else (e.g. subjectivist). The explanation often rests on making separations or distinctions, and in doing so there is both characterisation (making a concept with a particular definition) and reduction (through using a particular definition obscuring variety). This is a potential weakness of the writing assembled here, but also, and more generally, of our possibilities to make sense and form explanations within the sound patterns of our language systems. In Part 2 by exploring the three dilemmas we have spent some time considering the general challenges of language and using it for developing posthuman sensibilities. As we have considered these challenges are not straightforward to 'overcome' in imagining *witnessing-being-witnessed*. What we can do, and have been attempting through this book, is to critically engage with these potential issues by noticing them, and drawing them into conversation with the perspective(s) we are seeking to develop. Doing so is not to 'nullify the issues', or 'render them irrelevant', but try to thoroughly engage with the limitations of the positions and perspectives we may make claims to hold.

Somebodies constraints another's freedoms?

There is inevitable heterogeneity in concepts and how they may become mobilised, within all the contextual varieties and situations to which they can become associated. However, as we have been exploring throughout this book drawing upon sociomateriality and posthumanism is about seeking to 'break-with', 'unsettle' or 'reimagine' possibilities for being human in Anthropocene times. By suggesting this is the project of this book, we are asserting freedom-from the ways of thinking-being, set-up as 'dualist divides' which are implicated in planetary unsustainabilities. Chandler (2013) notices this tone when he writes about 'new materialism', a label which is used to refer to ideas which are variously associated with posthumanism and sociomateriality:

> "New materialism argues that we can emancipate ourselves once we throw off the shackles of humankind being endowed with divine purpose, reason or capacities for mastery. In recognising the limits of human capacities and appreciating the agency and effects of nonhuman others, we can then allegedly unleash our 'inner' human and become what we 'are', no longer alienated from each other and the world we inhabit." (2013, p. 522)

These are some of the complications of freedom that I was starting to flounder with early on in this chapter. One person's freedom-from 'nature', can be another person's idea of being dominated and divided from 'nature'. As ever we can bring things back to the underlying assumptions of theories and how these produce realities. If we are to assume human exceptionalism then we are likely to become focused on a project of being free through being able to be exceptional and distinct, by getting the most out of the 'others'. We can connect these concerns with ideas of (and sorry I am characterising!) humanist and anthropomorphic 'modernity'. As we started with back in Chapter 2, the Anthropocene thesis is that it is the dream of, and desire for, such exceptionalism that has made humans identifiably the most significant geological force on the planet, and in doing so threatening the sustainabilities of our continued existences. A pursuit of being free can be understood to curtail our freedom to continue to become exceptionally and independently free, mainly because of socio-ecological disruptions from increasing planetary volatility. It is the very denial of interdependences between human and nonhumans that enables what Bookchin describes as "consumerist and hedonistic" interpretations of freedom (1982, p. 245).

As was noted in Chapter 1 the globalising, or meta-narrative, of the Anthropocene can flatten out the variations in how different peoples' might be understood to be implicated in the climate emergency. For example, the historical and geographical emitting of carbon through burning fossil fuels is centred around the industrial revolutions in Britain and other 'western' countries. So how people are implicated in their own curtailment and the curtailment of others' 'potentialities', to use a term associated with ideas of Social Ecology which we will consider later is this chapter, is highly variable. Something stark in this regard is that the world's wealthiest 1% have been calculated to account for more than twice the combined carbon emissions of the poorest 50% (United Nations Environment Programme, 2020). We can imagine how actions in the pursuit of freedom-from any constraints through the accumulation of financial wealth and the spending of money, feeds-back into taking away freedoms from others through implications such as climatic changes and rising sea-levels.

Unknowing freedom

Our discussion can suggest that in adopting these posthuman impulses we are indeed 'on the way to freedom'. However, going back to Chandlers critique he writes that in a posthuman perspective "we are freed from the structures and laws of necessity (constitutive of human freedom) but only to be subordinated to the arbitrary and unknowable whims of blind necessity (to which only enslavement is possible)" (2013, p. 518). What is inferred here is quite the opposite to freedom, the self-imposed unknowability, which we have considered as core to taking a relational view, is instead understood as curtailing possibilities to becoming free. See I told you this freedom space is a challenge! Whilst I would likely not be trying to put a book together about posthumanism and sociomateriality if I was in agreement with Chandler's assertion, let us 'sit with it' for a while and see how this argument can prompt us to learn more about the dilemmas of *witnessing-being-witnessed.*

Let us go back to our river metaphor that we first explored in Chapter 2 when first introducing ideas of sociomateriality. As we considered we are 'in-the-flow', being mediated by what encounters us, as well as being physically shepherded through a landscape, which is acting upon us, and us upon it. Our potentialities for being and doing are inseparable from, and enabled by, the flowing. We contrasted this with a metaphor of separation whereby by we imagine ourselves in a boat a-top of the river, in control of the flow with others beneath. Consequently, ideas of sociomaterial entanglement, which give agency to 'others', through our assumed attachments do clearly raise questions about freedoms to be and do, related to notions of free-will. This is because we are understood to be produced, and able to become human, through our relations with the more-than-human. Indeed, we have explored through a range of examples on these pages how we can appreciate that others, species and technologies, 'act upon us' and in so doing transform possibilities by enrolling us into ways of doing and being.

By taking a posthuman approach we are very much muddying questions of responsibility and accountability, as the human is not understood to be 'sovereign' in that humanist or libertarian sense. As we explored in Chapter 3 a responsibility of entanglement asks for different appreciations, different ways of understanding being from the responsibilities associated with ideas of a sovereign being. Going back to Chandler's writing:

> "In a new materialist world, we no longer have the sense of a capacity to choose our own ends – a sense of freedom. Instead, we have merely a world of blind necessity, which appears to dictate to us how we should act in order to respond and adapt to our external environment. Politics then becomes merely a question of responsiveness – of ethical responsibility – not of freedom." (Chandler, 2013, p. 525)

From this quote we can appreciate that dilemmas of entanglement, and related unknowingness, are about a sense of losing control of ends (i.e. outcomes, destinations etc.). A situation where we are seen to be moved away from 'purposes', to 'responses', which is argued to be a way of making sense of being-in-a-world that relinquishes freedom. As I have repeatedly written about going through this book I am not trying to make *the* perspective, as I am aware that this speaking back to this text by Chandler, might come across as overly combative. However, my effort here is not to 'sure-up' these ideas about *witnessing-being-witnessed*, but as mentioned before show my attempts at developing a perspective 'warts-and-all' by seeking to tackle what I notice as the most probing dilemmas.

A main reflection on the above quote of Chandler is that from a posthuman perspective we could suggest that it is a 'sense of freedom', of a liberal modernist variety, that is considered to be a problematic imaginary. This is because it is an imaginary that is resistant to any contemplations about the mutual becoming of things, as the freedom for such imagining would be understood to sever us from being free. Remember, we are assuming the performativity of the theories and perspectives that we generate, as Law (2004) writes they inscribe as well and describe reality. Which means that we are attempting 'to deal with' assumed realities (i.e. planetary unsustainablities in Anthropocene times), but that we are socially constructing our understandings of our relationships to these realities of unsustainablity. Such construal is achieved through the invented categories of our language systems, which to reiterate the words of Bateson are not the "flesh and blood and action" of reality (1979, p. 27). Posthuman theory would appreciate the assumption of freedom, as human free-will to achieve our desired ends, to be a vocabulary from another world of theorising. In many ways the attempted getting out of those 'old boxes' purposely, and performatively, involves usurping ideas of freedoms with entanglements.

As Chandler points us to, and as we have been seeking to develop, a posthuman perspective involves 'jumping out of one fire in to another', because by seeking a 'new box' we become tasked with the imagining of the meanings of posthuman ethical responsibility. Although, remember we are not within a project of getting it right. There is no one best way to be found or understood. Our critical appreciation is hoping to open up the potential for more perspectives to ask new questions, as part of endeavours to unsettle us into more sustainable ways of being and doing. Doing so can even be appreciated as a form of freedom, by being "free to inquire, not accept, not look to a guide, to a system, to a saviour, to a guru" (Krishnamurti, 1997, p. 182).

The responsible-being that we have been trying to develop in *witnessing-being-witnessed*, involves a 'letting-be-of-things' to use the words of Introna (2013). An ethic that is searching for appreciations of being in mutual interaction within a world, where humans are not at its centre and the origination of the valuing of all others. As we have explored finding our way to imagining the possibilities for *witnessing-being-witnessed*, giving multifarious 'matter' rights on its own terms, are far from straightforward, and even if we glimpse some ways of articulating them they will not offer prescription. However, as with critical thought we can appreciate a free-ing sense of challenging ourselves with the possibilities of handling a slippery and elusive perspective. By having too 'tight a grip' we can interrupt possibilities for progressive thinking-being by becoming enchanted with a detachment of empty exceptionalism, which may well involve too much staring in the mirror. A significant challenge in *witnessing-being-witnessed* is that we try to avoid becoming defined by contemplating a determinist grip of 'others'. A place where any potential for choice has completely withered away.

Determinism in 'Anthropocene'?

There could appear to be an underlying determinism within Anthropocene narratives, this is to do with a sense of planetary decay or decline of a 'safe operating space' for living beings (Rockström et al., 2009). As we considered in Chapter 1, the Anthropocene is about transgressions of thresholds and passing of limits, a breaking apart from relative planetary stability of the Holocene over the past 10'000 years. The Anthropocene is associated with 'earthly volatilities' (Clark & Szerszynski, 2021). For example, McKibben wrote (evoking some 'straw person-ing', or in this case 'straw nature-ing') some years ago:

> "this new 'nature' may not be predictably violent. It won't be predictably anything, and therefore it will take us a very long time to work out our relationship with it, if we ever do. The

> salient characteristic of this new nature is its unpredictability, just as the salient feature of the old nature was its utter dependability." (McKibben, 1990, p. 88)

The Anthropocene narrative is determinist in the sense that humans' drive to taking control and becoming so planetary impactful, recognising there is much variation in the impacts of different humans beings and communities, has left us out of control of our destiny. Once again to have our future determined by the whims of a new 'nature'. However, these are not the whims of 'nature', but socio-cultural nature that, as we explored, most recently in Chapter 5, is far from an understanding of 'wild'. In the urgency of the Anthropocene narrative socio-culture nature is a whole lot uglier than before, because of excessive anthropo-meddling, which can imply a doomed sense of the possibilities for many of us to 'have a good life'. This because in this narrative we are going to be constrained and torn apart by climate extremes (e.g. unprecedented flooding), the accidents of our 'big picture' endeavours (e.g. deep sea oil spills), and the consequences of the removal of 'space' from other species (e.g. new deadly viruses). It is for sure a blockbuster Hollywood disaster movie of dystopia unleashed!

In the posthuman view we have been exploring I have suggested that we can not 'know the other', which means knowing what our shared planetary futures might or might not involve is far from reach. *Witnessing-being-witnessed* takes unknowing as a given which implies that moves to more ambitious planetary experimenting with-in-a-world (e.g. mega geoengineering projects) would not be an obvious way of moving forward. Although, some exploring Anthropocene thought have suggested that emerging earthly volatility implies that we are obliged to experiment with the ways that we can 'join forces with the earth' (Clark & Szerszynski, 2021). However, they may well be suggesting experiments with social thought more than mega-monolithic-material human interventions, such as the geoengineering just mentioned.

For *witnessing-being-witnessed*, which could be regarded as an experiment in social thought, a focus would be on grounding being-responsible with others, on a becoming planet, within the relational situations that we encounter at any given moment (for example, the window that we explored in Chapter 5). Where questions emerge such as: How might these others 'talk-back', and 'make-us' through our mutual interacting? And, what does it mean to take time and 'listen'? As Nigel Clark suggested in a recent webinar, about a newly published book 'Planetary Social Thought' that he had co-authored with Bron Szerszynski (2021), projects of the Anthropocene need to be involved in making Western thought strange enough to communicate on the same 'plateau' with other knowledges. 'Western thought' is broad terminology as is 'other knowledges', but this sentiment I find helpful to approaching and seeking to develop the posthuman perspective in this book. That a key quality criteria is that *witnessing-being-witnessed* needs to feel strange and quirky, as if it does not then we are likely not doing enough work to imagine ourselves out of those 'old box' perspectives.

Freedom and hierarchy

By roaming around with this dilemma of freedom we can consider strangeness in relation to Bookchin's (1982, 1996) ideas about Social Ecology. Bookchin and others, writing about Social Ecology, attempt to rethink human-being by considering issues of hierarchical relations due to how they can (re)produce patterns of domination between humans, and humans over nonhumans. In this writing it is suggested that freedom is a "word [that] is simply meaningless to many preliterate peoples" (Bookchin, 1982, p. 193). The argument is made that freedom is an idea that is related to institutions and the consequences of associated arrangements (e.g.

contracted working responsibilities in an organization). These institutional arrangements inscribe differences onto peoples' bodies through (social, economic or political) hierarchies, informing ideas about wanting to become free from whatever institutional processes we might have become enrolled into. For example, promotion processes to another 'grade' of being a worker.

Freedom could be understood as "an unstated reality in many preliterate cultures" (Bookchin, 1982, p. 196). The constraints related to "early community's material conditions of life" (p. 196), "choice, will, and individual proclivities could be exercised or expressed within confines permitted by the environment" (p.197). From a liberal modernist viewpoint, social, economic and political organization and associated hierarchies may well be argued to have liberated humans from some imagined drudgery of living with 'nature'. However, the point I want to make here is that in developing a posthuman perspective we are requiring ourselves to re-imagine the questions and challenges that we might raise about theory and thought. This is because doing so helps to open up possibilities to find new pathways of responsible-being that should feel strange from those which have been dominant in getting us to 'here'.

To pick up some more on ideas of Social Ecology and the questions they raise about freedom, a key thread is the focus on mutual relations, which are understood to be so by being non-hierarchical and non-dominating. Such mutual relations are seen to be crucial for humans to support the diversity and potentiality (understood to be about spontaneity, creativity and adaptation) in each other and natural processes (Bookchin, 1982). Relations of non-hierarchy and non-domination are suggested to foster and enable what are assumed to be natural tendencies towards ever-expanding socio-ecological complexity and diversity (Bookchin, 1982).

By taking our sociomaterial lens we can raise questions about the implied separation and dualisms which are maintained through Social Ecology, as it does seek to preserve forms of human exceptionalism and superiority to other beings. An exceptionalism which includes suggestions such as, that human consciousness is seen as the ultimate expression of natural evolutionary diversity and development (Bookchin, 1996). However, this does help us to consider how freedoms of mutuality could be extended to the more-than-human. What I mean by this is that the freedom for co-evolving within socio-ecological nature can be understood to come about through forms of mutual solidarity between things. By taking inspiration from Social Ecology it is through being with, and exploring the possibilities of, this mutuality, in the language of witnessing feeling the 'gaze of the other', that posthuman freedoms associated with diversities and potentialities can emerge.

Travelling

Let us consider some examples of travelling to try to better ground these discussions. Physical human mobility by using technologies such as cars and aeroplanes are likely motifs in tales of modernist enlightenment, the 'straw-person' we have been considering in this chapter (e.g. Miller, 2001). The associations of stories of freedom-to go to all 'corners of the world', at speed, when we want, are closely bound-up with these technologies. They are technologies that have become enrolled in ideas about helping us to surpass 'limits of nature', and particularly in the case of the aeroplane physically rise up to leave all others beneath. Or, as I mentioned in Chapter 5, the windscreen, and body, of a car enclosing us from that which is outside, the 'wilds of nature'. Our enclosure, in a car-body, giving us the freedom-to roam, overcoming 'the lack' of our bodily potential to move fast enough and for long enough across the earth.

These modes of travelling could be regarded as 'technologies of freedom' in which our living has become completely enrolled. They may well be presented, particularly through advertising, as having liberated us from the mundaneness and banality of the 'local' to be able to cover great swaths of the planet to 'live better', by being more widely present across 'global' space. As well as, in relation to the car, being able to reduce the amount of time we need to be moving within our locale so as to enable our attentions to be able to extend further afield. For example, the Covid-19 pandemic could be seen to have cut us off from this world of physical mobility. During lock-downs, the roads were quieter, and the numbers of aeroplanes in the air were vastly reduced. Many of us were severed from the our potential to move at speed, striped of our understood modernity. Unless perhaps you were part of some global elite that appeared to keep moving in their private jets during times of Covid-19 (e.g. Kommenda, 2021).

You are likely gathering, I am not a big fan of the car or indeed the aeroplane. As you can see from the previous paragraph through this text we are travelling, excuse the pun, in directions that are not going to be passionately embracing these technologies. However, in this exploration of the dilemma of freedom, I am hoping that by working through these examples, associated with modernist enlightenment as some kind of 'technologies of freedom', we can learn something more about the perspective of *witnessing-being-witnessed*. Both about the entanglement of bodies within these technologies, as well as how we might understand ourselves to encounter them from a posthuman perspective. Particularly, as we have been exploring, we are seeking to imagine new possibilities for responsible-being within the flow of mediatings, in which we are understanding our-selves to be immersed. We can see ourselves as caught in a tension of giving matter 'rights on its own terms', but with such technologies as cars and aeroplanes with cumulative effects on humans and other species, we can become concerned about a potential 'passivity' of letting-be, as such matter is implicated in the manufacturing of Anthropocene times.

The use of aeroplane travel to support academic work has been under increasing scrutiny in recent years. Like many other assessments of the intensity of anthropogenic influences on climate change calculations of carbon dioxide emissions have become the key metric for understanding the effects of aviation. Calculations like those of Kalmus (2016) who we considered in Chapter 2. Academia is a relatively flight intensive profession. Some examples of universities that have attempted to calculate their carbon emissions from flying include the University of Edinburgh, UK at 11 per cent and Ghent University, Belgium at 15 per cent.

What this means is that the focus on flying in academia is substantially about how emissions, which can be connected to flying, are cumulatively significant in calculations of a universities carbon footprint. As well as the sense that reducing flying appears relatively achievable in relation to making rapid carbon emissions reductions. Particularly, given that many academics have been forced to be 'grounded' during the Covid-19 pandemic. Whereas other aspects of university operations, associated emissions can be understood to be more 'hidden' within the supply of materials that are bought and consumed. However, attempts to reduce academic flight, like in other areas of society, can meet with complaints that doing so curtails freedoms, which as we have explored, we might connect to our identities as making us enlightened and modern.

Academics in flight

Parker and Weik (2014) have explored academic freedom and academic flying. They explained how "the notion of the free spirit has been associated with intellectual work for a long time, but mainly in the sense of being free from political interference in the research process" (Parker & Weik, 2014, p. 168). However, as they go on to describe "this 'freedom from' did not always translate into high amounts of geographical mobility" with "few scholars before World War II travell[ing] much" (p.168). In their analysis they explore how ideals about a 'freedom of the mind', as in images of a thinking academic, has been mingled with 'freedoms of the body' as expressed by hyper-mobility. They explain:

> "Nowadays, with relatively cheap and efficient global transport systems, the rise of the conference circuit and research travel budgets, the sense of 'freedom from' appears to have become a 'freedom to' pursue careers and academic capital from one international congress or top-ranked institution to another. But if such movement is expected, and lack of movement treated with suspicion, then there is some coercion here too. The professional academic is not free to move where they want or to not move at all, but softly compelled to move where they are expected to perform better. Indeed, their willingness to move is frequently being evaluated, and consequently so is their willingness to shrug off attachments and start packing." (Parker & Weik, 2014, p. 168)

The sense we have from this quote suggests to us the complexities of the multiple 'poles' of freedom which we have been considering. From this quote we can even infer that for some academics the potential to not-fly is freedom from the strength of constellations of cultural and institutional arrangements. Such, as criteria for being promoted, implicitly and explicitly recognising and celebrating the rapid and frequent movement of an academic body on an aeroplane. For example, notions of 'being international' in universities may well be translated into financial budgets for frequent flying to enable greater physical presence in far-off places by members of the university (e.g. Storme et al., 2013). As well as that, research funders have become enrolled to take-for-granted relations between research and flying, perhaps the people involved in the funding bodies identifying themselves as highly mobile academics, and partly selected as a reviewer of grant proposals due to such an identifier. What this can translate into is that a key dimension of 'good' and 'impactful' research will be understood as expressed by the inclusion of a significant research proposal budget-line-item for flying off to far away meetings and conferences.

University finances in Britain have become much more uncertain in an era of Covid-19 and that B-word that I mentioned at the start of this chapter. However, prior to these heightened uncertainties if you worked at a university that was 'doing okay' then often 'research stimulation' was about travelling to meet new people face-to-face to make new connections to do more 'internationally excellent' work. With unseemly undertones of western universities spreading their 'enlightened' forms of 'knowledge production' to solve the problems of those in places of a more 'backward' orientation. We can also understand that the patterning of 'hubs' of travel infrastructure, and associated flows of capital investment, like airports, can be connected with (historical) distributions of colonial wealth (Knowles, 2006). To be free of flying, particularly if you are in location of former imperialist activities, as per Parker & Weik's (2014) discussion, requires some 'ducking and diving', I can tell you this from my own experiences!

To add further into this exploration of academic flying, freedom and what it may mean for *witnessing-being-witnessed*, is the uneven distribution of those who participate in flying. In general and in academia. For instance it is estimated that more than 80% the world's population has never flown (e.g. Farrier, 2013). At a country level, in Britain, for example, it has been calculated that 15% of the population is responsible for 70% of the flights (Klöwer et al., 2020). In universities, a study of the University of British Columbia found that 50% of emissions were from flights of 8-11%

of academic staff, with senior professors more likely to be in that category than junior academics (Wynes & Donner, 2018). Based on some analysis by University of Glasgow, one return flight to New York from Britain is calculated to be more than half what is regarded to be a sustainable annual carbon footprint for a person. These statistics and carbon footprint calculations do help to give us some texture to the human relations with aeroplanes, and in particular how unevenly distributed the participation in flying is across human populations, as well as the carbon 'intensity' of flight. Consequently, not only are we able to develop some appreciations of how the academic body, as is our particular focus here, is entangled into being moved by aeroplanes. But also, if flying is conceptualised as freedom-to roam, how this free-spiritedness can understood to be implicated in the suffering and un-freedom of the lives of other humans and more-than-humans.

Freedoms colliding

I do not want to go on too much about academic flying, as you can tell is a topic that has got me and others quite 'hot under the collar' (e.g. Nevins, Allen, & Watson, 2022). However, what I want to explore here is the collision of various forms and interpretations of 'freedoms'. What I mean by this, as we have been considering in this chapter about understanding dilemmas of freedom in relation to *witnessing-being-witnessed*, is we can appreciate how these multiple versions of freedom are in tension. This is because the meaning of one concept of freedom can be understood as in relation to another, which can be regarded as part of taking a critical position that there is no serene and correct 'place to stand'.

The definition of a position is somehow inevitably defined in relation to other likely contrasting position(s). For example, the straw-persons notion mentioned earlier in this chapter, such as with humanism and posthumanism. The construal of the category of posthumanism is in large part about a rejection of the category of humanism. To imagine ideas of posthumanism without noticing, or ignoring, the relation to humanism would be to miss quite a lot of 'the point'. Indeed such thinking can raise general criticisms of aspects of 'critical thought' that can be largely about an opposition and departure from something suggested to be 'uncritical'. However, as we are attempting to work through, yes we are of course criticising other positions and categories, but we are attempting to do so within the pursuit of developing an alternative perspective as part of imagining other possibilities. The criticality we are engaging in, as has been explored, is an awareness of multiple perspectives and how all, including our own, will have its limitations.

In relation to competing tensions of freedoms the example of academic flying our freedoms-to, include aspects such as the following. The freedom for rapid movement of the travelling academic. The freedom for universities to pursue agendas of internationalisation. The freedom of the travelling academic to develop their career by being widely present at meetings and conferences. Indeed even perhaps the freedom of the academic to not to live in the place or country where the university they work is located, so being able to commute to work via aeroplane. Such freedoms-to can be understood to be in tension with others freedoms-from including aspects such as follows. The freedom-from having 'western academics' promoting their ways of knowing and researching, as well as having your lives represented and commodified through the eyes of others. The freedom-from having to live with the climatic and planetary effects of others high consumption of fossil energy which enable their hypermobile ways of living and working. The freedom-from the possibilities of 'western' universities reformulating imperialisms into the 'good intentions' of investing in 'internationalisation' to enlighten and develop others' worlds. The freedom-from images of 'success' and 'status' being associated with high consumption and ever more long distance travelling to 'exotic' places. Such shadow-sides of 'western academia' can be found in the writing of decolonial scholars of 'the South' including Mignolo (2007) and Quijano (2007).

This 'balance sheet' example of competing freedoms does make me wonder about ideas of 'zero-sum-game'. What I mean by this is the thought that notions of humanity, and more particularly some parts of humanity, displaying their exceptional characteristic of 'free will' can be seen to take away or constrict the potential for 'free will' of other people or beings. Such a thought is cast within understandings of socio-ecological embeddedness with consequent interdependencies and relationalities, all 'that stuff' which we have been attaching to posthuman and sociomaterial sensibilities. However, I studied Accounting as part of my undergraduate degree and I could never get the damn balance sheets to balance! And the other part of my degree was Economics with all its funny ideas about 'rational economic beings' etc. That was probably when zero-sum-game was mentioned.

These subjects, Accounting and Economics, in their 'traditional' forms, are not the ground from which I am working in trying to imagine this posthuman perspective. Indeed looking back they were likely very much 'grist to the mill' in helping to put my attentions in other directions. Given those historical associations I am not into such Newtonian laws of motion, albeit that Physics could never be suggested to be a great strength of mine! I suppose what I am saying is not so much cause-and-effect, more relational ricochets in the perspective we are exploring. The freedoms we may claim, are claimed within a web of sociomaterial relations, which means there are consequences. In which technologies such as associated with flight, that we can become tightly enrolled, can significantly amplify the potential of our bodily affects. Of course my slightly deft get out here is that as we have looked at earlier, in particular in Chapter 3, that these consequences and relations are unknowable in the figuring it all out sense. Although we can pay attention to others by noticing how 'voices' may be excluded and attempt to bring them into dialogue.

In writing about posthumanism and progressive political projects Cudworth and Hobden suggest "that 'freedom' is both embodied and embedded" (2015, p. 144). Given the discussion so far in this chapter these seem to be conducive qualities to associate with the dilemmas of freedom in relation to *witnessing-being-witnessed*. In the sense that freedom is something that is located and specifically construed and felt within and between bodies. As well as inescapably immersed within our entangled sociomaterial relations with other things and beings. Although, there may well be disconnects between a social felt sense of freedom, and the material accomplishments of 'being free'. To explain this, going back to the example of academic flying, one person-body may feel free from not flying due to Covid-19 pandemic travel restrictions. Which means that they are not 'drawing' upon matter such as the fuel to propel an aeroplane to its destination in far away places. Whereas another person-body may feel very differently, a removal of the freedom to fly and potential to consume air travel with the associations of 'using' matter and related pollution. For example, as reported about some people's willingness to take flights to 'nowhere' during the pandemic (e.g. Havelock, 2020). Indeed seeking 'freedom' from imposed restrictions via lockdowns and social distancing in attempts to deal with the Covid-19 pandemic have been significant narratives. Of course, if you are not able to physically go out of your home, and you have the pressure of homeschooling children your sanity may well be associated with the potential to be free again!

Passively-active

It may well be that freedom, or at least freedom as we generally know it, is the 'wrong' language to bring into making sense of the possibilities of developing a posthuman perspective with the backdrop of unsustainability. As well as not overly productive for seeking pathways to freedom, away from futures of pernicious challenges associated with changing climates and species extinctions. It can be wrong in the sense that 'freedom' is somehow other-worldy, in this case in the worlds of humanism and neoclassical ideas about human exceptionalism and independence. Although we might, dare I write, separate, as in the above paragraph, some sense of felt social freedom from that of physical material freedom. As with the above example, and earlier examples in this chapter, freedom is a matter of perspective!

If as we are assuming in taking a sociomaterial approach, that we are becoming in an emerging material world, then the rights and fates of matter are not so much about what and how we think about them, but more about how we co-act upon them and they upon us. Questions of the potential for making choices then come into view, which we can associate with ideas of freedom i.e. 'the freedom to choose'. Often a maxim and rallying cry of 'free-market' and neoclassical economics, which have already had a few mentions in this book. However, in a posthuman perspective we are decentring human-will as the key ingredient for action.

By remembering our river metaphor what is really achievable from all our desperate flailing within our unknowable entanglement? Also, to make it more challenging, the earthly volatility of the Anthropocene implies that the riverbanks are unstable. This is of course the moment to play my second 'trump card', the first was unknowability, the second is 'modesty'. As with engaging in, and considering these dilemmas, we are not doing so with the arrogant idea that we can 'figure it all out'. Au contraire! The point is we cannot, but equally important is that figuring it all out is not a prerequisite for ethical and moral being. Instead a requirement for ethical and moral action in this flowing and shape-shifting world of being is an embodying of modesty. A freedom to imagine and become in ways that might currently be construed as alien. Although, importantly, ways that we do not become too proud about.

In many respects from the perspective of *witnessing-being-witnessed* we might well be better off replacing ideas, and ideals, of freedom with those of solidarity. As was mentioned earlier in this chapter, a mutual solidarity between things. We can understand a further potential implosion of forms of freedom. Whereby freedom-to-be is based on understandings of mutual responsibility with connected support between members (human and nonhuman) of a community. Which means that freedom is based within an appreciation and acceptance of interconnectedness. Solidarity underpins the potential for futures in which being free-to-do are possible. Some questions do emerge. Such as, what makes up a global-local sociomaterial community? As well as, what about relations of power in solidarity, because as we have explored social relations (related to aspects including race and gender) are not symmetrically equal? Neither question has a straight forward reply, that would be far too boring!

In relation to community, this may well be in-the-moment of being in solidarity, but as with the discussion of chains-of-supply which support the creation of things, in Chapter 5 about the proximity dilemma, many of these relations are untraceable. Particularly untraceable, to have some significant awareness of them, within a brief moment of action. As for the second question on the power between beings and things, this is an enormous question. If in very general terms we can understand power as about "a capacity to get things done" (King & Lawley, 2019,

p. 500). Then taking a relational perspective we might assume that power is produced through relationships between human and nonhuman entities "as a network of social boundaries that constrain and enable action for all actors" (Hayward, 1998, p. 2). So as Latour suggests "power is not something you can hoard and possess, it is something that has to be made" (1986, p. 274). Power is understood as a relational effect, a hybrid of human and nonhuman actors (Latour, 2005), because "actors are afforded by their very ability to act by what is around them" (Mol, 2010, p. 258).

Whilst we might be able to gain some purchase on how power between people is made, discursively and physically, we of course started the chapter with mentioning histories of slavery(!), how power is made between peoples-animals-technologies feels a much more complex undertaking. An undertaking which is not going to be undertaken here! However, the significant point is that we can not assume that solidarity is a similarly felt and lived solidarity for all. Consequently, to have any ethical legitimacy it is likely any solidarity will involve 'dialogues' with a melange of 'voices', particularly those who might generally be considered as under-represented or voiceless.

A solidarity of a 'letting-be-of-things', as we have explored in relation to the other dilemmas of centrality and proximity, is about being passively-active rather than actively-passive. What I mean by actively-passive is that it is not about seeking something of an exceptionalism via human 'withdrawal' from active participation in the world. That image of humanity as a virus or disease whereby any movement or breath is condemned as being against the other-than-human. This 'retreat' rests on those ideas of a wild nature, which as we have explored has been understood as sociocultural nature for some time (McKibben, 1990).

Passively-active involves an attentiveness to being in the flow-of-beings. In many ways the river, going back to our metaphor, has carved new unimagined channels, possibly cutting deeper and flowing faster through the world, and simply bobbing along in those could be understood as complicity in the raging Anthropocene currents involved in creating 'something new under the sun' (to mention again that book title of McNeill (2000)). Complicity, such as collective unquestioning human enrolment in technologies such as cars and aeroplane travel, is assumed to accumulate in producing Anthropocene times. The currents and rapids may compel us to follow a flow, by consuming and accumulating more matter, pulling us toward imaginaries that we can find our way out of the water, to have our own place in the sun, on the banks. An issue is that the sun feels like it is getting hotter, much hotter, and all that stuff, from the consuming and accumulating, is not going to stop it. In the words of the previously mentioned poet Kae Tempest "..all this stuff is blocking us".

In passively-active, the passive is about decentring the human-being, and the active is about attention to our entanglements with those proximate beings-and-things. What this means, as we will explore in Part 3, is that we can hope to become more attentive about our tusslings in the flow, more skilled and deft in our attempted (dis)entanglings. However, with the realisation that we cannot transcend others or remove ourselves.

PART THREE: Witnessing possibilities

Chapter 7

Witnessing-as-being

Disturbing bag

In the final part of this book we will explore some possibilities and potentialities for *witnessing-being-witnessed*. This chapter considers about how each of us might try to make sense of ourselves and our-doings – *witnessing-as-being*. Chapter 8, the final one, will consider how organizing, getting things done together, can be conceptualised within the assumptions of *witnessing-being-witnessed*.

We begin this chapter with an example, which is prompted by being interrupted by a plastic bag in a tree. In this example the three dilemmas discussed in Part 2 are drawn upon and explored to discuss the implications for *witnessing-as-being*. In particular, questions of what it could mean to be in dialogue and solidarity with more-than-human-others are considered. By drawing us towards my 'disciplinary home' of Organization Studies I use debates about leading and leadership to position some possibilities for understanding and translating *witnessing-as-being*. An example,

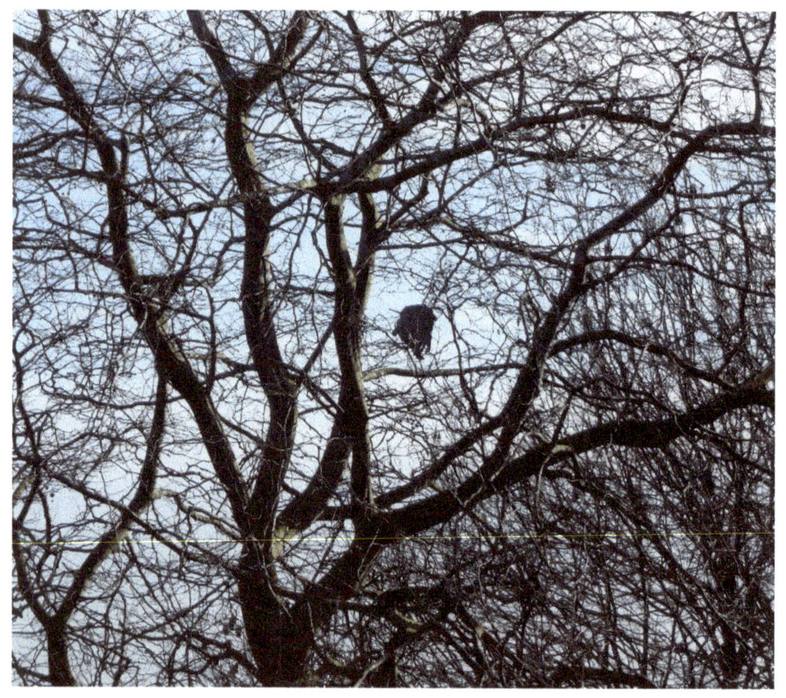

Considering the three dilemmas: A photo of the 'disturbing' bag in the tree outside our window

from an artist's work is used to suggest some potentialities for developing creative dialogues and alliances with matter.

The good news is that the plastic bag has gone! Not all of them, just the one that had lodged itself in the tree outside the window that I am sitting next to when I started to draft this chapter. Actually no, when I look again it is still there but much lower down. That it is moving is a good sign that it will become detached from the tree.

It is one of the trees that I can see when I am typing, this one is a large London plane tree. It was in the top of this tree, on one of the coldest days this winter, that I saw a flock of eight redwings. I was not sure what they where at first, definitely not blackbirds but about that size. About the shape of song thrush, if that means anything to you. When I got my binoculars I could see their 'orange-red flank patches' which is described as making them distinct on the Royal Society for the Protection of Birds website (RSPB). It is the website that always seems to come top in the web-searching when I look for information about British birds.

We previously 'spent some time' with windows, back in Chapter 5, which involved considering the dilemma of proximity and exploring the separating and enclosing that windows afford our bodies. A window understood through the lens of *witnessing-being-witnessed* transforms the potential for my assembling of text to be 'all-weather', as well as being a barrier to the feral. And also, unless open, a part of the skin of our privately-owned home. A reality of ownership that is produced via a Building Society's regulated financial loan capacities, which are expressed through financial digits on screens run by computer programmes, and contractual texts, or scripts, which articulate the financing arrangements. We can add to this reading of the window the mediating potential of glass, as we explored in Chapter 5, enabling my bodily potential to see the screen on to which the words I am typing are appearing, and the London plane tree outside. However, apart from the affordances of the window, a term which 'came on the scene' in Chapter 3, there are some particular reasons for starting this chapter with the plastic bag in the tree. Reasons which are beyond my general attempts, mentioned at the end of Chapter 2, to bring regular glimpses of aspects of sociomaterial relations that can be appreciated as involved in assembling this contingent and situated text.

The appearance of the plastic bag to my visual awareness felt like quite a disturbance to a sense of the naturalness of the tree. This London plane tree has been a perch and food source for those redwing that came by in varying numbers quite a few times over the winter months. The plastic bag feels to glare back, following close contact with human hands, like the one-use cups and plastic lids mentioned in Chapter 4, it is similarly consigned to many years of painfully slow decomposition. Although, perhaps this bag may decompose more quickly than the cups. To update you, the plastic bag did become dislodged from the tree and fell to the ground. I went out and got it, and put it in our kitchen bin with the other used things, mostly plastic that have entered our house under various guises. The bag is not associated with the category of recyclable where we are and so is repelled from joining other things (e.g. paper, tins and glass) which are allowed into our coloured recycling bins, a first step in their imagined metamorphosis.

I did not inspect the bag too closely, it was pretty torn to shreds, I did grab a gardening glove to deal with it so that I avoided any fleshy contact. However, it may well have been one of those 'poo bags', the ones that if you are a dog owner you will be well acquainted with for 'managing' your animals excrement. The bag was unused and empty, if you were wondering. It appeared a slightly bigger bag, than a 'poo bag', quite like one of those that you can get given at the local off-licence, which you really didn't want, when you are in need of grabbing an impromptu few cans of beer. Your lack of attention, probably from searching for some cash or a payment card, meant that the cans unexpectedly disappeared inside the bag before you were able to mount any resistance.

There are of course an array of connected imaginaries about the doings and happenings of this bag. It might have a much shorter 'life expectancy' than those one-use cups and plastic lids. Who knows, it could be made of some form of 'natural' material like cellulose which would mean that it will not be hanging around in its current form for too long. I am not sure if my enrolment of it into our household waste collecting processes, by putting it into our kitchen bin, will have any effects on its potential for decomposition. It may well be incinerated into some other molecular form. However, the bag is now outside of my field of vision, and away from species which could have found it problematic to encounter.

The disturbance that I mentioned at the start of the previous paragraph can be regarded as a bit of an alien reaction from a posthuman viewpoint. As we have considered throughout this book, going all the way back to Chapter 1, we are attempting to appreciate being in a socio-ecological world. A world in which it is understood that how reality is construed is based on the interpreting and valuing imposed by human beings, and that humans-being is interdependent with an extensive diversity of nonhumans. We have developed appreciations of these interconnections and interdependencies through drawing upon ideas of sociomateriality and posthumanism. It is my bifurcating, which we have explored, particularly in relation to the writing of Introna (2009, 2013), of the 'natural' tree and the 'unnatural' bag that prompted a sense of incongruence and my expression of dissatisfaction. The incongruence involved imposing valuing associated with pristine ideas of that tree in winter, naked of it leaves, as a place for those endearing redwings to rest and feed, with the appearance of a carrier, made out of extracted hydrocarbons, that supports human consumption.

If I look up some information about trees, strangely via the algorithms of Ecosia a search 'engine' in which my searching is somehow translated to the planting of trees, I find out some interesting things about the tree known as London plane. Incidently, Ecosia first found me via a community newspaper that I thumbed through as a reflex to it being on the table at a cafe I visited. My change in search 'engine' reconfiguring the possibilities for what I might be able to find. It is the Woodland Trust's website that appears high on the search list of my screen when I look for information about trees. On these webpages the London plane is described as a 'non native' and a 'new hybrid' (Woodland Trust). Bruno Latour would be delighted, as he is very much into hybridity, as we considered early on in Chapter 2 in relation to actor-network approaches! The concept of hybridity, to which Latour is connected, seeks conceptualisations beyond 'self-contained' things and beings. For example, a human with gun or walking stick in which the later acts as 'mediator', a concept introduced in Chapter 2. A mediator is understood to actively contribute to the ways in which action unfolds, reshaping action possibilities in such significant ways that understanding them, the person and the gun or walking stick, separately makes little sense. However, for the London plane, it is 'genetic hybridity' that it is associated with. This is because it:

> "is thought to be a cross between the Oriental plane and the American sycamore – both of which had been introduced to Britain. By chance, one of each species had been planted in the London nursery garden of John Tradescant, the younger which cross-pollinated to produce a new hybrid. It was first noticed by Tradescant – a famous botanist – in the mid-

> 17th century and named after the city where it originated." (Woodland Trust).

I do not want to rehearse again the naturalness arguments that we have covered earlier, for example in Chapter 5, and is woven through many sustainability debates (e.g. McKibben, 1990). However, starting this chapter with my perceived desecrating collision between tree and bag can help us to learn about some possibilities for *witnessing-being-witnessed*. Some brief looking has opened up questions about the presence of this tree, "the most common tree in London" (Woodland Trust), nearby our house in urban Sheffield in northern England. Questions such as: how has it come to be their in all its Eastern-North American accidental genetic hybridity? And, in what ways are those redwings of the nature of this place if they spend the largest proportion of their time in parts of Scandinavia, Iceland and Russia (RSPB)?

We are indeed entangled in complex multifaceted situations, that require more than a second look. Doing so to consider diffuse realities of what we are witnessing and being witnessed by. What can be the purposes of our being passively-active (as discussed at the end of Chapter 6)? Or, are purposes beyond reach, too grand, too ambitious, meaning that we can at best only seek momentary attentiveness? For instance, on the topic of trees and caring for them, in her posthuman related explorations Tsing (2015) mentions attempts to conserve the ponderosa pine trees after they had been 'logged out' in Oregon in the United States of America. As part of the conservation efforts the Forest Service had taken care to stop any forest fires (Tsing, 2015). However, stopping the fires led to an understanding that the ponderosa pine trees needed the periodic fires to reproduce. As well as the lack of fires enabling other species to spread which created "ever denser more flammable thickets of live, dead and dying trees" (Tsing, 2015, p. 30).

Considering the t(h)ree dimensions

Let us follow through this tree-bag happening in relation to the three dilemmas which we considered in Part 2. First is centrality, which is about exploring the anthropocentric tendencies of understanding humans as "the unquestionable value from which all other values derive their meaning" (Introna, 2014, p. 8). We started with my perception of 'the situation', the tree-bag collision, being produced through my sensory-perceptual array – the inscription of 'a problem' is one of human centred-ness. Although as suggested part of the ascribed value of those branches on that tree is connected with the redwing flock which had spent time there, who may well be put off their perching and feeding by some plastic bag flapping in the wind. Consequently, we could consider some valuing of this tree on 'bird terms', of course it is not just redwings who frequent it, for example a feral pigeon landed in it when I was first drafting the paragraph that you have just read.

What about the tree? This understood contributor to the 'lungs of a city', what might be the 'speaking of the tree'? In what way might the tree be understood as witnessing other beings. We were told by a neighbour that where that tree stands, and the others next to it, at some stage there were houses. I have not researched that urban history, but this appears a planted tree, it has likely not found its own way there, as in a seed in a woodland setting. It is a tree occurring due to human-sapling-planting. Granted the tree has put in more effort to exist over the years than those people-shovels who dug the hole to plant it. Could I be understood to be enrolled as a valued constituent part of the trees surrounds now that I have moved that bag so that it cannot get into its branches again? The bag could be regarded as a minor concern to it, particularly as it appears that its fruits are gone and the potential for birds to eat and spread this years seeds are no more. Likely my greatest value to the tree would be associated with its preservation, its letting-be.

The mentioned history of the patch of land that decades ago had houses on it, may become a very unfortunate dimension of its past for preventing any future house building on it. Indeed, there has been much activity in the city of Sheffield in relation to its urban trees and making sure that they are not chopped down (e.g. Bramley, 2018).

As we considered in relation to the centrality dilemma in Chapter 4 our imaginings of *witnessing-being-witnessed* are unavoidably encased within our human languages, which work hard to hold us at their centre. They are human languages after all! Much about issues of human centrality was explored to be about supporting the 'rights of matter' and 'rights of the more-than-human', connected with the challenge of "matter being used flagrantly and hurriedly in the service of efficiency and convenience in human-only terms" (Allen & Marshall, 2019, p. 104). I do not want to get overly self-congratulatory here, about my rather pathetic momentary bag exploits, but I am just trying to work through this example, and of course it is going to have its problems. For instance, there is a tendency, or desire, which I have mentioned before in another text (Allen, 2019c), for writers to portray themselves as orientated to 'the good' through a crafted presentation of self (Taylor, 1989). A heroic humanist narrative of 'doing the right thing', in this case paying attention and taking care of the bag. Whilst it might be impossible to entirely displace our-selves and all things human from centre stage in our narratives, we can raise questions about human valuing as 'the centre' of all valuing of beings. Indeed, doing so is likely to be a necessity, as it is the other-than-human which mediate and transform the possibilities of our humanity. This is because, as we have considered in this perspective, our bodies are defined by, and kept alive through, their sociomaterial entanglements. As with the current RSPB tagline 'giving nature a home', we can add to it the recognition of the mutuality of 'nature' giving us a home.

Speaking of a tree? Photo of a 'Save Me' tree in a road nearby to our home that has become enrolled into campaign activity to protect urban trees

The second dilemma is proximity. This dilemma, explored in Chapter 5, is to a large degree about ideas of 'affect'. Whereby 'affective' contact with others, was suggested to offer possibilities for somehow circumventing the net of human language that is caste over to define the world within its threads. Affect, as has been explored, is about a bodily feeling-being 'in the flesh' (Introna, 2014). Connected with the centrality dilemma, proximity is involved in prompting different ways of understanding human-being. The being in 'fleshy' proximity, to become into 'affective' contact, is about feeling an entanglement that is somehow not named or construed in language. So for example, the tree is not conveniently reduced to the category of 'London plane', or the bird to 'redwing'. This is because, doing so flattens a living being into something of a commodity, to be 'the same' as all the others to which that word is given. By doing so we make others countable and measurable, able to become (re)presented as a numerical value within some anthropocentric 'storehouse' of nature.

We first considered in Chapter 2 how these makings of linguistic boundaries between things can 'block' potential appreciations of our sociomaterial vulnerabilities and interdependencies. The tree in question is visible through the window which I am sat next to typing these words, it is in that sense proximate to my body. For instance, I was able to nip out of the house and grab the bag that had been attached to the branches to 'dispose' of it in our kitchen bin. I could go out and touch that tree, feel its bark. To wonder about what is going on 'in there', heading out of winter to warmer months, it may well be 'awakening' to move towards some leafy state. Although, with this particular tree I have not touched it, and felt it in my flesh. Perhaps I should try it. It is not that I have avoided such a close encounter, but rather that it has not ever really occurred to me.

I admit to having touched may other trees, either as part of an inquiring prod, or as a support to help to keep me on my feet as I move across ground next to it. In those moments of physical support my being able to stand-up is enabled and maintained by a tree which was graspable. In these times, some of my fleshy contact was likely on the aggressive side as I may have been attempting to work against a slippery muddy ground to avoid the full effects of gravity on my body. So in that way, on the occasions when I did physically touch a tree, it was quite a purposeful or reactionary contact which involved appropriating the tree for my human needs of stopping my bum from meeting the ground. Perhaps, on some occasions, I fulfilled the needs of the tree by its seeds becoming attached, following my close contact, to my clothes to help to enable their wider dispersion.

We keep returning to 'things' not being straightforward, and for all our sanity I would suggest necessarily so. My contact with the London plane outside the window might be better understood as one of metaphorical touch. What I mean by this is that it is in-touch, close-by, particularly, when I am first drafting this chapter, in times of pandemic and being at home in some form of lock-down. We have been heavily mediated in our movements due to the emergence and detection of a deadly virus. The tree could be thought of as 'standing-for' all those other trees to which I have been in close touch. Trees of multifarious species, so their naming and word-category associations blur and matter little beyond their tree-like-ness. Although, perhaps paradoxically, this 'local' of tree I could be affectively related to its embodying of a global concern for trees which has become interwoven in narratives of global sustainability. Processes of making sense that are not easily able to severe cognitive mind from bodily being. I can not touch and feel the tree to be somehow in support of my breathing, but I can conceptually believe it to be so. However, making such a bio-physical human-centred association is likely robbing the tree of it own rights. Although referentially the tree 'breaths', at least in part, from the expelling of 'air' from my body. We are perhaps each others dependents.

The third dilemma is about freedom. In Chapter 6 we explored the multiple meanings, interpretations and inter-connectivities of different ideas about freedom. In seeking to make sense of posthuman freedoms this included some distinctions between 'freedom-to' and 'freedom-from'. As we have explored this particular proximately located tree's presence has agency. So much so that it has been directing our attentions over recent pages. Sorry if you are getting, or have got, a bit bored with this example, but we are on to the third and final dilemma now, and I really better follow this through for completeness. Once we have done that I promise we will 'move on'. As I have already mentioned, the tree has agency, so blame this London plane tree!

Agency and the mutuality of 'it' between the human and more-than-human was a significant area for inquiry in relation to freedoms in Chapter 6. It was the lead into this whole tree-bag saga, how the tree was 'acting-upon' and enrolling us, well me, into offering some support in doing what I physically could with the 'removal' of that plastic bag. There was something of a 'gazing' of the other, *witnessing-being-witnessed*. In an example in Chapter 6 we considered flying, in relation to which I suggested that being passively-active in the flow-of-beings involved grappling to resist some strong undercurrents of associated modernist imaginaries. In that case, an imaginary of the being-successful knowing hyper-mobile academic. In this example, the tree likely has less of a heavy undertow, although as we have considered its being can be closely associated with global-local discourses that are infused with human concerns of trying to avert climate emergencies.

Neither I nor the tree are free from potential planetary climate threats, albeit that we will 'know' them in different ways. However, where as my *witnessing-being-witnessed* in relation to flying is likely more active than passive, in relation to the tree it seems more passive than active. The sociomaterial networks that we could associate with the tree are less likely, than those of flying, to entangle us in narratives and connected doings of enlightenment, progress and being modern. And, more importantly a letting-be of the tree (and trees in general), I suppose unless they are somehow 'invasive' and 'disease ridden', seems more graspable and doable. Whereas, the letting-be of the accumulated Anthropocene infrastructure of aeroplane technologies appears less viable if we are seeking not to incite Earthly volatilities related to changing climates. Although, if we did not have gas piped to the house to enable our boiler to pump heated water around our central heating system, we might well interpret the tree as a good source of heat for the house if chopped up and burnt. Unfortunately, and perhaps ironically in this case, gas boilers are calculated to be a major source of carbon emissions (e.g. Carrington, 2021), with tree burning sometimes labelled as 'carbon-neutral'. Also, we could consider the various particulate matters, and associated polluting of air, which are traceable from our burnings of both gas and wood.

The earlier discussion on freedoms in respect of entangled sociomateriality in Chapter 6 took us towards thoughts that solidarity may be a more helpful concept for posthuman-being. This was due to the aforementioned interconnected 'poles' of freedom, whereby beings might be understood to compete for their relative freedoms. Solidarity, because of the attention to the embodied embeddedness of beings, appears more suited to encompassing the mutuality of *witnessing-being-witnessed*. In terms of the organic relations between our bodies and a tree, it is a solidarity towards each-others ongoing potential to become and breathe. However, outside of this mutuality when a 'third-party' is added in to our attention, such as an aeroplane flying above us both, the tree and I, things can become more difficult. As in very simplistic terms, as I can be accused of here, the tree is cast in positive terms (i.e. for the sustainability of humanity) and the flying in negative terms (i.e. against the sustainability of humanity). Which means that it becomes hard to find ways in which the tree and I may find solidarity with the flying plane. These are of course the inevitable complexities of the 'rights of matter', even if the locus of valuing can be displaced to a tree, matter can potentially be seen to be embattled in its own hierarchies of matter-ing the most. Fortunately, I never suggested that I was going to 'resolve' such wonderings, quite the opposite. However, if we seek some 'strange' and 'new box' posthuman knowing then we have to expect getting into quite an (en)tangle. By, considering 'when species meet', such as the tree and I, Haraway suggests how creatively exploring such interdependencies "is the play of companion species learning to pay attention" (Haraway, 2008, p. 19). She suggests:

> "Once 'we' have met, we can never be 'the same' again. Propelled by the tasty but risky obligation of curiosity among companion species, once we know, we cannot not know. If we know well, searching with fingery eyes, we care. That is how responsibility grows." (Haraway, 2008, p. 287)

Answering to..

Back when I was studying for my PhD researching on organizations and environmental sustainability one of my supervisors, Judi Marshall, once wrote in her feedback a question – 'who did I answer to?' It is one of those short simple looking questions, which when you start considering it you realise that it is rather profound, in the 'deep understanding' sense of the word. It is a question that is more than about to asking 'to whose benefit?' do you think you are doing this researching. This is because, it is also asking 'who do you identify as important?' from your/our history of being. And, more specifically, if that being or being(s) were in front of you right now 'who would you feel compelled to provide a fulsome justification to about your work, and care about them seeing what you are doing as valuable?'.

At the time I remember making connections about my 'answering to', back to people and places that I had encountered, such as the family we, I am my partner-wife, had stayed with in Nicaragua in Central America for three months in 2008. A situation afforded by technologies including that of aeroplane travel. I suppose in that sense 'answering to' was about some notion of feeling guilty. Guilty about the naivety of how we had come to be with those other people, our paths woven into conversation by narratives of us 'developed' peoples helping them with their 'poor', and by inference 'under-developed' lives. That situation is a whole chapter on its own (do not worry I will spare you on that here!), but the reason why I mention it is because we are seeking to consider such ideas with posthuman attentions. What this means is that the 'answering to' can be understood as also encompassing the more-than-human. So for example, that tree outside my window, sorry I know I wrote that we will move on from it, but all such forms of 'matter' (alive and dead) may be part of some imagined 'jury' on our being and doing in-a-world. And, as with the discussions about dilemmas of freedom from a posthuman perspective, these are not imagined to be about interdependencies of constraint, but more dialogues of solidarity, which hopefully means that we can become more attentive to our entangled being.

In this exploration of the 'answering to', we must not, however, forget our the river metaphor for our sociomaterial being. As we have repeatedly returned to, with *witnessing-being-witnessed* we are not understanding our-selves as 'in control' of all this stuff. In many ways the imagining that we are 'in control' can impede possibilities for freedoms. A conception of being in control is tightly meshed with fully-knowing the other, a concern that *witnessing-being-witnessed* attempts to destabilise. This is because, as previously typed, witnessing is about being present and responsible in relation to some aspects of being in a world, but with an awareness of an inability to fully appreciate what you are being present and responsible towards (Haraway, 1997, 2008, 2016). Also, that is not to say that we are totally out-of-control and unable to thrash about enough to dissociate our bodies from certain ways of doing things. Such as the flying that we may have construed, via its associated effects, as involving breaking apart some boarder solidarity between beings. So reflecting on this 'answering to' question within a *witnessing-being-witnessed* perspective, it can be understood to be more about 'who (human and nonhuman) you are recognising yourself as being in dialogue with?'. In doing so opening up questions such as 'if you are in dialogue how are appreciations of the mutual witnessing taking place?' and 'how might you become aware if this mutual witnessing breaks-down?'.

Needing to go 'home'?

My current job title is 'Lecturer in Organisation Studies', and as I have mentioned before I work in the department of a university called the 'Management School'. Why do I mention this again now? Well, maybe you are sticking with me through these pages and that I have such disciplinary and subject attachments, mainly via a job contract and associated role title, is meaningless to you. In a 'post-disciplinary world', as I remember the late Sociologist John Urry once referring to in a research seminar, such a label and attachments are pretty irrelevant. So if you are a reader who is 'down' with those kind of ideas, then great, and maybe I need to stop worrying. However, as I tap the keys on the keyboard in front of me and these words appear on the screen I do worry that you might be feeling that I am, and have been, a little 'off-piste' in how you might see my subject specialisms. Although, if we have made it this far together to be in the final part of this book then I may well be worrying unnecessarily.

My concern here is that if you pick up a book by somebody who has been associated with an area such as Organization Studies, then you may well feel that it is in relation to that subject area that you want to know about *'witnessing-as-being'*. This seems pretty fair enough give the 'modesty' which we have considered on earlier pages, initially in Chapter 3. I suggested that modesty was about an appreciation that we are limited entangled beings, and whilst there are many wonderful things we can achieve we are more than a bit vulnerable, and quite puny, within a worldly habitat. Such modesty and associated limited-ness may well need to extend to claims about our grasps on reality and how they relate to a particular area of academic debate. I do not want to feel like I am in some particular 'academic or subject box', indeed this posthuman project is about unsettling boxes and imaging something other. Anyway, I do see that I should try and draw the streams of gatherings of ideas in this book, as we attempt to bring things together in these final chapters, towards some Organization Studies type areas. To do this I am going to attempt to come into conversation with some of the writing associated with leadership.

Entangled leadership

When I have written about leadership, which was a topic briefly mentioned early on in Chapter 5 (in connection with activism), I have been particularly interested in ideas that question the notion of an individual self (leader) as at the centre of concerns about leadership. As we have explored in respect of sociomateriality and posthumanism the idea of an independent humanist person-self is destabilised. Such a conceptualisation of 'unbounded beings' as we explored in Chapter 2, particularly in relation to authorship, is at the centre of new possibilities that appreciate entanglements. For many ideas about 'hero' leaders and leadership a sovereign human-self is assumed and placed at the centre of attention. Whereby, for example, a person possessing some traits or behaviours is understood as the primary basis for leader(ship) effectiveness. However, when leadership is approached from a relational perspective, as with sociomaterial and posthuman sensibilities, the meanings of, and potential for, leadership is reconfigured. By considering leadership I am seeing this very generally as referring to "processes of connecting people, things and places that are attempted with the purpose of taking action to address socio-ecological issues" (Allen, 2019a, p. 176).

Before we consider some of the relational ideas about leadership and their potential significant to making sense of *witnessing-as-being*, it is important to notice something about the 'capture' of ideas of leadership in relation to particular ways of organizing. For example, back in 1999, by Kathleen Allen and co-authors in an early contribution to developing ideas of an 'ecological approach' to leadership – that paid attention to complexity, interdependence and a long-term orientation – suggested that:

> "Leadership based on position and authority is inadequate for the challenges we face today. We need leadership which increases our capacity to learn new ways of understanding, defining, and solving the complex problems we are facing. ... Waiting for great individual leaders to guide and direct organizations as well as guarantee our safety and security is no longer possible." (Allen, Stelzner, & Wielkiewicz, 1999, p. 63)

These ideas resonate with more recent writing about leadership and sustainability such as that of Western (2010) in relation to 'eco-leadership'. He suggests that this perspective involves "a radically distributed leadership – in an attempt to harness the energy and creativity in a whole system" by promoting diversity and interdependence within organizations (Western, 2010, p. 44). Or, Satterwhite's 'systemic leadership' (2010) which draws upon ideas from cultural biology. She argues that her approach "helps establish our biological relationship and interdependence with our environment, as well as pushing us to consider what we choose to conserve together" (Satterwhite, 2010, p. 239). I am not going to review many ideas here – I have briefly reviewed some ideas about leadership and sustainability elsewhere (Allen, 2019a) – but I want to notice that most writing which connects ideas of leadership to socio-ecological sustainability attempts to decentre 'the individual' person-leader. Doing so can be regarded as associating with a 'post-heroic' leadership perspective i.e. not romanticising the actions of some 'great man' (e.g. Collinson, Smolović Jones, & Grint, 2018).

These ideas about leadership can be informative to considering and conceptualising *witnessing-as-being*, as we will consider next. However, predominant languages and meanings of 'leadership' are tightly woven into being about hierarchy and control in the pursuit of capital accumulations (e.g. Learmonth & Morrell, 2017). What I mean by this is that it can be hard to disassociate leadership from these connections which can be understood to appropriate the term in particular ways. Ways that are at odds with the relational perspective we have been developing. This is because the languages and meanings (with 'performative' consequences – see Chapter 2) are associated with hierarchies of associations and valuing that are centred around particular human-ends. As Achille Mbembe spoke about at a virtual seminar titled 'Post-development and decolonial perspectives' on Tuesday, October 13th 2020, a fundamental challenge for ethical being and organizing is to prioritise the living world over private property.

Relational leadership is a stream of work which in various ways seeks to place relationality and interdependency at the centre of understandings of leadership. Relational leadership has been suggested to offer the potential to understand ways of fostering sustainable and equitable forms of organizing to help to address complex, pressing and conflict ridden socio-ecological challenges (Nicholson & Kurucz, 2017). In this perspective leadership is understood not to be a property or trait of any person but as occurring within dynamic relations between people (Hosking, 2011). "Consequently, relational leadership involves a relational understanding of the world – that is, that people and things are given meaning only in relation to, and through interaction with, other people and things" (Allen, 2019b, p. 253). Which means that "leadership [is] not given, but [is] always in the process of becoming, on the way in or out" (Wood & Dibben, 2015, p. 39), an "event in the making" (p. 41). I previously wrote that:

> "In this view leadership is about processes of people interacting in which, at various moments, some people may be 'taking leadership'- that is, being influential in informing what is discussable, how the current situation is understood and what can be acceptable action – or 'giving leadership'- that is, permitting or promoting the views or actions of other people as figural in what is relevant and important at that moment." (Allen, 2019b, p. 252)

When leadership is understood in this processual and becoming sense we can appreciate its potential connections with the sociomaterial view that we have been considering on these pages. This is because with leadership, as mentioned above, about relating to purposeful acts of connecting people, things and places, we can explore how *witnessing-being-witnessed* can help us to appreciate forms of entangled leadership. What I mean by this is that it can give us some more 'texture' to trying to make sense of what *witnessing-as-being* involves. As we have explored a central idea of witnessing is that you are attempting to be present and responsible in relation to other-forms-of-life, but with the awareness of an inability to fully appreciate what you are being present and responsible towards. Or, also as we first considered at the end of Chapter 3, drawing on the ideas of Latour (2005), being as 'mediator', transforming and being transformed by that which you are being witness to.

When we consider 'leadership', and it being relational, we are doing so within a viewpoint of sociomateriality. A viewpoint that as we explored in Chapter 2, involves appreciating language and knowing as interrelated and interdependent with the materiality of the situation or circumstance (Carlile & Dionne, 2018). It was these ideas of sociomateriality in Chapter 2 that first took us towards working with and developing Dale's (2005) metaphor of a river, with the mutual enacting of river (social) and riverbanks (material). Whereby the riverbanks, are both being reshaped by the flow of the river, but simultaneously shaping as the "formation of the river itself is created by the shape and configuration of the landscape; as it moves over different forms of structure, over different types of rock, it is also shaped and changed" (Dale, 2005, p. 664).

Witnessing leadership

With our adopted appreciations of posthumanism and sociomateriality we could outright reject 'leadership' as a potentially productive space for theorising. For sure it is tempting, as we have already noticed, much leadership theorising-writing is drenched in ideas of hierarchism, heroicism, individualism and capitalism, to just mention a few -isms! Leadership and our images of "flailing in a torrent of sociomaterial mediatings" (Allen, 2019c, p. 73) or "vulnerable and confused refugee" (p. 74) do not appear obvious potential 'cousins'. However, this does offer us opportunities to 'talk back' to some of these leadership ideas with the learning about *witnessing-as-being* from this learning-writing project.

We embarked on this leadership thread, within this chapter, as I felt that I needed to come back to my 'home' discipline, as we have at times seemed to have wandered quite far and wide. As I mentioned already (when I moved away from that tree and bag example), associating more closely with things organization-like, might be disappointing for some readers, but possibly a bit of a blessed relief for others. Perhaps, to make some productive connections, we may need to 'step back' from the general view of leadership I have presented. A view which positions leadership as being about purposeful connecting of people, things and places. Indeed that definition, one that I assembled for some earlier writing on 'leadership and sustainability' (Allen, 2019a), appears quite devoid of the 'nature' that is fundamental to this inquiry into possibilities for witnessing. Also, we can appreciate the purposefulness is likely enveloped in humanist inclinations. We can though, 'step back' to consider a broader conception of leadership. For example, a 'classic' definition considers leadership as a "process of power-based reality construction" (Smircich & Morgan, 1982, p. 270).

This Smircich and Morgan (1982) definition is one that it rooted in leadership being a process between people. However, given our sociomaterial appreciations we would likely want to extend this view of leadership to be about a mutual process, between the human and more-than-human, in all its variety. Power is a key appreciation in this definition. We briefly considered power in Chapter 6, as about "a capacity to get things done" (King & Lawley, 2019, p. 500), when exploring the dilemma of proximity for *witnessing-being-witnessed*. Our consideration of power was within a 'relational view' in that it was something that can be understood to be made between human and nonhuman actors (Latour, 1986). A relational view includes appreciating that "actors are afforded by their very ability to act by what is around them"

(Mol, 2010, p. 258). As we considered at the time, in Chapter 6, 'extending' an understanding of power beyond human interactions is an ambitious endeavour. However, what we can take away from making these connections, is that leadership, as "process[es] of power-based reality construction" (Smircich & Morgan, 1982, p. 270), can be understood from a posthuman view to be about boundary making between 'things'.

The potential forms of reality construction with associated boundary making will differ between humans and more-than-humans. For example, a table is not going to 'tell us how it is', whereas we might find it hard to avoid the designated role based leader of an organization (such as a President) doing so. However, the table can become enrolled into possible constructions of reality. For example, Donald Trumps appearance at a 'mini-table' whilst he was President of the United States (Carroll, 2020). Of course the staging of such a situation can not be underestimated, as governments and organizations seek to 'manage impressions'. Although, we could say in this case that the 'mini-table' became active within producing realities through its associations, such as a child at school being told to sit behind their desk.

We can also go back to Chapter 3 where we considered the array of potential mediators involved in the example of writing-up-researching (including, a research stream called 'Science and Technology Studies', transcriptions of the research interviews, a voice recorder device, search engine algorithms and a 'Management School' building-edifice). What our relational view directs us towards is understanding a possible posthuman leadership that involves appreciations of more-than-human leadership influences on how action unfolds. This does raise questions, about 'stretching' notions of leadership in this way, such as – are we evacuating the term of any explanatory potential? For instance, we might ask questions such as 'In this view what is not leadership?' and 'How might we distinguish conceptions of leadership from organizing?'.

Just a moment

In the pursuit of possibilities for *witnessing-as-being*, by drawing on ideas of leadership we may perhaps 'muddy' our discussion, as the term is quite differently grounded to our adopted notion of witnessing. However, as I mention a few paragraphs back, we are not seeking to 'sort out leadership' but 'speak back' to debates in imagining some 'new boxes'. In particular, as we struggle with our entanglement, how might we find ways to gain some worthwhile purchase on making power to inform leadership influence for socio-ecological sustainabilities? Also, what ways of conceptualising *witnessing-as-being* are modest enough to respect the unknowability of being-in-a-world? As well as appreciating that leadership in a sociomaterial world is not simply a human preserve? One possibility is to understand the potential to take relational leadership as 'a moment' (Ladkin, 2017).

> "The 'leadership moment' includes leader/follower relations, but extends beyond that focus to consider the purposes to which a leader directs his or her efforts, as well as the role context plays in achieving leadership. 'Context' is understood to be subjectively deter-mined and as such, to have an affective element which is overlooked by relational approaches." (Ladkin, 2017, p. 396)

In our posthuman perspective 'the moment' is perhaps more textured by the interactings of variegated materialities (such as the mediators mentioned above). However, what is particularly promising here for our imaginings is that we can try to 'contain' our understanding of reverberating mutual witnessings to moments. The moments have histories, but the potential and possibilities for comprehending something as ephemeral as *witnessing-being-witnessed* can feel more doable as it is 'just a moment'. A transient space that perhaps through its disconnection from other moments means that we could help to find our way to some poise in that moment, with out pressure to do it in the next coming 'moment'. Ironically, in grasping for this writing of Ladkin (in this moment as it were!) her understanding of a moment, "does not refer to a temporal quality" (2017, p. 396). So I want to be clear that perhaps I am at cross purposes with Ladkin's intentions and approach. However, in this unsettling posthuman re-imagining I am gathering upon them, in partial ways, in the pursuit of 'going somewhere else'. The temporal 'moments' that I have reached towards here is to help our grasping of the possibilities for *witnessing-as-being* in the chapter. It is likely about an imaginary moment, but seems to offer some potential for some modest leadership-power reality making. Indeed 'a moment' is sufficiently pliable for us. For example, when our daughter suggests that she will hang her coat up in 'a moment' the possibilities are endless as to the time period we are being referred to! The benefit of attaching a notion of 'a moment' to *witnessing-being-witnessed* is that in all the unknowability of our entanglement we can feel some possibility for worthwhile action. I suppose we could call it 'hope'. Although in some sense that 'we need' hope perhaps draws use back to a purposing of matter for our humans ends. Anyway, this is about giving us something to think and write about!

Back in Chapter 2 I mentioned some researching that I completed with colleagues about how action emerged on sustainability at an urban regeneration project (Allen, Brigham, & Marshall, 2018). Our analysis explored how nonhuman mediators were much more significant to how action emerged than the expressions of visions of sustainability by organizational actors and positional leaders. The understanding of the potential 'scene' of mediators involved in shaping how sustainability became enacted was a retrospective analysis of materials gathered. Mediators was a term adopted from Latour (2005), first mentioned in Chapter 2, about how different human and nonhuman actors can be understood as enacting mutual agency, and in doing do transforming and being transformed. The materials included "interviews, project meetings, email exchanges, telephone conversations and document tracking with a wide range of actors associated with, or seeking to become associated with the Brownfield initiative" (Allen, Brigham, & Marshall, 2018, p. 32). I do not want to go into the details here, the point of mentioning it is that whilst this research could perhaps be regarded as 'a moment', it was not about witnessing or relational leadership 'in the moment'. Also, the range of gathered materials, as mentioned above, is way beyond what could be imagined to be marshalled 'in a moment'. A moment of the other-than-human becoming involved in the 'gazing back' that we have associated with *witnessing-being-witnessed.*

What I am trying to communicate here is that in the analysis mentioned above, which was drawing upon an actor-network lens, we positioned it as not representing some "God's eye view" (Whittle & Spicer, 2008, p. 619). By this I mean understanding ourselves to be above and apart from the spaces of researching, so the related image of peering down like Gods to understand and be 'in control' of and able to comprehend all that was going on. Instead, we positioned ourselves (as researchers) as being produced by, and embedded within, the sociomaterial interdependencies that we sought to explore. This is because the 'social' and 'material' are understood as only becoming meaningful through their interrelationships, a core assumption of sociomateriality. Such a sensibility is woven through this posthuman learning-writing endeavour. However, this recognition helps to bring us to consider how our potential for *witnessing-being-witnessed* can be appreciated as being partial in both an awareness (as just mentioned), and also in a temporal sense. Hence it is this fleetingness that could well offers us some modest possibilities. We might be able to imagine some moments of poise amongst all our flailing in the river of our entanglements. Poise being about an attention to the mutual interactings in which we are immersed, offering us potential to make some associations as part of shaping the boundaries for co-actings.

In the case of Brownfield, for example, the urban regeneration initiative mentioned above, we suggested the need for rethinking ideas of 'relational work' (Allen, Brigham, & Marshall, 2018). Relational work being about developing attentions to the different relations in which we become enrolled, and transform and are transformed by. Doing so was about: "expanding attention to the challenges and dynamics involved in forming alliances with (non)human mediators so that possibilities can be opened up for creatively enrolling them into enacting progressive visions for sustainability" (Allen, Brigham, & Marshall, 2018, p. 37). A general message was that leadership on sustainability needed to look 'beyond' the pronouncements of leaders. To do so by considering how the translation of sustainability into actions would benefit from attentions to how nonhuman mediators converge and diverge from human intentions. In this analysis our consideration of nonhuman mediators did not extend to other species and living beings. However, a version of this relational work to which we (myself and the colleagues in the article I am referring to) were gesturing towards could be developed with witnessing and associated dilemmas. Although, by suggesting such an 'expanded attention' could well be considered to be more in the vein of posthumanism as some new "teleological evolutionary stage" (Gane, 2006, p. 140), which as we have explored early on in this book is not where we are hoping to head.

Breathing space

There is a danger that modesty used here becomes a convenient overlay to 'opening up a can of [sociomaterial] worms'. This is because every-thing as mediator dead or alive, human or nonhuman, makes our *witnessing-being-witnessed* an unattainable impossibility. Let us work our way through an example to try to make sense of *witnessing-as-being* as a moment of power-based reality construction. The example I am going to use is 'close to home' so my apologises for any romanticising. My partner-wife is a visual artist and in recent years created a range of paintings as part of work about making the invisible air pollution (particularly in cities), and its consequences, visible. This involved an online and physical exhibition 'Breathing Space' which was in collaboration with others (particular academic researchers) as part of 'The Festival of the Mind' event in Sheffield which took place between September 17th and 27th 2020 ('Breathing Space').

What makes this an interesting example for *witnessing-being-witnessed*, is that through this art project we could consider that various 'alliances' are made with matter to produce the exhibition. Its beginning, in terms of the art work development, can be traced back to having her, my partner-wife's, awareness transformed by a reported story of the death of a young girl (Kissi-Debrah, 2018). Ella Kissi-Debrah tragically died in 2013 from breathing difficulties associated with an asthma attack, which followed ongoing respiratory issues that had required her to be admitted to hospital with life-threatening asthma 27 times over a three-year period (Kissi-Debrah, 2018). We could make some connections with the death of Ella at nine-years-old with the utterances of 'I can't breathe', which were that last words of Eric Garner, an unarmed black man who was killed in 2014 after being put in a chokehold by a member of the New York City Police (Baker, Goodman, & Mueller, 2015). A moment that is central in stories about the development of the Black Lives Matter movement (mentioned in Chapter 2). Although, very different forms of human violence.

A story that can be told about this example, was of my partner-wife being affected by this news story and associated imaginary, as well as through her later contact with Ella's mum who was campaigning about air quality, and for an inquest into Ella's death. The inquest did later occur and a landmark legal decision was made that translated a history of events and data into a relationship that established 'air pollution was a factor' in Ella's death (BBC News, 2020). There are many facets to this situation and interesting sociomaterial interdependencies to consider, as well as associated forms of leadership from an array of actors, human and nonhuman. Such as the unexpected happenings of air pollution monitoring devices in the areas near Ella's home, which provided measurements that were able to be later related to the timings of Ella's asthma attacks. However, I want to focus on an alliance with matter that my partner-wife made through using dirt and grime. She collected the dirt and grime from the exhaust pipes and wheels of cars to use as the material to create paintings and drawings of Ella. We can understand ourselves to swept along (back to our river metaphor), with the landscape (being-in-a-world) creating and affording the possibilities for the flow of mediatings, the meetings between social meanings and physical beings. What I want to explore here is a potential moment of poise in a conceptualisation of *witnessing-as-being*. A moment in which the matter of dirt or grime car exhaust pipes and wheels is transformed by its presence as marks on canvases. Canvases that were later hung within a space designated as gallery, and displayed as digital images on an associated website, tightly enrolling them it as objects of art and culture.

The transformation of 'invisible' matter in the form of air pollution from car exhausts, as well as minute particulate matter from tyres and break pads, into something visible and meaningful to observers is 'the moment' we are considering. We can consider the mediation of my partner-wife through interactions with texts (news reports) and associated humans (Ella's mother and family). These mediations set within histories of personal experiences, including being inscribed as asthmatic, and being a mother of our daughter, who at the time was of a similar age to that at which Ella died. As well as being immersed in broader flows of narratives and assembled texts about air pollution and environmental unsustainably. Texts both part of the 'everyday' brought into attention via websites with associated internet connections and device screen viewing technologies, as well as through past enrolments such as within a university Master degree in Science of the Environment. A located degree assemblage of aspects including people, public-academic discourses, academic publishing systems, and searching technologies. Arrays of mediators that can be understood to be intermingled within streams of my wife-partner being 'with' and 'in' different spaces to be affectively involved with sociocultural natures.

This is a story of a complex interactional flow within which alliances were formed with the 'dirt and grim' associated with the motion and propulsion of cars. To transform this 'dirty matter' into a charcoal-like mark making material for painting-drawing involved processes of physically 'collecting' this dirty matter, with old rags, from parked cars outside of our house. Matter that can be often overlooked through its invisibility, only fleetingly perceptible via smells from being in proximity to the expulsions from an internal combustion engine. An alliance with this unexpected mark making matter emerged out of various forms of affective and non-affective 'contact' from being-in-a-world. Consequently, we can appreciate this as 'a moment' of poise to re-make the matter into art works with potentialities for affecting human-others.

The canvases hanging in the gallery representing some marks of 'relational leadership', artefacts with the power for creating new realities from those who find themselves as observer. In some ways giving leadership to car grime to be some-thing more figural in our imaginings.

Another fascinating artistic example of creating alliances with the more-than-human is associated with Teemu Lehmusruusu who is based in Finland. His 'House of Polypores' work can be understood to enable the 'speaking of decaying trees'. In this artwork a highly sensitive sensor system monitors changes and movements in the decomposing tree/wood, which through coded microprocessors changes the data feed into a musical soundscape that is played by nine organ pipes ('House of Polypores, 2021'). Connectedly, Michael Prime a musician and artist in Britain uses devices to collaborate with plants and fungi by mapping and amplifying their bioelectrical sounds. He suggests that the sounds generated reflect the fluctuations of the bioelectrical field of the organism, which is constantly changing in response to its environment (Morgan, 2021). His work by making life processes audible, like the work of Teemu, seeks to challenge ideas of plants and fungi as being part of an inanimate backdrop to human life.

As I mentioned when I began the above 'Breathing Space' example, as with the discussed researching at Brownfield, 'I' am being produced by and embedded within the sociomaterial interdependencies being brought into this book-text. Hence, within this perspective of *witnessing-being-witnessed*, and the assumed performativity (see Chapter 2) of describing and inscribing realities, romanticising a field of action is quite possible. As others such as Introna (2014) notices in his example of a 'letting-be-of-things'. However, we are seeking some glimpses and images of possibilities for posthuman appreciations, which as we have considered come with an unavoidable unknowability.

However, as we are exploring our potential for tracing and forming alliances, or prompting dialogues of solidarity offers possibilities. What we are hoping for here is to find 'some purchase' or 'some texture' which can help us towards ways of understanding being that offer us potential to productively act-upon socio-ecological sustainabilities. Because as Braidotti suggests:

> "… the posthuman is both situated and partial – it does not define the new human condition, but offers a spectrum through which we can capture the complexity of ongoing processes of subject-formation. In other words, it enables subtler and more complex analyses of powers and discourses." (Braidotti, 2019, p. 36)

By exploring *witnessing-as-being* in this chapter I have endeavoured to make some sense of how we might act from an awareness of the 'gazing back', or 'speaking back', of the more-than-human in all its variety. To attempt this we have particularly considered *witnessing-being-witnessed*, along with all its sociomaterial flowings, as 'a moment'. Whereby we might find some momentary poise to give/take some leadership, assemble some boundaries or make some power. A poise where we do not make ourselves as 'the centre', as our posthuman poise is only imaginable by understanding ourselves as part of an interdependent periphery.

Chapter 8

Witnessing-as-organizing

Printing problems

This final chapter explores the potential implications of *witnessing-being-witnessed* for how we organize – *witnessing-as-organizing*. It begins by attempting to express more about the contingency and situatedness of this learning-writing which, as suggested at the very beginning of the book, is key to experimenting with *witnessing-being-witnessed*. I try to consider some of the sociomaterial interactings of the voiceless 'others' in the flowings-together which have assembled this text. Questions about potential anthropomorphizing (previously mentioned in Chapter 4 in relation to the dilemma of centrality) are surfaced and considered in relation to seeking to give voice to the more-than-human. These discussions lead us into exploring issues of alienation and commodification which are understood as needing to be addressed in imagining possibilities for *witnessing-as-organizing*. In doing so, notions of, and debates about, 'alternative organizing' are engaged with. An example, of an alternative organization is explored, and critiqued, as part of extending visibility on how we might seek to translate *witnessing-being-witnessed* into the ways we can get things done together. A key aspect of these discussions involves considering, from a posthuman perspective, 'goals' and 'languages' related to organizing. Finally, some attempted drawing together is done to try to leave us with some gathered sense of the streams of messages from across these pages.

In the previous chapter we where thinking more 'personally' about *witnessing-as-being*. In this final (!) chapter, as just introduced, I will be specifically considering *witnessing-as-organizing*. Given that I am currently inscribed with the job label of 'Lecturer in Organisation Studies', I guess this is where I need to show my specialism. By the way the '!' a couple of sentences ago was that, yes, we are here in this final chapter of the book. In the early chapters I shared my wonderings about whether the words I was assembling would actually 'make it', and be part of some whole called 'a book'. I do feel a lot more relaxed about things now – a possible ending is in sight. We are on the final chapter. Well, okay, as I first type this sentence the seven chapters that will proceed this one to be a book are in some initial state of draft, they are going to need some more work. However, in this marathon learning-writing project it does appear that I am on something of a homeward stretch! From all those hours of typing has come this text. Of course this sense of having assembled a book when I am first drafting this chapter may be premature, as getting to a book will involve lots of responding to feedback and completing multiple rounds of revisions.

My attempt at a book, going back to my the first sentence from Chapter 1, by assembling letters into words, words into sentences, sentences into paragraphs and paragraphs into chapters, has materialised into some-thing. Now that I have got this far I might even feel able to tell colleagues about my book writing endeavours, as any potential eye-rolling about why on earth I would want to write a book can no longer deter me. I have all these pages of words to show for it, which are wrapped up into computer code, that taken together makes something called a file, that I know of by 'file exploring' on the screen of my computer. 348 kilobytes of file apparently when I check its 'properties'. That kilobytes count does not include photos, so that will bulk it up, give it more of a metaphorical thud. Then, if I can win my disagreement with our printer, which does not currently recognise the inkjet cartridges that I did a home refill job on then I may be able to print it into some greater physical being.

The home cartridge refilling can be partly explained to be about trying to avoid the escalation of the prices of ink cartridges in Covid-times. Imposed homeworking has meant an inability to access the printers at work. Also, cartridge refilling is about exploring a potential reuse, instead of replacement 'regime', to how our home printing is organized. Although, in attempting to take care of matter, I do not want to 'give birth', via printing stuff out, to any more 'unnecessary' matter. However, I have been stashing paper on which only one-side is printed, some of it collected some years ago (I wrote earlier that there is always a danger of heroism with attempting to trace relational entanglements!). Some of the making of paper with one-side printed on, was my doing, the rest I picked up at work finding it along the way in teaching rooms, or next to printers as relics of a 'print job' that did not quite go to plan. Some of the paper even goes back to studying a Masters degree in 2003-4. What this means is that if I do print out this text it will not be so much creating more matter, but reforming those sheets of paper in the cupboard, by (hopefully!) getting our printer to print the ink on to the paper that I syringed into its cartridges. However, my syringing has seemingly caused some indigestion, or a 'U051 error' as the printer tells me, a diagnosis that I have so far been unable to permanently cure.

I am trying to 'lighten things up a bit' at the start of this final chapter as it may well have got a bit 'heavy going' reading about *witnessing-as-being*, particularly in the second half of the last chapter. As well as, as I have tried to do throughout this book, experiment with, and explore how, my practical engagement in learning-writing can be understood as being mediated and transformed through my 'contingent' and 'situated' relationality within a becoming world. And also, having a moment here to take it in that, yes, I did get to the last chapter! How the hell did that happen? When I started tapping away at a keyboard in the pursuit of book writing back in February 2020, amongst doing all other working related commitments – all of which felt a more publicly legitimate 'use of my time' – actually creating a 'whole' book did feel quite far fetched. In the beginning I comforted myself with the thought that worst case, if I only managed a few draft chapters before giving up on my clandestine book writing endeavours, I could try to rewrite them into the more accepted academic currency of journal articles (see discussion in Chapter 1 on this topic). Although, what is perhaps more surprising is that on first drafting this chapter my general view is that this learning-writing book assembling has been pretty enjoyable. Whilst the opening vignette about my printer-cartridge exploits is somewhat frivolous, and for a bit of 'light relief', I do want to notice an 'issue' which can help us to find our way into this chapter on *witnessing-as-organizing.*

Questions of anthropomorphizing

Based on the description about the printer we have at home, perhaps for some comedic effect, sorry, yes, I was trying to be a bit humorous in case you missed it, I could well be accused of anthropomorphizing. By, for example, using words like 'indigestion' which is referring to a human condition. Given all the discussions throughout this book on possibilities of decentring humans in processes of being and valuing in-a-world, such a move of anthropomorphizing might be understood to be a potential 'strategy' for witnessing (something I briefly mentioned in Chapter 4). Anthropomorphizing does, however, offer up some potential problems.

A posthuman perspective is reaching for 'something else', other ways of understanding and being human. An elsewhere which is about possible 'communions' with matter or the-other-than-human, to have 'value in its own right' (Allen & Marshall, 2019). We noticed earlier on in this book that there is a lot 'lumped-in' under notions of more-than-human. In such a category there are a plethora of wide-ranging and variegated beings and things, including animals and technologies. As Puig de la Bellacasa has written the posthuman "speaks in one breath of nonhumans and other than humans such as things, objects, other animals, living beings, organisms, physical forces, spiritual entities, and humans" (2017, p. 1). Consequently, to make a common 'thread' or 'language' which anthropomorphizes the other-than-human, particularly given the infinite array of possible communions, is problematic.

We might imagine that 'making' others as reflecting humanity could be a part of a 'levelling up', in which through the meanings we inscribe to a soft-toy we transform it into something with human personality and life. We may seek comfort in such toys due to the continuity of their presence throughout our lives, an ability to 'listen' and not talk back, as well as their softness to our touch. However, in relation to the notion of witnessing, doing so seems to deny the mystery and otherness of matter because it centres human purposes. Although, it may well mean that we 'take care' of that teddy bear and 'look after' it for many years, unlike perhaps those one use one-use coffee cups, that first got a mention in Chapter 4. Apparently, the name 'teddy bear' is most frequently traced to a story of the late President (Teddy) Roosevelt who refused to shoot a captured bear while hunting in Mississippi ('Real Teddy Bear Story - Theodore Roosevelt Association'). Celebrated as a moment of sparing the life of a nonhuman other!

In Chapter 6 I mentioned the television programme the Repair Shop in relation to ideas of affective contact. We considered how objects are repaired in the programme using 'traditional' techniques and materials, teddy bears are not uncommon. Upon being presented the repaired item the owners can be brought to tears. Whether or not such affective contact can be understood as relating to such objects being either anthropomorphized, or standing for the memories of deceased humans, is beyond explanation. We are a remote and distant viewer who can understand themselves as being 'manipulated' to become involved in some emotional journey as television entertainment. In a way though we could consider that associated care for these things is about them somehow 'being human'. An 'overcoming' of human centrality, explored in Chapter 4, by inscribing an imagined human exceptionalism onto nonhuman-others. However, this is an ethical project that does not seem to reflect the socio-ecological challenges of the Anthropocene times that have informed my interest in attempting to develop the perspective of *witnessing-being-witnessed*. This is because I have been generally interested in exploring how to loosen 'human grip' on others, allowing them to be variously other on their 'own terms', rather than trying to assimilate them into our gaze.

We have repeatedly reminded ourselves that we are not about 'figuring it out', rather noticing the dilemmas, and engaging within the inevitable limitations of a perspective. Perhaps the printer meets teddy bear example was a slightly incompatible intersection. The teddy-bear has 'eyes', unless they have fallen off following much contact and cuddling, or abuse. Consequently, we are helped in our imagining of the teddy bear witnessing us, gazing back. The printer, whose suggested 'indigestion' started this chapter has a box-like appearance that is less easily associated with bodily images of humanity. Indeed, when in early chapters, such as Chapter 4, we have considered the 'gazing back' or 'speaking of things' such language is undeniably overlaying human sensory awareness onto heterogeneous nonhuman others. There appears to be a potential tight-rope of seeking to develop languages of relations and entanglement, and cloaking others within capes of anthropomorphism. As Sheldrake writes in his explorations of fungi:

> "If you repurpose a human concept to make sense of the life of a non-human organism, you've tumbled into the trap of anthropomorphism. Use 'it' and you've objectified the organism, and fallen into a different kind of trap" (Sheldrake, 2020, p. 46)

In our sociomaterial relatings such things (teddy bears and printers) are likely less consequential to our being-alive than our mutual 'breathing' in the tree example in Chapter 7. Although, the relations which bring about a window (as in Chapter 5), or a book (as in Chapter 4), involve drawings together of matters through 'processes of production' or 'supply chains' which have consequences, albeit often hard to significantly trace. Such process of object creation could be enrolled into a web of violence making to other beings. For example, if a teddy bear is partly constituted of a chemical such as formaldehyde, a 'naturally occurring' compound, that is likely harmful to both maker and owner (Clarke, 2008). Also, we can appreciate that technologies such as printers, might give us agency to reproduce messages for displaying (for example, when printing presses where first used they were seen to be revolutionary (Eisenstein, 1983)), but through our association with them, they organize us. For example, through the already mentioned regimes of ink-replacement and associated activities to keep them at our service. We do, however, maintain the ability to take them out of our homes and lives, in acts of removing 'unnecessary' matter. I do not need to go far from our house to encounter skips of accumulated matter for disposal, because it has no perceived value to the humans that had kept it, such as the ones pictured below. The skips might represent an 'extreme form' of alienating matter. Alienation is a notion that I want to move to next as we consider *witnessing-as-organizing*.

Alienating and commodifying others

In Tsing's (2015) fascinating posthuman informed exploration she considers the importance of notions of alienation in her following of the flows associated with matsutake mushrooms. She describes alienation as follows:

> "In capitalist logics of commodification, things are torn from their life-worlds to become objects of exchange. This is the process I am calling 'alienation', and I use the term as a potential attribute of nonhumans as well as humans" (Tsing, 2015, p. 121)

The notion of commodification was briefly mentioned in Chapter 7. Here it was referred to as involving a 'flattening out' of some-thing (be it a 'tree' or 'slave') to become 'the same' as all the others to which that word is given – a commodity. The concept of commodification is often prominent in critiques of capitalism in general, and associated organizational responses to socio-ecological unsustainabilities such as 'carbon markets' (e.g. Böhm et al., 2012). The general argument, which is connected with a Marxist standpoint, is that commodification ('real' or 'proxy') is central to the potential for opportunities for accumulation by human-

Alienating matter? Photos of some skips accumulating matter in roads nearby our house

individuals. Whereby the accumulation of capital is understood to be a key logic to, and for, the creation of forms of capitalist market economies. By commodifying 'things' possibilities are created to own, rent, sell etc. for profit. Or, as Tsing (2015) states in the above quote, make others into 'objects of exchange'.

Tsing (2015) connects ideas of commodification with alienation. Alienation is a term that is also most typically related to Marxist ideas. In general, alienation is about the experience of being isolated from a group or an activity. In relation to organizing and work, 'the worker', as opposed to 'the owner', can be understood to become isolated from "their skills, the final product and their coworkers" (King & Lawley, 2019, p. 64). From a Marxist viewpoint it is suggested that "capitalism would increase levels of alienation generally and that, as collective consciousness increased, workers would increasingly resist their exploitation" (Clegg et al., 2019, p. 443). The images of organization which are mostly associated with these notions of alienation can be regarded as 'rational' or 'machine-like' approaches. 'Rational' in the sense that effective organization is understood to involve clear direction with associated goal clarification, and an overriding focus on "the [financial] bottom line" (Quinn et al., 2014). 'Machine-like' in the sense that 'good' organizing is about the effective control of orderly relations between clearly defined parts (i.e. people as 'cogs') that have some determinate order (Morgan, 2006). Such ideas about organizing can be related to assumptions about 'workers' as being: predictable and comprehensible, lazy and disinterested, passive and dependent, and reactionary.

Tsing (2015) sees 'alienation' as particularly important in her posthuman informed study of matsutake mushrooms, this is because she understands alienation as a process of disentanglement. As with the above quotation 'torn from their life-worlds', referring to the mushrooms, to "serve as counters" as part of capital accumulations, which "converts ownership into power" (Tsing, 2015, p. 133). She goes onto suggest that "capitalism is a translation machine for producing capital from all kinds of livelihoods, human and non-human" (p. 133). Consequently, when we are trying to explore possibilities for posthuman or entangled organizing, we are doing so in light of such concerns about processes of disentanglement. However, at this late stage, the final chapter of this book, I am not planning some major 'broadside' on processes involved in varieties of capital exchange and accumulation.

Notions of capital and capitalism are significant for many of us who live within societies and economics which have become substantially defined by associated labels. This means that many of us may well have to live with the associated systemic weaknesses of these ideologies and associated arrangements. These weaknesses may likely include: that capitalism confers economic power on a category of people, owners of capital, who have an active economic interest in keeping large segments of the population in an economically vulnerable and dependent position (e.g. emergence of zero hours contracts); pricing by the present economic cost of producing things means that markets are largely incapable of accounting for long term socio-environmental costs; and, systemic biases towards turning increases in productivity into increased consumption via advertising, marketing and promotion of consumerist lifestyles, rather than increased 'free time' (Wright, 2010).

We can be generally aware of some 'issues' associated with processes of capital accumulation as a dominant 'logic'. However, as has been suggested by other writers "the posthuman perspective would not envisage a programmatic overthrow of capitalism, but rather change through small actions particularly as a result of increased awareness about forms of intra and inter-species domination" (Cudworth & Hobden, 2015, p. 145). Consequently, considering *witnessing-as-organizing* is about efforts to redress such alienations and dominations. What this means is that in this chapter we are going to place our attentions at a more 'micro-level' of organization than 'macro-level' politics. By suggesting such a categorisation I am not suggesting that they are separate, but indicating that a more modest project with organizing likely involves considering what we might regard as 'alternative organizations' that could be 'prefigurative' of possible futures. Two concepts that we will explore over the following paragraphs.

Some quick comments on organization

In a general sense 'organizations' can be understood "as goal orientated collectives" (Clegg et al., 2019, p. 4). An important assumption is that forming an organization can enable the effective assembling of people, processes and materials which can 'extend human agency'. The term organizing can be used in preference to organization, as the former is a more processual term relating to sociomaterial 'comings together'. Where as 'organization' can sound quite thing-like in the sense that you can 'touch it', which could be a distraction as identifying where an organization begins and ends can be challenging. This is because ideas about what an organization is could include: contracts with workers and suppliers, legal articles of association, organizational policies and processes, organizational communications (such as websites and reports), buildings and other physical 'assets', people who work at or who are somehow involved, and reputation. Consequently, considering organizing as about people 'getting things done together' may well be a more productive framing for making sense of what might be encompassed in collective endeavours. Particularly, given that collective endeavours can involve connections becoming formed and organized between heterogeneous beings and entities. As well as, particularly in relation to exploring *witnessing-being-witnessed*, opening up more expansive spaces for imagining possibilities.

Spaces in which we can take the subversion of alienations and dominations as a key concern.

In Chapter 6, we considered some of the work of Bookchin and others writing about Social Ecology. In particular, the attentions of Social Ecology to considering issues of hierarchical relations, which include social, political and economic inequities (e.g. Bookchin, 1982, 1990). In this writing hierarchy is understood to (re)produce patterns of domination between humans, which can be reflective of, and reflected in, relations between humans over nonhumans. In theories of organizing and managing, notions of hierarchy can often be understood to have become naturalised. This is because they are taken-for-granted in how to 'do organizing'. For example, classical notions of bureaucracy, written in textbooks about organizations and organizing, assume that the creation of authority between people is necessary, and that this is achieved and controlled through hierarchies (e.g. King & Lawley, 2019).

We can understand hierarchy as about enabling some people to be able to hold power over others by giving them formal authority to direct others. Doing so with the potential to administer sanctions or penalties if directions are deviated from, as well as give (financial) rewards when their directions are followed. Ideas about hierarchy can be related to ideas of 'managerialism'. Managerialism assumes the necessity for organizational superiors, or 'managers', who are characterised as acting with "rationality and neutrality", and "have the right to make decisions and give instructions to employees without seeking their consent" (Cunliffe, 2014, p. 14). These assumptions about how to get things done, dominate in what we might call 'traditional organizations'. Consequently, what can be particularly interesting for us to consider for *witnessing-as-organizing* is what are termed 'alternative organizations', because they subvert these interests and assumptions.

Alternative organizing

Alternative organizations, like 'traditional organizations', include much variety. A key criteria for identifying an alternative organization is that its core purpose contrasts with the mainstream or dominant purpose of economic profit or growth (Reedy & Learmonth, 2009). This means that alongside the discussed aspects of hierarchy and managerialism, alternative organizations can be generally regarded as forms of organizing which cannot be described by the dimensions capitalist, managerialist and hierarchical. Alternative organizations have been defined as involving "forms of organizing which respect personal autonomy, but within a framework of co-operation", with a core purpose for taking responsibility for enabling futures of individual and collective flourishing (Parker et al., 2014, p. 32). What this implies is that the means of organizing in ways that are not capitalist, managerialist or hierarchical is attempted to be connected to the ends of individual and collective flourishing. We can understand flourishing as connected with freedom from forms of domination and alienation, which can be more easily associated with 'traditional organizations' (Kociatkiewicz, Kostera, & Parker, 2021). Flourishing has been described as a "means not only to grow, but to grow well, to prosper, to thrive, to live to the fullest", which associates it with ideas of positive emergence (Ehrenfeld & Hoffman, 2013, p. 6). This is growth in a 'human improvement' sense, rather than growth in 'financial wealth'.

We are moving quickly here, very quickly, with some broad brush strokes through some ideas about organizing that in my teaching, in a Management School, would likely be considered over many weeks and months. Interesting though, that this brisk pace is connected with exploring an area, 'Organization Studies', in which I could claim to have some 'specialist knowledge', in contrast to some earlier sections of the book where I was staggering around searching for some ways forward in text (e.g. the opening of Chapter 6). However, what I am trying to articulate is that when we approach organizing we are attempting to do so in a way that is considering new possibilities. A way that is beyond understanding organizations being some corporate form, of which the primary purpose is to accrue and direct human agency in the pursuit of accumulating capital and the making of (excessive) profits.

I have tried to briefly explain and justify a general assumption that hierarchy in organizing can be connected with ideas of domination, whereby a person has formalised power over another (Bookchin, 1996). These processes of domination can be related to alienation, as with Tsing's (2015) writing, whereby humans, and nonhumans, are made to become isolated so that they are understood to be disentangled. Although, Tsing (2015) explains, in her analysis of the collection and trade of matsutake mushrooms, that alienation can be understood as relating to transitory moments for humans and nonhumans, rather than some permanent state associated with particular ways of organizing. However, overall we can suggest that sociomaterial organizational processes of commodification and alienation may well be very much at odds with posthuman sensibilities.

The potentials for *witnessing-as-organizing*, that we will explore in this chapter, understands alternative organizations as offering some possible glimpses of being 'prefigurative'. Prefigurative meaning that alternative organizing can be understood as involved in creating potentialities for informing and bringing new more equitable and just ways of organizing social relations into being (Parker et al., 2014). This is not to inscribe all traditional organizations to be totally enveloped in commodification and alienation, that would be a very bold suggestion. However, in seeking to move out of the 'old boxes' in this posthuman imagining it is notions of alternative organizing that appear to be the most congruent. This is primarily because, as introduced they are by definition brought in to being with intentions of equity and democracy through "frameworks of cooperation" (Parker et al., 2014, p. 32). Like any forms of organization there are inevitable potential tensions and contradictions, in the case of alternative organizing these are likely between individual autonomy and collective solidarity (Parker et al., 2014). Which means that we need to be careful to not become overly utopian and rose-tinted about such 'alternative' possibilities. However, such tensions and contradictions can likely be understood to be relatively 'minor' compared to, for example, those that we can consider in 'traditional organizations' which highlight some severe fault-lines between capital accumulation and taking actions to substantially address sustainability concerns.

There is a range of work, including some of my own with colleagues, about the tensions and contradictions expressed by people who work for organizations which are capitalist, managerialist and hierarchical (e.g. Allen, Marshall, & Easterby-Smith, 2015; Wright, Nyberg, & Grant, 2012). Contradictions which have been understood as relating to ideas of 'self-alienation' (Costas & Fleming, 2009), which "speaks to moments when we become discomforted by seeing ourselves as being who we do not want to be" (Allen, Marshall, & Easterby-Smith, 2015, p. 331). The general point I am trying to make here is how peoples' expressions of contradictions, between what they are expected to do working as part of an organization, and acting on their concerns about sustainability, helps suggest to us the potential substantial limitations for traditional forms of organizing. Or, the problems associated with what might be more generally described as an 'ecological modernization' perspective to addressing sustainability issues. As such a perspective relies on an often "unacknowledged contradiction ... that sustainability may be combined with perpetual growth in human consumption of products and services, because innovation will sufficiently reduce the material and energy inputs involved in production and distribution" (O'Reilly, Allen, & Reedy, 2018, p. 220). Forms of innovation that are likely predicated on the 'scaling-up' of organizing to expand the reach of processes for commodifying 'nature', as well as seeking to 'replace it' with technologies (O'Reilly, Allen, & Reedy, 2018).

I have already mentioned that in this final chapter I am not about to go out 'all-guns-blazing' wrought with some anti-capitalist angst. As we can understand from the discussion over the chapters, in particular our 'straw-man/person' consideration in Chapter 6, we can quickly get into immodest troubles by seeking to make some unhelpful imaginaries that we attempt to 'defeat'. So, in some slightly cack-handed-way, what I am trying to tell you is that we are best looking at alternative forms of organizing if we are attempting to develop ideas about *witnessing-as-organizing*. Remember this is a perspective with which we are hoping to extend some visibility for being responsible, solving whatever we might imagine as *the* problem is of a very different realm of writing.

A Friends example

To consider possibilities we are going to explore a particular example of alternative organizing that I have been researching over the past five or so years. I will very briefly introduce this form of alternative organizing. Quakers (or Religious Society of Friends) are an international community of about 340,000 people, and tend to be understood as nonconformist Christians (Dandelion, 2008). Quakers see living as sacramental where all life is appreciated as sacred, which means that concepts such as God or the divine relate to (aspects of) people and living beings, not a remote (human) spirit (Durham, 2010). The focus of Quaker organizing within each local group is substantially about developing and supporting a worshipping community of people, which can involve the development of community initiatives (e.g. campaigning for particular local-global issues), and the maintenance of any buildings in which they might meet and worship together. There is no creed or statement of belief as with many other religious groups, which means that there can be much variety between Quakers and Quaker Meetings (the name for the local groups). In general, Quakers in Britain are guided by four testimonies: equality, simplicity, truth and peace – of which equality tends to be seen as the most important. As written elsewhere as an introductory explanation to Quaker organizing:

> "There are different national, regional and local aspects, and associated roles in Quaker organization. However, the overriding principle is that nobody is 'in charge' (Bradney & Cownie, 2000, p. 71), and to avoid the development of hierarchies and protectiveness over people's positions, roles are expected to be rotated every three years. The 'business method', the key decision-making process, has been developed over the past 350 years. There are many dimensions to the 'business method', but a core ideal, expressed in secular terms, is that 'everyone must feel it right to let the decision go ahead, even if there are bits of it which they might have expressed differently, or changed in some way' (Bradney & Cownie, 2000, p. 71)." (Allen, 2019b, p. 254)

For considering *witnessing-as-organizing* a particularly interesting aspect of Quaker organizing is that it can be understood as embracing individual 'unknowing' (Allen, 2017; Law & Mol, 2003). Unknowing as we previously defined in Chapter 3, is the "realisation of inadequacy to anything approaching full and comprehensive understanding" (Zembylas, 2005, p. 142). We explored how an appreciation for unknowing can be understood to be important when considering a relational ontology, where ontology refers to "philosophical assumptions about the nature of reality" (Easterby-Smith, Thorpe, & Jackson, 2013, p. 18). Relational ontology was first mentioned in Chapter 2, as related to assumptions that every being and thing is only meaningful and/or alive because of its relations with other beings and things. Consequently, the relations between entities are understood to be "ontologically more fundamental than the entities themselves" (Wildman, 2010, p. 55). And, when I write about 'entities' these are regarded as having permeable boundaries. For example, in Chapter 2 human skin was mentioned as being understood as "a permeable zone of intermingling", "an entanglement" (Ingold, 2008, p. 1806). Assumptions about unknowing, based on taking a relational ontology, informed our move towards the more tentative and reciprocal idea of *witnessing-being-witnessed.*

In Quaker organizing I have suggested that: "unknowing, where nobody individually understands the meaning of the situation or has an answer, is an accepted and core aspect of being in conversation, which supports a patient and frequently silent searching for how to go on together" (Allen, 2017, p. 135). The waiting and searching for a collective way forward is related to assumptions about God being immanent in human affairs – including Quaker commitments to 'God in everyone' and that Quaker decision-making is about 'discerning the will of God'. However, conceptions of God in Quaker contexts tend to be diverse and diffuse, but not understood as a defined human deity. There is much that could be introduced, but I am attempting to give you just enough 'ground' from which to see how Quaker organizing can be understood to be an 'alternative' form of organizing. Doing so, so that we might be able to imagine something of *witnessing-as-organizing* in this final chapter.

Law and Mol have suggested that Quaker processes can offer possibilities to engage in the often elusive and diffuse character of knowing how to organize in "heterogeneous worlds" (2003, p. 35). They have considered how Quaker organizing can be understood as about 'fluidity', because it involves "giv[ing] up the habits of distinction", which, for example, challenge views that see individuals as distinguishable self-contained subjects (Law & Mol, 2003, p. 24). The fluid qualities which Law and Mol associate with Quaker organizing is related to appreciating an indeterminacy of knowing how to go-on-together. As mentioned above there is an assumption of the need for dialogue out of which the 'sense of the meeting' or 'will of God' will emerge (Ambler, 2013).

By finding ways forwards amidst the diffuseness of notions of 'God' it has been suggested that Quakers are about understanding "that there is more than can possibly be put into words", which involves an apprehension "to naming, delineating, dividing and measuring" (Law & Mol, 2003, p. 25). For example, in her analysis of Quaker organizing Molina-Markham examines the roles of different types of silence in achieving a collective 'sense of the meeting', arguing that silence can be understood "not as an absence or as the opposite of speech, but as a deeply meaningful communicative event" (2014, p. 171). She suggests that in both the presence and absence of speech, collective meaning is made (Molina-Markham, 2014). It is in these ways that Quaker organizing can show fluidity, which Law and Mol explain as seeing the 'Other' or 'Otherness' (e.g. relating to indistinguishable boundaries between bodies) as "never mov[ing] away from the margins of vision, the corner of the eye, just unknowable, just beyond" (2003, p. 34).

For *witnessing-being-witnessed* we can start to understand how Quaker organizing could be productive to explore, because of the possibilities to consider how it might support images of entangled organizing. However, so far the story of Quaker organizing has had quite a humanist tone i.e. an understanding developed by focusing on the intentions of human-beings. Going back to Tsing's (2015) comments, mentioned above, we are searching for some glimpses of how we might understand ourselves to be involved in organizing which subverts alienation and commodification. Consequently, we are attempting to imagine how immersed in torrents of sociomaterial flowings we may find ways to purposefully come together, humans and other-than-humans, without being torn or implicated in the tearing of others – socially and materially ripped from being-entangled. Or, returning to the words of Introna (2013), which we explored particularly in Chapter 4, 'letting-be' of others.

Posthuman intentionality?

If as defined above organizing is understood to be generally about "goal orientated collectives" (Clegg et al., 2019, p. 4). We can appreciate that notions of organizing and organization are defined as existing by their collective human intentionality. Which means they can be mainly regarded as projects of humanism. So whilst as with Quaker organizing we may search for ways of being and doing together that attempt to work against processes of alienation, through the focus on things 'greater than humans' (i.e. diffuse notions of God), we can find some challenges for *witnessing-as-organizing*. In particular, the goal orientation of gathering people together to hear humans speak and be silent, typically indoors protected from 'outside' by walls, roofs and heating arrangements, can be understood to be involved in avoiding the gaze of living others. Consequently, we can notice that concerns for buildings and their maintenance, which are in close proximity to the collective bodies, can gain significant attention in Quaker organizing. As I was once told buildings can be understood as 'the tail that wags the dog', inferring that the meanings and affordances of these constructed spaces are significant mediators of Quaker organizing.

In the previous paragraph and I not seeking to cast some general assertions about Quakers, as from my studies and involvement some kind of 'environmental consciousness', or 'concern for sustainability', can receive substantial attention and action. However, associated with awareness of different ways of (un)knowing which are enabled through Quaker's documented 'framework of cooperation' my question is: How might a posthuman intentionality emerge? A shared intentionality toward collective goals that make organizing something meaningful for all involved. Whereas in the previous chapter, about *witnessing-as-being*, we moved towards considering possibilities related to finding some momentary poise to give/take some leadership, assemble some boundaries, or make some power. In this chapter trying to consider organizing we might envisage 'it' as about a collection of these 'moments of poise' amongst the assembled bodies. Perhaps given the suggested 'fluidity' that has been associated with Quaker organizing any collective goal making is necessarily fluid (Law & Mol, 2003). Although, to develop these ideas by exploring this example of Quaker organizing we likely need to make the distinction between processes of collective decision-making through the mentioned 'business method', and processes of Quaker worshipping.

The distinction between collective decision-making and worship is, at its most simple, that decision making involves an agenda of what will be discussed, minutes that are created and agreed for each agenda item, and an expectation that actions will be undertaken related to each minute. Where as, in 'liberal' or 'unprogrammed' worship (Dandelion, 2008), there are other varieties, has been described as:

> "All gather together in an unadorned room and sit in silent worship. After a while, one or another may stand and speak of a religious insight he or she feels called upon to share. The meeting ends, perhaps an hour after it began, with the general shaking of hands." (Sheeran, 1983, p. 4)

The collective decision-making associated with the 'business method' in a 'Meeting for Business' (typically monthly) is also understood to be a process of worship, as it is seen to be about seeking the 'will of God' like a 'Meeting for Worship' (typically weekly). However, the important aspect for our exploration of Quaker organizing, is that in Meetings for Worship the collective goal can be understood to be about gathering and being together. This is distinctive from considering specified agenda items and associated issues (such as building maintenance matters, or how to locally support campaign groups such as Extinction Rebellion) in order to make a decision or come up with a collectively agreeable response (represented by a written minute). Consequently, the 'fluidity' associated with Quaker worships and its suggested apprehension "to naming, delineating, dividing and measuring" and knowing (Law & Mol, 2003, p. 25), can be understood to become interrupted by 'an agenda' filled with human intentions. Albeit as mentioned above that Quaker buildings can have significant agency in determining what is on the agenda. In this sense the framework for collaboration to support human-ends appears to diminish the potential to allow 'the speaking', or feel 'the gaze', of the-more-than-human. This is because, as with our considered dilemmas, the presence of an agenda organizes 'human affairs' to be at the centre of interactions. So whilst we might imagine attention to be paid, for example with the ethics of what is purchased by the community, such as benches for sitting on during a meeting, as with the dilemma of centrality in Chapter 4, the locus of valuing seems anchored in relation to human-beings.

From our consideration of *witnessing-being-witnessed* we continue to realise that it is a perspective, like all perspectives, that is fraught with questions and dilemmas. Questions that become even more pronounced when we try to conceive of *witnessing-as-organizing* in relation to making sense of collective endeavours. We might hope that notions of collective could become an inevitably broadened term to include the more-than-human, but the organizational 'moves' to open a dialogue with such variegated 'voices', or indeed the 'voice-less', as we have been considering, is neither obvious nor straightforward. Indeed the very notion that we can organize our-selves from a posthuman perspective could well appear dubiously arrogant. This is because, as we have explored, posthuman appreciations involve considering how we are being organized through our sociomaterial entanglements.

What these explorations so far may suggest is that *witnessing-as-organizing* might be more associated with the disorganization of that which is amplifying human associations towards unsustainabilities. For example, going back to air travel, mentioned in Chapter 6 this may well involve disorganizing or disassembling the flying infrastructures into which we have become enrolled. Although, some have suggested that Anthropocene narratives encourage us 'to join forces with' and take advantage of 'earthly volatility' (Clark & Szerszynski, 2021). However, this sentiment could suggest that we have some potential to choose and know our entanglements, so that we can pursue effective appropriations of volatility. In *witnessing-being-witnessed* the assumption of unknowability, due to our relational entanglement, and that we are in flows, drenched in continual mediations (technological and ecological) is fundamental. To assume we might be able imagine rationalised 'choices' is already a potential move of human separation which denies assumptions of sociomateriality. As we are considering in relation to 'alternative organizing', we are seeking to imagine a process of being as 'becoming-communion', instead of 'overcoming adversity'.

Languages of entangled organizing

A challenge to the alternative form of organizing that we have considered is that, as mentioned, the very act of seeking to organize to a collective purpose seems to anchor the valuing to being in human-only-terms. Although we might see how an alternative organizational form might be potentially less alienating to those humans involved, it appears that the more-than-human is still an after-thought, once the 'agendas for action' are written. Whilst in *witnessing-as-being* we could imagine possibilities for moments of poise to join forces with matter and redraw boundaries in creative ways (e.g. the car grime art example in Chapter 7). It can seem that an act of 'organizing' or 'organization', in very general terms as "goal orientated collectives" (Clegg et al., 2019, p. 4), insert a humanism, from which in this exploration, we have sought other possibilities. Indeed, histories of organization tend to begin from a narrative of finding ways for humans to free themselves from the scarcity and hostility of 'nature' (Wren, 2005). However, humanist exceptionalism being inevitably involved in any form of organizing is far from some kind of straightforward assertion. This is because, as we have considered from a posthuman perspective, human acting and by association, human purpose-ing, is understood to emerge from relational entanglements. Which means that a separation of 'human', takes us back towards the dualisms and bifurcations that we have been attempting to circumvent. For instances, as Fox and Alldred remind us:

> "Rather than focusing upon humans as 'individuals' (literally: 'indivisible'), what we may term a 'posthuman' is an

> assemblage of biological, sociocultural and environmental elements, whose capacities to affect and be affected are contingent upon setting and emergent in its relations with other matter" (Fox & Alldred, 2020, p. 124).

What does this mean for how we can (re-)think about notions of organizing from a posthuman view? We could possibility understand ourselves as moving into a problematic territory by seeing humans, and their purposes, as a 'natural' derivation of 'nature'. Something like the Anthropocene as the next 'natural' evolution of the Earth. However, given as we have explored with the defining qualities of the Anthropocene (climatic change, species extinction, declining reproductive potential for many beings etc.) being harmful to many forms of life, this does not appear particularly 'natural'. However, we cannot dismiss any marks of humanity as 'the problem', simply because they are cast through human languages, and so in close association with our beings. We are part of entanglements, and so have both a responsibility to witnessing, along with being witnessed and valued by nonhuman others. As mentioned in Chapter 7, searching for way to become parts of 'dialogues' of solidarity.

In Chapter 4 the importance of language was mentioned due to the boundaries it draws and the potential to 'block' possibilities. In particular, the writing of Kimmerer (2013) was referred to in relation to the grammatical 'rules' of English and inscriptions of inanimate-ness to the more-than-human. Her work explores different streams of knowledges classed as 'indigenous' and 'scientific' and considers the potential separations and connections. What this writing can suggest is that searching for some 'processes' of *witnesses-as-organizing* is based within the meanings and possibilities of the languages through which they are made sense of. Some specific linguistic explorations, for example in relation to animacy in 'indigenous' ways of speaking and (un)knowing, are beyond the scope the pages. However, Kimmerer does suggest, for example, that "indigenous ways of understanding recognize the personhood of all beings as equally important, not in a hierarchy but a circle" (2013, p. 385). Also, that the capitalization tendencies of English associated with human-names reproduces "a certain distinction, the elevated position of humans and their creations in the hierarchy of beings" (Kimmerer, 2013, p. 385).

We might well want to be careful to avoid romanticising (seeing them to be overwhelmingly positive) the exotic potential of 'indigenous' knowledge (e.g. Jackson, 2014), but there are likely possibilities for informing entangled organizing. However, if we are to imagine non-alienating and non-dominating forms of organizing which could be appreciative of *witnessing-being-witnessed* we could do with other vocabularies. Vocabularies that can help us to pay attention to the rights, 'gazing', and 'speaking' of matter in all varieties. Doing so in ways that, as we considered early on in this chapter, do not cloak nonhuman others within some bizarre cape of anthropomorphism. For example, some have explored the indigenous knowledges associated with the Cree in North America, which are understood to involve "engag[ing] in respectful and reciprocal dialogue with other living creatures" (Whiteman & Cooper, 2000, p. 1272).

Streams of ways of (un)knowing

In this exploration of posthuman organizing, as a prompt to another way of knowing-being, it is important to remind ourselves that it does not shut down conversations with other knowledges. What I mean by this is that whilst as with the above paragraph we might look to indigenous ways of knowing for alternative possibilities, which do not assume human exceptionalism, it does not mean an all out rejection of everything else. For example, in this book a number of the references would be regarded as 'scientific' which may well be associated with ideas of objective and 'detached positions'. Such references have given texture to issues of sustainability (climate change, biodiversity loss etc.) which as we have explored is at the 'centre of this book' as well as being an ambitious normative notion. We have engaged with the idea from the early parts of this book that all perspectives can be understood to be underpinned by assumptions, and so variously limited. Consequently, we can appreciate a need to be careful to the claims to knowing that we may make from any perspective, as well as any possibilities for versions of 'truth' (see Chapter 1). The assumption for unknowing which emerges from a relational ontology, that underpins *witnessing-being-witnessed*, is not some magical 'card' to get-out of truth conundrums. This is because as we have explored unknowing is about encouraging a more tentative and reciprocal sense of how we might understand being-in-a-world. A sense that we can carry with us when confronted by different knowledges which might inform any organizing, be they precise and specific, or more ambiguous.

As we come to towards the end of this book, of course there is not going to be some cleared up sense of how to do *witnessing-as-organizing*. No neat punch lines, or something of a souped-up stakeholder mapping tool, that can 'capture' all these nonhuman others. Although, by now you will likely not be expecting it. Where we are going now, is to come back to our metaphor of the river, originally inspired by writing of Dale (2005) about sociomateriality, which I think has 'served' us reasonably well, going back to when it was first introduced in Chapter 2. Many different metaphors have been associated with seeking to make sense of organizing, for example the 'machine' that was mentioned earlier in this chapter associated with 'traditional organizations'. Some of the more exotic organically orientated organizational metaphors include 'rhizomatic' (Yu, 2006). However, we are going to return to our river in considering *witnessing-as-organizing*.

One of the interesting dimensions of a river metaphor that I have so far not brought attention towards is that for any flowing, the water needs to be heading downhill, sometimes gradually, sometimes rapidly. This is perhaps an unfortunate aspect of this metaphor as connotations of 'going downhill', has been given meanings of things gradually getting worse. In all our flailing within a torrent of sociomaterial relatings, with some potential for poise, we are on a downward path! For a perspective that is seeking to get out of some 'old boxes' to explore some alternative possibilities, this does not come across as an overly attractive prospect. Perhaps in trying to live with realities of Anthropocene times we might feel a nagging sense of things 'getting worse'. However, perhaps we can seek comfort from understanding 'the flow' to be about a continual renewing, rather than decline. Indeed eventually a river meets a sea and with it a new 'horizon' of possibilities for renewal. Let us for the moment put aside the upsetting state of many water ways and seas. For example, the images of accumulations of plastic within oceans and within the bodies of sea creatures, as well as many British rivers being treated as no more than an 'industrial drain' (e.g. Brown, 2021). As I mentioned I am trying to come to some kind of closing that offers a sense of enticing possibilities.

Reflecting on the river photos that have been included in this book, as part of attempting to show some of the situatedness and contingency of my relational entanglements, a more fitting view may well have involved an underwater camera. What I mean

Returning to the river metaphor: A third photo of the 'flowing' of the Riverlin Valley a few miles from our house where we walk and jog most weeks

by this is that the photo is taken from above the flowing river, as if to see it all, peer down upon, be separated from, which is incongruous from understanding us as flailing within a torrent of sociomaterial mediatings. The technology of an underwater camera, which I am not in proximity to, could have presented a more appropriate view. However, the enrolment of additional technologies in support of this book-writing endeavour, based on the matter involved, could well feel incongruous with the attentions that we have been exploring with *witnessing-being-witnessed*. Perhaps the plastic bag in the tree from the beginning of Chapter 7 could have been reimagined as a waterproof skin for a camera to afford it waterproof-ability!

In the river we are understood to be part of the flowing of the social, shaping and being reshaped by the riverbanks (the materiality). Although with the mutual-inacting (sociomateriality) we can appreciate that parts of the riverbanks, as 'rocks and sediment' are present within the flow (Dale, 2005). Any attempts at organizing are within this co-mingling flow. Consequently, our imagined organizing becomes related to how we seek to make connections with similarly vulnerable human others, to bring them into some productive but sympathetic combining of energies. Whereby any potential for collective agency or power, that might be understood as embodying 'organization', is open to the 'gazing' and 'speaking' of nonhuman others.

The varying intensity of, and turmoil in, the flowing will ask of us different ways of *witnessing-being-witnessed*. We may well become acted upon in disturbing and disorientating ways, a metaphorical waterfall may appear exciting, but can potentially 'knock the stuffing out of us'. However, we are acting within the flowing, variously together in suspension, understanding ourselves as part of an interdependent periphery. Due to a constantly changing flowing and emerging of circumstances, what might be productive and sympathetic for the collective efforts of the entangled human-beings is in ongoing need of revision and reimagination. However, the agility to find poise within the flow requires of us to be able to 'hear' others, which means we need to resist becoming, and being, alienated and dominated. Additionally, the river flow and the envisaged 'circularity' of its constituents allow us to imagine how things are understood to be "endlessly emerging, changing, fragmenting and fracturing, opening up both (post)human and non-human possibilities rather than closing them down" (Fox & Alldred, 2020, p. 126).

Something that I wanted to achieve through this learning-writing is a book that for a reader was not painful to engage with. What I mean by this is assembling a text which can help to prompt some posthuman imaginings that can feel promising and worthwhile. To do so I have attempted to make things as entertaining as I can, by trying to be creative, in the genre of 'academic', with how I show something of my 'contingent' and 'situated' relationality which I notice in producing this text. In doing so finding myself on something of a type-rope teetering between moments of possible excitement, associated with 'extensions of visibility' on realities, and becoming lost into a banality of the every-day. If you have made it this far then perhaps you might understand that I have shown some glimmers of success along-the-way. In this writing-learning process where we have tried to engage in a perspective of possibilities related to sociomateriality and posthumanism, maybe you have joined me fleetingly for some parts of the text, or for quite of lot the text. Sociomateriality and posthumanism are terms, of supercilious appearance, but as we have encountered can be seen to offer possibilities to be able to prompt our imaginations. I have hoped to explain these two terms, with examples, in ways that make some sense, and so they are not words that can leave you cold with their potential for giving people a snooty 'brush off'.

The 'critically speculative' approach that I have tried to uphold has taken us to an acceptance of unknowing, and a close attention to some key dilemmas which can be associated with *witnessing-being-witnessed* (Puig de la Bellacasa, 2017). By considering the three dilemmas of centrality (Chapter 4), proximity (Chapter 5) and freedom (Chapter 6) we noticed some of the challenges that emerge in attempting to bring together a posthuman perspective in relation to sustainability in Anthropcene times. These associated dilemmas will not drift away, continuing to acknowledge and explore them is integral to 'modest' learning-writing. As explored it is unknowability and unresolvability that imbues *witnessing-being-witnessed* with possibilities. Such learning-writing has perhaps been some-kind of act of denial (as mentioned in Chapter 5), or at the very least a form of escapism. An escapism of imagination that it is hoped can in some round-about-ways materialise into (moments of) flourishing beings and organizings. By doing so this text hopes to escape its own designation of 'academic', with connected definitional concern for 'not real life' (considered in Chapter 1), by finding some performative associations that make its assembling worthwhile, in whatever ways that might be understood.

Epilogue

A key tension in writing this book has been a personally felt pressing need to 'do something' about the unsustainabilities which I have given as context for this learning-writing, and assembling thought in a way that respects my appreciations of being in a relational world. In many ways for a reader a sense of elusivity of a categorical answer to that 'so what?' question might still be nagging. It is a question which haunts much academic writing requiring it to be immediately relevant, or even somehow actionable. We have navigated connected issues by considering how dimensions of modesty and unknowability are important signifiers of *witnessing-being-witnessed*. These have become significant motifs for the sociomaterial and posthuman perspective that has been developed on being and organizing in an entangled world. However, prompted to write this brief epilogue by the Editors, I want to leave us with a few 'fragments of rock' to indicate some of the main eddies of what has been gathered in this book.

Firstly, the guiding metaphor, and associated vocabulary, of a river has drawn together an array of concepts and been used to anchor the diverse examples which have been explored. The river metaphor has been productive both due to its flowing-ness, as this reflects in particular the key notion of sociomateriality, but also that the English language offers a wealth of words in relation to rivers and associated processes and motions. Also, being in the city of Sheffield, amongst five rivers, the Rivelin which is one of them was pictured in several of the included photographs, was fitting to ground my experimenting in situated and contingent learning-writing.

Secondly, as part of seeking to 'open up' debates on the typically inscrutable sociomateriality and posthumanism three key dilemmas have been noticed and explored which are at the heart of possibilities and potentialities for – as I mentioned at the very beginning in a very broad brush stroke – finding our ways to something better and something hopeful for us all. Centrality, proximity and freedom have been brought to the fore in how we might seek to reimagine possibilities for our beings and doings. These dilemmas have particularly been considered in relation to the challenges of bringing in mutuality in making sense of being reciprocally witnessed by voiceless more-than-human others.

Thirdly, the conceptualisations, dilemmas and examples have been brought into conversation with my 'home discipline' of Organization Studies. This is perhaps not the easiest, or most obvious, academic territory to be modestly and vulnerably approaching sociomateriality and posthumanism. However, possibilities for *witnessing-being-witnessed* were considered in relation to debates of leading and organizing. The relative novelty of this disciplinary approach may well offer glimpses of potentialities for understanding responsible-being in an entangled world.

That really is 'it'. I have found it quite rare to be contacted about things written, maybe a book may matter more, but please do get in touch if you are mediated to do so. By enrolling an array of devices and algorithms to search you should be given a means of contact. I look forward to possible dialogues.

References

Abram, D. (1996). *The Spell of the Sensous: Perception and Language in a More-than-Human World.* Pantheon Books: New York.

Akrich, M. & Latour, B. (1992). A Summary of a Convenient Vocabulary for the Semiotics of Human and Nonhuman Assemblies, in: Law, J. and Bijker, W. (Eds.), *Shaping Technology / Building Society: Studies in Sociotechnical Change.* Cambridge, MA: MIT Press.

Alaimo, S. (2010). *Bodily Natures: Science, Environment, and the Material Self.* Bloomington: Indiana University Press.

Allen, K. E., Stelzner, S. P. & Wielkiewicz, R. M. (1999). The Ecology of Leadership: Adapting to the Challenges of a Changing World. *Journal of Leadership & Organizational Studies,* 5(2), 62–82.

Allen, S. (2012). Making-Sense of Sustainability: Seeking to Enact Modesty and Humility in (Re) Searching. Retrieved from 10.13140/RG.2.2.11185.28000

Allen, S. (2017). Learning from Friends: Developing Appreciations for Unknowing in Reflexive Practice. *Management Learning,* 48(2), 125–139.

Allen, S. (2019a). Leadership and Sustainability, in: Leal Filho, W. (Ed.), *Encyclopedia of Sustainability in Higher Education,* (pp. 1067–1073). Cham, Switzerland: Springer Nature.

Allen, S. (2019b). Exploring Quaker Organising to Consider the Possibilities for Relational Leadership. *Quaker Studies,* 24(2), 249–269.

Allen, S. (2019c). The Unbounded Gatherer: Possibilities for Posthuman Writing-Reading. *Scandinavian Journal of Management,* 35(1), 64–75.

Allen, S., Brigham, M. & Marshall, J. (2018). Lost in Delegation? (Dis)Organizing for Sustainability. *Scandinavian Journal of Management,* 34(1), 29–39.

Allen, S. & Marshall, J. (2015). Metalogue: Trying to Talk about Sustainability–a Reflection on Experience. *Tamara Journal for Critical Organization Inquiry,* 13(1–2).

Allen, S. & Marshall, J. (2019). What Could Happen When Action Research Meets Ideas of Sociomateriality? *International Journal of Action Research,* 15(2).

Allen, S., Marshall, J. & Easterby-Smith, M. (2015). Living With Contradictions: The Dynamics of Senior Managers' Identity Tensions in Relation to Sustainability. *Organization & Environment,* 28(3), 328–348.

Allen, T., Tainter, J. & Hoekstra, T. (2003). *Supply-Side Sustainability.* New York: Columbia University Press.

Ambler, R. (2013). *The Quaker Way a Rediscovery.* Winchester: Christian Alternative.

Ameye, M., Allmann, S., Verwaeren, J., Smagghe, G., Haesaert, G., Schuurink, R. C. & Audenaert, K. (2018). Green Leaf Volatile Production by Plants: A Meta-Analysis. *New Phytologist*, 220(3), 666–683.

Ashley, S. What Is the Anthropocene? *National Trust.* Retrieved March 4, 2020, from https://www.nationaltrust.org.uk/features/what-is-the-anthropocene

Baker, A., Goodman, J. D. & Mueller, B. (2015). Beyond the Chokehold: The Path to Eric Garner's Death. *The New York Times.* Retrieved March 4, 2021, from https://www.nytimes.com/2015/06/14/nyregion/eric-garner-police-chokehold-statenisland.html

Barad, K. (2003). Posthumanist Performativity: Toward an Understanding of How Matter Comes to Matter. *Signs: Journal of Women in Culture and Society*, 28(3), 801–831.

Barad, K. (2007). *Meeting the Universe Halfway: Quantum Physics and the Entanglement of Matter and Meaning.* Durham & London: Duke University Press.

Bateson, G. (1979). *Mind and Nature: A Necessary Unity.* London: Wildwood House.

Bateson, G. (2000). *Steps to an Ecology of Mind.* London: The University of Chicago Press.

BBC News. (2020). Ella Adoo-Kissi-Debrah: Air Pollution a Factor in Girl's Death, Inquest Finds. *BBC News.* Retrieved March 4, 2021, from https://www.bbc.com/news/uk-england-london55330945

Bennett, J. (2010). *Vibrant Matter: A Political Ecology of Things.* Durham, Durham, N.C.: Duke University Press.

Bhasker, R. (1979). *The Possibility of Naturalism.* Harvester, Hassocks.

Blake, J. (1999). Overcoming the 'Value Action Gap' in Environmental Policy: Tensions between National Policy and Local Experience. *Local Environment*, 4(3), 257.

Bloomfield, B. P., Latham, Y. & Vurdubakis, T. (2010). Bodies, Technologies and Action Possibilities: When Is an Affordance? *Sociology*, 44(3), 415–433.

Böhm, S., Misoczky, M. C. & Moog, S. (2012). Greening Capitalism? A Marxist

Critique of Carbon Markets. *Organization Studies*, 33(11), 1617–1638.

Bookchin, M. (1982). *The Ecology of Freedom: The Emergence and Dissolution of Hierarchy*. California: Palo Alto: Cheshire Books.

Bookchin, M. (1990). *Remaking Society: Pathways to a Green Future*. Boston: South End Press.

Bookchin, M. (1996). *The Philosophy of Social Ecology: Essays on Dialectical Naturalism*. Montreal: Black Rose.

Borgerson, J. (2010). Witnessing and Organization: Existential Phenomenological Reflections on Intersubjectivity. *Philosophy Today; Charlottesville*, 54(1), 78–87.

Bradney, A. & Cownie, F. (2000). *Living Without Law: An Ethnography of Quaker Decision-Making, Dispute Avoidance, and Dispute Resolution*. Dartmouth Publishing Company.

Braidotti, R. (2013). *The Posthuman*. Cambridge: Polity.

Braidotti, R. (2019). A Theoretical Framework for the Critical Posthumanities. *Theory, Culture & Society*, 36(6), 31–61.

Bramley, E. V. (2018). For the Chop: The Battle to Save Sheffield's Trees. *the Guardian*. Retrieved February 25, 2021, from http://www.theguardian.com/uk-news/2018/feb/25/for-the-chopthe-battle-to-save-sheffields-trees

Breathing Space. *Festival of the Mind 2020*. Retrieved March 4, 2021, from http://festivalofthemind.sheffield.ac.uk/2020/futurecade/breathing-space/

Brown, D. (2021). Sewage Discharged into Rivers 400,000 Times in 2020. *BBC News*. Retrieved March 31, 2021, from https://www.bbc.com/news/science-environment-56590219

Burke, S. (2008). *The Death and Return of the Author: Criticism and Subjectivity in Barthes, Foucault and Derrida*. Edinburgh: Edinburgh University Press.

Butler, J. (2005). *Giving an Account of Oneself*. New York: Fordham University Press.

Carlile, P. R. & Dionne, K.-E. (2018). Unconventional yet Consequential, in: Bryman, A. and Buchanan, D. (Eds.), *Unconventional Methodology in Organization and Management Research*, (pp. 233–254). Oxford University Press.

Carlile, P. R., Nicolini, D., Langley, A. & Tsoukas, H. (Eds.). (2013). How Matter Matters: Objects, Artifacts, and Materiality in Organization Studies, in: *How Matter Matters: Objects, Artifacts, and Materiality in Organization Studies*. Oxford University Press.

Carrington, D. (2021). UK's Home Gas Boilers Emit Twice as Much CO2 as All Power

Stations – Study. *The Guardian*. Retrieved October 11, 2021, from https://www.theguardian.com/environment/2021/sep/29/uks-home-gas-boilers-emit-twiceas-much-co2-as-all-power-stations-study

Carroll, R. (2020). 'Mini Desk. Tiny Hands. Small Soul': Trump Mocked for Giving Speech at Little Table. *the Guardian*. Retrieved March 3, 2021, from http://www.theguardian.com/usnews/2020/nov/27/mini-desk-trump-mocked-speech-little-table-diaperdon-twitter-presidentfurniture

Chandler, D. (2013). The World of Attachment? The Post-Humanist Challenge to Freedom and Necessity. *Millennium*, 41(3), 516–534.

Charlton, N. (2008). *Understanding Gregory Bateson: Mind, Beauty and the Sacred Earth*. Albany: State University of New York Press.

Cielemęcka, O. & Daigle, C. (2019). Posthuman Sustainability: An Ethos for Our Anthropocenic Future. *Theory, Culture & Society*, 36(7–8), 67–87.

Clark, N. & Szerszynski, B. (2021). *Planetary Social Thought: The Anthropocene Challenge to the Social Sciences*. Cambridge: Polity Press.

Clarke, J. (2008). Harrods Recall Danger Teddy Bears. *Press Association*. Retrieved March 9, 2021, from https://advance.lexis.com/document/?pdmfid=1519360&crid=e48d4105-d66c-4020b567-fd-dc865a339a&pddocfullpath=%2Fshared%2Fdocument%2Fnews%2Furn%3AcontentItem%3A4T7V-S3T0-TX4T-70YV-00000-00&pdcontentcomponentid=8170&pdteaserkey=sr0&pditab=allpods&ecomp=Lzgnk&earg=sr0&prid=b0490757-6208-4ce6-93ce-a5d938ba3e8a

Clegg, S. R., Kornberger, M., Pitsis, T. & Mount, M. (2019). *Managing and Organizations: An Introduction to Theory and Practice*. London: Sage.

Clough, P. T. (2009). Reflections on Sessions Early in an Analysis: Trauma, Affect and "Enactive Witnessing". *Women & Performance: a journal of feminist theory*, 19(2), 149–159.

Colebrook, C. (2014). *Death of the PostHuman: Essays on Extinction, Vol. 1*. Ann Arbor: Open Humanities Press.

Collinson, D., Smolović Jones, O. & Grint, K. (2018). 'No More Heroes': Critical Perspectives on Leadership Romanticism. *Organization Studies*, 39(11), 1625–1647.

Costas, J. & Fleming, P. (2009). Beyond Dis-Identification: A Discursive Approach to Self-Alienation in Contemporary Organizations. *Human Relations*, 62(3), 353–378.

Crane, A. & Matten, D. (2010). *Business Ethics: Managing Corporate Citizenship and Sustainability in the Age of Globalisation*. Oxford: Oxford University Press.

Cregan-Reid, V. (2018). Anthropocene: Why the Chair Should Be the Symbol for Our Sedentary Age. *The Conversation*. Retrieved December 1, 2020, from http://theconversation.com/anthropocene-why-the-chair-should-be-the-symbol-for-oursedentary-age-105319

Cudworth, E. & Hobden, S. (2015). Liberation for Straw Dogs? Old Materialism, New Materialism, and the Challenge of an Emancipatory Posthumanism. *Globalizations*, 12(1), 134–148.

Cunliffe, A. L. (2004). On Becoming a Critically Reflexive Practitioner. *Journal of Management Education*, 28(4), 407–426.

Cunliffe, A. L. (2014). *A Very Short, Fairly Interesting and Reasonably Cheap Book about Management*. Sage.

Cunliffe, A. L. & Luhman, J. (2012). *Key Concepts in Organization Theory*. London; Thousand Oaks, Calif.: SAGE.

Dale, K. (2005). Building a Social Materiality: Spatial and Embodied Politics in Organizational Control. *Organization*, 12(5), 649–678.

Dale, K. & Burrell, G. (2008). *The Spaces of Organisation and the Organisation of Space: Power, Identity and Materiality at Work*. Basingstoke: Palgrave Macmillan.

Dandelion, B. P. (2008). *The Quakers: A Very Short Introduction*. Oxford University Press.

Devall, B. (2001). The Unsustainability of Sustainability. *Culture Change Magazine*, (19). Retrieved from http://www.culturechange.org/issue19/unsustainability.htm

Diamond, J. (2006). *Collapse - How Societies Choose to Fail or Survive*. London: Penguin Books.

Dickens, P. (1996). *Reconstructing Nature: Alienation, Emancipation and the Division of Labour*. London: Routledge.

Dresner, S. (2002). *The Principles of Sustainability*. London: Earthscan.

Easterby-Smith, M., Thorpe, R. & Jackson, P. R. (2013). *Management Research*. London: Sage.

Ehrenfeld, J. & Hoffman, A. (2013). *Flourishing: A Frank Conversation about Sustainability*. Stanford University Press.

Eisenstein, E. L. (1983). *The Printing Revolution in Early Modern Europe*. Cambridge: University Press.

Elias, N. (1991). *The Symbol Theory*. London: Sage.

Eshun, E. (2021). White Mischief - The Background Hum - BBC Sounds. Retrieved October 8, 2021, from https://www.bbc.co.uk/sounds/play/m00106by

Eskilson, S. (2018). *Age of Glass: A Cultural History of Glass in Modern and Contemporary Architecture*. Bloomsbury Publishing.

Faraj, S. & Azad, B. (2012). Materiality and Organizing: Social Interaction in a Technological World, in: Leonardi, P., Nardi, B. A., and Kallinikos, J. (Eds.), *The Materiality of Technology: An Affordance Perspective*. Oxford University Press.

Farrier, T. (2013). What Percent of the World's Population Will Fly in an Airplane in Their Lives? - Quora. Retrieved July 29, 2020, from https://www.quora.com/What-percent-of-the-worldspopulation-will-fly-in-an-airplane-in-their-lives

Ferrando, F. (2013). Posthumanism, Transhumanism, Antihumanism, Metahumanism, and New Materialisms. *Existenz*, 8(2), 26–32.

Feyerabend, P. (1978). *Against Method*. London: Verso.

Fotaki, M., Metcalfe, B. D. & Harding, N. (2014). Writing Materiality into Management and Organization Studies through and with Luce Irigaray. *Human Relations*, 67(10), 1239–1263.

Fox, N. J. & Alldred, P. (2020). Sustainability, Feminist Posthumanism and the Unusual Capacities of (Post)Humans. *Environmental Sociology*, 6(2), 121–131.

Franco, L. & Wentzel, M. (2019). Brazil Dam Disaster: How Do You Clear Tonnes of Toxic Sludge? *BBC News*. Retrieved November 27, 2020, from https://www.bbc.co.uk/news/world-latin-america-47061559

Gaertner, D. (2014). Sehtoskakew: "Aboriginal Principles of Witnessing" in the Canadian TRC. *Novel Alliances*. Retrieved September 27, 2021, from https://novelalliances.com/2014/07/09/sehtoskakew-aboriginal-principles-of-witnessing-inthe-canadian-trc/

Gallagher, S. & Jong, E. de. (2019). 'One Day We'll Disappear': Tuvalu's Sinking Islands. *The Guardian*. Retrieved October 25, 2021, from https://

www.theguardian.com/globaldevelopment/2019/may/16/one-day-disappear-tuvalu-sinking-islands-rising-seas-climatechange

Gane, N. (2006). When We Have Never Been Human, What Is to Be Done? Interview with Donna Haraway. *Theory, Culture & Society*, 23(7–8), 135–158.

Gergen, K. (2009). *Relational Being: Beyond Self and Community*. Oxford: Oxford University Press.

Gibson, J. J. (1977). The Theory of Affordances, in: Shaw, R. and Bransford, J. (Eds.), *Perceiving, acting and knowing: Toward an ecological psychology*. Hillsdale, New Jersey: Lawrence Erlbaum Associates.

Givoni, M. (2014). The Ethics of Witnessing and the Politics of the Governed. *Theory, Culture & Society*, 31(1), 123–142.

Goldsmith, E. (1996). *The Way: An Ecological World View*. Totnes: Themis Books.

Gore, T. (2015). *Extreme Carbon Inequality: Why the Paris Climate Deal Must Put the Poorest, Lowest Emitting and Most Vulnerable People First*. Oxfam. Retrieved from https://policypractice.oxfam.org/resources/extreme-carbon-inequality-why-the-paris-climate-deal-mustput-the-poorest-lowes-582545/

Gourlay, L. (2015). Posthuman Texts: Nonhuman Actors, Mediators and the Digital University. *Social Semiotics*, 25(4), 484.

Grey, C. & Sinclair, A. (2006). Writing Differently. *Organization*, 13(3), 443–453.

Guardian Research. (2010). BP Oil Spill Timeline. *the Guardian*. Retrieved August 10, 2020, from http://www.theguardian.com/environment/2010/jun/29/bp-oil-spill-timeline-deepwaterhorizon

Haraway, D. (1992). The Promises of Monsters: A Regenerative Politics for Inappropriate/d Others, in: Grossberg, L., Nelson, C., and Treichler, P. (Eds.), *Cultural Studies*, (pp. 295–385). New York: Routledge.

Haraway, D. (1997). *Modest Witness @ Second Millenium : FemaleMan Meets OncoMouse : Feminism and Technoscience*. New York ; London: Routledge.

Haraway, D. J. (2008). *When Species Meet*. Minneapolis: University of Minnesota Press.

Haraway, D. J. (2016). *Staying with the Trouble: Making Kin in the Chthulucene*. London, England: Duke University Press.

Havelock, L. (2020). Qantas Seven-Hour 'flight to Nowhere' Sells out in 10 Minutes. *inews.co.uk*. Retrieved February 24, 2021, from https://inews.co.uk/news/world/qantas-flight-tonowhere-tickets-sell-out-scenic-australia-652262

Hayles, N. K. (2008). *How We Became Posthuman: Virtual Bodies in Cybernetics, Literature, and Informatics*. Chicago: University of Chicago Press.

Hayward, C. R. (1998). De-Facing Power. *Polity*, 31(1), 1–22.

Hill, D. W. (2019). Bearing Witness, Moral Responsibility and Distant Suffering. *Theory, Culture & Society*, 36(1), 27–45.

Holt, B. (2020). The Return of Jane Elliott. *New York Times*. Retrieved August 5, 2020, from https://advance.lexis.com/document/?pdmfid=1519360&crid=f2bccb89-5ceb-459f-9e009eb543bef551&pddocfullpath=%2Fshared%2Fdocument%2Fnews%2Furn%3AcontentItem%3A60C2-TX61-JBG3-64R0-00000-00&pdcontentcomponentid=6742&pdteaserkey=sr0&pditab=allpods&ecomp=gzJ3k&earg=sr0&prid=539a501b-646f-4ecc-838e-a2c01743cfa9

Hosking, D. M. (2011). Telling Tales of Relations: Appreciating Relational Constructionism. *Organization Studies*, 32(1), 47–65.

Hotten, R. (2020). University Staff Urge Probe into E-Book Pricing 'Scandal'. *BBC News*. Retrieved March 18, 2021, from https://www.bbc.com/news/business-54922764

House of Polypores, 2021. Retrieved October 11, 2021, from https://www.tellingtree.fi/house-of-polypores-2021

Hughes, J. A. (1981). *The Philosophy of Social Research*. London: Longman.

Hunt, N. (2019). The Great Green Expansion: How Ring-Necked Parakeets Took over London. *The Guardian*. Retrieved December 10, 2020, from https://www.theguardian.com/cities/2019/jun/06/the-great-green-expansion-how-ringnecked-parakeets-took-over-london

Hunt, S. (2021). Unsettling Conversations on Climate Action. *The Professional Geographer*, 0(0), 1–2.

Hutchby, I. (2001). Technologies, Texts and Affordances. *Sociology*, 35(2), 441–456.

Ingold, T. (2002). *The Perception of the Environment: Essays in Livelihood, Dwelling and Skill*. London: Routledge.

Ingold, T. (2008). Bindings against Boundaries: Entanglements of Life in an Open World. *Environment and planning A*, 40(8), 1796.

Introna, L. D. (2009). Ethics and the Speaking of Things. *Theory, Culture &*

Society, 26(4), 25–46.

Introna, L. D. (2013). Otherness and the Letting-Be of Becoming: Or, Ethics beyond Bifurcation, in: Carlile, P. R., Nicolini, D., Langley, A., and Tsoukas, H. (Eds.), *How Matter Matters: Objects, Artifacts, and Materiality in Organization Studies*. Oxford: Oxford University Press.

Introna, L. D. (2014). Ethics and Flesh: Being Touched by the Otherness of Things, in: Olsen, B. (Ed.), *Ruin memories: materialities, aesthetics and the archaeology of the recent past*, (pp. 41–61). Oxford: Routledge.

IPCC. (2018). *Global Warming of 1.5 °C: An IPCC Special Report on the Impacts of Global Warming of 1.5 °C above Pre-Industrial Levels and Related Global Greenhouse Gas Emission Pathways, in the Context of Strengthening the Global Response to the Threat of Climate Change, Sustainable Development, and Efforts to Eradicate Poverty*. Geneva, Switzerland: IPCC. Retrieved October 12, 2018, from http://www.ipcc.ch/report/sr15/

Jackson, T. (2014). Cross-Cultural Management from the South: What a Difference Global Dynamics Make. *International Journal of Cross Cultural Management*, 14(1), 3–5.

Jones, M. (2014). A Matter of Life and Death: Exploring Conceptualizations of Sociomateriality in the Context of Critical Care. *MIS Quarterly*, 38(3), 895-A6.

Kalmus, P. (2016). How Far Can We Get Without Flying? *Yes! Magazine*. Retrieved March 10, 2020, from https://www.yesmagazine.org/issue/life-after-oil/2016/02/11/how-far-can-weget-without-flying

Kimmerer, R. W. (2013). *Braiding Sweetgrass: Indigenous Wisdom, Scientific Knowledge and the Teachings of Plants*. Minneapolis, Minnesota: Milkweed Editions.

King, D. & Lawley, S. (2019). *Organizational Behaviour*. Oxford: Oxford University Press.

Kissi-Debrah, R. (2018). Air Pollution Killed My Daughter – and Now I Can Prove It. *the Guardian*. Retrieved March 4, 2021, from http://www.theguardian.com/commentisfree/2018/aug/31/proof-air-pollution-killed-mydaughter-ella-new-inquest

Klöwer, M., Hopkins, D., Allen, M. & Higham, J. (2020). *An Analysis of Ways to Decarbonize Conference Travel after COVID-19*. Nature Publishing Group.

Knowles, R. D. (2006). Transport Shaping Space: Differential Collapse in Time–Space. *Journal of Transport Geography*, 14(6), 407–425.

Kociatkiewicz, J., Kostera, M. & Parker, M. (2021). The Possibility of Disalienated Work: Being at Home in Alternative Organizations. *Human Relations*, 74(7),

933–957.

Kommenda, N. (2021). Wealthy UK Flyers Opt for Private Jets to Evade Covid Lockdowns. *the Guardian*. Retrieved March 22, 2021, from http://www.theguardian.com/business/2021/jan/21/wealthy-uk-flyers-opt-for-private-jets-toevade-covid-and-lockdowns

Krishnamurti, J. (1997). *Kirshnamurti : Reflections on the Self* (R. Martin, Ed.). LaSalle, Ill: Open Court.

Ladkin, D. (2017). How Did That Happen? Making Sense of the 2016 US Presidential Election Result through the Lens of the 'Leadership Moment'. *Leadership*, 13(4), 393–412.

Latour, B. (1986). The Powers of Association, in: *Power, action and belief : a new sociology of knowledge?* London: Routledge & Kegan Paul.

Latour, B. (1987). *Science in Action: How to Follow Scientists and Engineers through Society*. Cambridge, Massachusetts: Harvard University Press.

Latour, B. (1988). The Politics of Explanation, in: Woolgar, S. (Ed.), *Knowledge and reflexivity: New frontiers in the sociology of knowledge*. London: Sage.

Latour, B. (2005). *Reassembling the Social: An Introduction to Actor-Network Theory*. Oxford: Oxford University Press.

Latour, B. (2011). Love Your Monsters: Why We Must Care for Our Technologies as We Do Our Children. *Breakthrough Journal*, 2(Autumn), 8.

Latour, B. & Venn, C. (2002). Morality and Technology. *Theory, Culture & Society*, 19(5–6), 247– 260.

Law, J. (1994). *Organising Modernity*. Oxford: Blackwell.

Law, J. (2004). *After Method: Mess in Social Science Research*. Abingdon: Routledge.

Law, J. & Mol, A. (1995). Notes on Materiality and Sociality. *The Sociological Review*, 43(2), 274– 294.

Law, J. & Mol, A. (2003). On Metrics and Fluids: Notes on Otherness, in: Chia, R. (Ed.), *Organized Worlds: Explorations in Technology and Organization with Robert Cooper*. Routledge.

Learmonth, M. & Morrell, K. (2017). Is Critical Leadership Studies 'Critical'? *Leadership*, 13(3), 257–271.

Lovelock, J. (2006). *The Revenge of Gaia*. London: Allen Lane.

Malm, A. (2018). *The Progress of This Storm: Nature and Society in a Warming World*. Verso Books.

Mao, F. (2020). Coronavirus Panic: Why Are People Stockpiling Toilet Paper? *BBC News*. Retrieved March 19, 2021, from https://www.bbc.com/news/world-australia-51731422

Marcus, J., Kurucz, E. C. & Colbert, B. A. (2010). Conceptions of the Business-Society-Nature Interface: Implications for Management Scholarship. *Business & Society*, 49(3), 402–438.

Marshall, J. (1981). Making Sense a Personal Process, in: *Human Inquiry*. London: Wiley.

Marshall, J. (1995). *Women Managers Moving on: Exploring Career and Life Choices*. London: Routledge.

McKibben, B. (1990). *The End of Nature*. London: Penguin Books.

McNeill, J. (2000). *Something New under the Sun: An Environmental History of the Twentieth Century World*. London: Penguin Books.

Mignolo, W. D. (2007). Delinking: The Rhetoric of Modernity, the Logic of Coloniality and the Grammar of de-Coloniality. *Cultural Studies*, 21(2–3), 449–514.

Miller, D. (2001). *Car Cultures*. Oxford: Berg.

Mills, C. W. (1959). *The Sociological Imagination*. New York: Oxford University Press.

Mol, A. (2010). Actor-Network Theory: Sensitive Terms and Enduring Tensions. *Kölner Zeitschrift für Soziologieund Sozialpsychologie*, 50(1), 253–269.

Molina-Markham, E. (2014). Finding the 'Sense of the Meeting': Decision Making Through Silence Among Quakers. *Western Journal of Communication*, 78(2), 155.

Morgan, G. (2006). *Images of Organization*. Thousand Oaks, Calif; London: SAGE.

Morgan, J. (2021). Autumnwatch - 2021: Episode 3. Retrieved November 2, 2021, from https://www.bbc.co.uk/iplayer/episode/m00111j0/autumnwatch-2021-episode-3

Mutch, A. (2013). Sociomateriality — Taking the Wrong Turning? *Information and Organization*, 23(1), 28–40.

Mytton, D. & Ashtine, M. (2021). We Are Ignoring the True Cost of Water-Guzzling Data Centres. *The Conversation*. Retrieved October 20, 2021, from http://theconversation.com/we-areignoring-the-true-cost-of-water-guzzling-data-centres-167750

Nevins, J., Allen, S. & Watson, M. (2022). A Path to Decolonization? Reducing Air Travel and Resource Consumption in Higher Education. *Travel Behaviour and Society*, 26, 231–239.

Nicholson, J. & Kurucz, E. (2017). Relational Leadership for Sustainability: Building an Ethical Framework from the Moral Theory of 'Ethics of Care'. *Journal of Business Ethics*, 156(1), 25–43.

Norgaard, R. (1994). *Development Betrayed: The End of Progress and a Coevolutionary Revisioning of the Future*. London: Routledge.

Oliver, K. (2000). Beyond Recognition: Witnessing Ethics. *Philosophy Today; Charlottesville*, 44(1), 31–43.

O'Reilly, D., Allen, S. & Reedy, P. (2018). Reimagining the Scales, Dimensions and Fields of Socio-Ecological Sustainability. *British Journal of Management*, 29(2), 220–234.

Orlikowski, W. J. (2006). Material Knowing: The Scaffolding of Human Knowledgeability. *European Journal of Information Systems*, 15(5), 460–466.

Orlikowski, W. J. (2007). Sociomaterial Practices: Exploring Technology at Work. *Organization Studies*, 28(9), 1435–1448.

Orlikowski, W. J. (2010). The Sociomateriality of Organisational Life: Considering Technology in Management Research. *Cambridge Journal of Economics*, 34(1), 125–141.

Orlikowski, W. J. & Scott, S. V. (2008). Sociomateriality: Challenging the Separation of Technology, Work and Organization. *The Academy of Management Annals*, 2(1), 433–474.

PA Media. (2020). There Is Such a Thing as Society, Says Boris Johnson from Bunker. *The Guardian*. Retrieved October 8, 2020, from https://www.theguardian.com/politics/2020/mar/29/20000-nhs-staff-return-to-service-johnson-says-from-coronavirus-isolation

Parker, M., Cheney, G., Fournier, V. & Land, C. (2014). *The Routledge Companion to Alternative Organization*. Abingdon: Routledge.

Parker, M. & Weik, E. (2014). Free Spirits? The Academic on the Aeroplane: *Management Learning*, 45(2), 167–181.

Plumwood, V. (2002a). *Environmental Culture: The Ecological Crisis of Reason*. London: Routledge.

Plumwood, V. (2002b). Decolonisation Relationships with Nature. *PAN: Philosophy Activism Nature*, (2), 7.

Polanyi, M. (1962). *Personal Knowledge: Towards a Post-Critical Philosophy*. London: Routledge & Kegan Paul.

Porritt, J. (2007). *Capitalism: As If the World Matters*. London: Earthscan.

Princen, T. (2010). *Treading Softly: Paths to Ecological Order*. London: MIT Press.

Puig de la Bellacasa, M. (2011). Matters of Care in Technoscience: Assembling Neglected Things. *Social Studies Of Science*, 41(1), 85–106.

Puig de la Bellacasa, M. (2017). *Matters of Care: Speculative Ethics in More than Human Worlds*. Minneapolis: University of Minnesota Press.

Quijano, A. (2007). Coloniality and Modernity/Rationality. *Cultural Studies*, 21(2–3), 168–178.

Quinn, R. E., Bright, D., Faerman, S. R., Thompson, M. P. & McGrath, M. R. (2014). *Becoming a Master Manager: A Competing Values Approach*. John Wiley & Sons.

Ravetz, J. R. (2006). Post-Normal Science and the Complexity of Transitions towards Sustainability. *Ecological Complexity*, 3(4), 275–284.

Raymond, W. (2000). Social Darwinism, in: Offer, J. (Ed.), *Herbert Spencer: Critical Assessment*, (pp. 186–199). London ; New York: Routledge.

Real Teddy Bear Story - Theodore Roosevelt Association. Retrieved March 9, 2021, from https://theodoreroosevelt.org/content.aspx?page_id=22&club_id=991271&-module_id=333084

Reedy, P. & Learmonth, M. (2009). Other Possibilities? The Contribution to Management Education of Alternative Organizations. *Management Learning*, 40(3), 241–258.

Rheinberger, H. J. (1997). *Toward a History of Epistemic Things*. Stanford: Stanford University Press.

Rockström, J. et al. (2009). A Safe Operating Space for Humanity. *Nature*, 461(7263), 472–475.

RSPB. Redwing Bird Facts | Turdus Iliacus. *The RSPB*. Retrieved February 25, 2021, from https://www.rspb.org.uk/birds-and-wildlife/wildlife-guides/bird-a-z/redwing/

Sainato, M. (2020). 'I'm Not a Robot': Amazon Workers Condemn Unsafe, Grueling Conditions at Warehouse. *the Guardian*. Retrieved March 18, 2021, from http://www.theguardian.com/technology/2020/feb/05/amazon-workers-protest-unsafegrueling-conditions-warehouse

Sandywell, B., Silverman, D., Roche, M., Filmer, P. & Phillipson, M. (1975). *Problems of Reflexivity and Dialectics in Sociological Inquiry : Language Theorizing Difference*. London ; Boston: Routledge & KPaul.

Satterwhite, R. (2010). Deep Systems Leadership: A Model for the 21st Century, in: Redekop, B. W. (Ed.), *Leadership for Environmental Sustainability*. Abingdon: Routledge.

Sayer, A. (2015). *Why We Can't Afford the Rich*. Policy Press.

Schumacher, E. F. (1982). *Schumacher on Energy*. London: Cape.

Sheeran, M. (1983). *Beyond Majority Rule: Voteless Decisions in the Religious Society of Friends*. Philadelphia: Philiadelphia Yearly Meeting of the Religious Society of Friends.

Sheldrake, M. (2020). *Entangled Life: How Fungi Make Our Worlds, Change Our Minds and Shape Our Futures*. London: The Bodley Head.

Simpson, C. (2012). The Deadly Tin Inside Your Smartphone. *Bloomberg.com*. Retrieved September 7, 2018, from https://www.bloomberg.com/news/articles/2012-08-23/the-deadlytin-inside-your-smartphone

Sinclair, A. (2010). Placing Self: How Might We Place Ourselves in Leadership Studies Differently? *Leadership*, 6(4), 447–460.

Smircich, L. & Morgan, G. (1982). Leadership: The Management of Meaning. *The Journal of Applied behavioral science*, 18(3), 257–273.

Solnit, R. (2010). *A Paradise Built in Hell: The Extraordinary Communities That Arise in Disaster*. London: Penguin Books.

Stead, V. & Elliott, C. (2009). *Women's Leadership*. Springer.

Steffen, W., Richardson, K., Rockström, J., Cornell, S. E., Fetzer, I., Bennett, E. M., Biggs, R., Carpenter, S. R., Vries, W. de, Wit, C. A. de, Folke, C., Gerten, D., Heinke, J., Mace, G. M., Persson, L. M., Ramanathan, V., Reyers, B. & Sörlin, S. (2015). Planetary Boundaries: Guiding Human Development on a Changing Planet. *Science*, 347(6223), 1259855.

Steier, F. (Ed.). (1991). *Research and Reflexivity*. London ; Newbury Park, Calif: Sage.

Storme, T., Beaverstock, J. V., Derrudder, B., Faulconbridge, J. R. & Witlox, F.

(2013). How to Cope with Mobility Expectations in Academia: Individual Travel Strategies of Tenured Academics at Ghent University, Flanders. *Research in Transportation Business & Management*, 9, 12–20.

Stubbs, W. & Cocklin, C. (2008). Teaching Sustainability to Business Students: Shifting Mindsets. *International Journal of Sustainability in Higher Education*, 9(3), 206–221.

Szerszynski, B. (1996). On Knowing What to Do: Environmentalism and Modern Problematic, in: *Risk, environment and modernity: towards a new ecology*. London: Sage.

Taylor, C. (1989). *Sources of the Self: The Making of the Modern Identity*. Cambridge, Mass: Harvard University Press.

Tsing, A. L. (2015). *The Mushroom at the End of the World*. Oxford: Princeton University Press.

United Nations Environment Programme. (2020). *Emissions Gap Report 2020*. Nairobi.

United Nations Secretary-General. (2018). UN Secretary-General's Remarks on Climate Change. Retrieved March 9, 2020, from https://www.un.org/sg/en/content/sg/statement/2018-09-10/secretary-generals-remarksclimate-change-delivered

Valtonen, A. & Pullen, A. (2021). Writing with Rocks. *Gender, Work & Organization*, 28(2), 506– 522.

West, S., Haider, L. J., Stålhammar, S. & Woroniecki, S. (2020). A Relational Turn for Sustainability Science? Relational Thinking, Leverage Points and Transformations. *Ecosystems and People*, 16(1), 304–325.

Western, S. (2010). Eco-Leadership: Towards the Development of a New Paradigm, in: Redekop, B. W. (Ed.), *Leadership for Environmental Sustainability*. Abingdon: Routledge.

Whiteman, G. & Cooper, W. H. (2000). Ecological Embeddedness. *Academy of Management Journal*, 43(6), 1265.

Whittle, A. & Spicer, A. (2008). Is Actor Network Theory Critique? *Organization Studies*, 29(4), 611–629.

Wildman, W. J. (2010). An Introduction to Relational Ontology, in: Polkinghorne, J. (Ed.), *The Trinity and an entangled world: Relationality in physical science and theology*, (pp. 55–73). Cambridge: Eerdmans.

Williams, J. (2013). *Understanding Poststructuralism*. Durham, Cambridge: Acumen Publishing, Cambridge University Press.

Williams, R. (2012). Edith Garrud: A Public Vote for the Suffragette Who Taught Martial Arts. *the Guardian*. Retrieved December 16, 2020, from http://www.theguardian.com/lifeandstyle/2012/jun/25/edith-garrud-suffragette-martial-arts

Wood, M. & Dibben, M. (2015). Leadership as Relational Process. *Process Studies*, 44(1), 24–47.

Woodland Trust. London Plane (Platanus x Hispanica) - British Trees. *Woodland Trust*. Retrieved February 25, 2021, from https://www.woodlandtrust.org.uk/trees-woods-and-wildlife/british-trees/a-z-of-britishtrees/london-plane/

Woolgar, S., Coopmans, C. & Neyland, D. (2009). Does STS Mean Business? *Organization*, 16(1), 5–30.

Wren, D. A. (2005). *The History of Management Thought*. Hoboken: John Wiley and Sons.

Wright, C., Nyberg, D. & Grant, D. (2012). "Hippies on the Third Floor": Climate Change, Narrative Identity and the Micro-Politics of Corporate Environmentalism. *Organization Studies*, 33(11), 1451–1475.

Wright, E. O. (2010). *Envisioning Real Utopias*. London: Verso.

Wynes, S. & Donner, S. D. (2018). *Addressing Greenhouse Gas Emissions from Business-Related Air Travel at Public Institutions: A Case Study of the University of British Columbia*. Victoria, BC: The Pacific Institute for Climate Solutions. Retrieved from https://pics.uvic.ca/sites/default/files/AirTravelWP_FINAL.pdf

Yu, J. E. (2006). Creating 'Rhizomatic Systems' for Understanding Complexity in Organizations. *Systemic Practice and Action Research*, 19(4), 337–349.

Zalasiewicz, J., Williams, M., Steffen, W. & Crutzen, P. (2010). The New World of the Anthropocene. *Environmental Science and Technology*, 44(7), 2228–2231.

Zembylas, M. (2005). A Pedagogy of Unknowing: Witnessing Unknowability in Teaching and Learning. *Studies in Philosophy and Education*, 24(2), 139–160.

Zylinska, J. (2018). *The End of Man: A Feminist Counterapocalypse*. University of Minnesota Press.

www.ingramcontent.com/pod-product-compliance
Lightning Source LLC
Chambersburg PA
CBHW042314210326
41599CB00038B/7119

* 9 7 8 1 9 0 6 9 4 8 5 7 3 *